WOMEN WRITERS OF THE FIRST WORLD WAR

Didn't women have their war as well?

The notion of 'women's writing' during the First World War is still often seen as a contradiction in terms. The conflict, the story goes, was a masculine domain: as women did not fight, they were necessarily excluded from the experience of war.

This bibliography challenges that view by listing and annotating hundreds of published and unpublished books, articles, memoirs, diaries and letters written by women during and after the First World War. Included are:

- Virginia Woolf, Katherine Mansfield, G.B. Stern, Brenda Girvin, Vera Britain, Storm Jameson, Rose Macaulay and Berta Ruck
- known and unknown autobiographers and diarists
- writers of pro- and anti-war propaganda
- journal and magazine articles
- literary, cultural and historical criticism
- archival material.

An invaluable resource for both researchers and the general reader, this is the first detailed bibliography of its kind, providing a vast range of reference to, and commentary on, both the larger (political, science) issues of the war and its more localised topics (the Serbian Front, peace organisations). 'Experience of war', we quickly learn is not the exclusive province of the fighting man.

Sharon Ouditt is Senior Lecturer in English at The Nottingham Trent University.

WOMEN WRITERS OF THE FIRST WORLD WAR

An Annotated Bibliography

Sharon Ouditt

London and New York

First published 2000
by Routledge
11 New Fetter Lane, London EC4P 4EE

Simultaneously published in the USA and Canada
by Routledge
29 West 35th Street, New York, NY 10001

Routledge is an imprint of the Taylor & Francis Group

© 2000 Sharon Ouditt

Typeset in Sabon and Futura by Routledge
Printed and bound in Great Britain by MPG Books Ltd, Bodmin

British Library Cataloguing in Publication Data
A catalogue record for this book is available from the British Library

Library of Congress Cataloging in Publication Data
Ouditt, Sharon, 1963–
Women writers of the first World War: an annotated bibliography/
Sharon Ouditt.
     p. cm.
Includes bibliographical references (p.   ) and index.
1. English literature–20th century Bibliography. 2. World War,
1914–1918–Great Britain–Literature and the war Bibliography.
3. Women and literature–Great Britain–History–20th century Bibliography.
4. English Literature–Women authors–History and criticism Bibliography.
5. English Literature–20th century–History and criticism Bibliography.
6. Women authors, English–20th century–Biography Bibliography. 7. World
War, 1914–1918–Women–Great Britain Bibliography. 8. English
Literature–Women authors Bibliography. I. Title. II. Title: Women writers of the
1st World War.
Z2014.W37093   1999
[PR478.W65}
016.8208'0358–dc21   99–20102
                                                                              CIP

ISBN 0–415–04752–8

CONTENTS

CONTENTS

ACKNOWLEDGEMENTS

Many people have provided help and encouragement with this project, and I must begin by thanking Martin Stannard for unfailing support during the entire process.

My colleagues at The Nottingham Trent University have provided a friendly and sustaining intellectual environment: thanks are due to all, but particularly to Leonora Nattrass for sharing problems, and to Dick Ellis for generating and maintaining a stimulating research culture.

For various combinations of intellectual and practical support, thanks are due to the following: Sylvia Ouditt, Reno Ouditt, Rick Rylance, Judith Boddy, Claire Tylee and Caroline Zilboorg. The staff at Cambridge University Library have been helpful, as have the staff of the Departments of Documents and Printed Books at the Imperial War Museum. Peter Liddle, Keeper of the Liddle Collection, has been extremely generous in both sharing his extensive knowledge, and providing opportunities to meet and work alongside other First World War scholars. Finally, I must say thanks to Zuli and Leo for putting up with this for so long.

ABBREVIATIONS

ASC	Army Service Corps
BEF	British Expeditionary Force
BRCS	British Red Cross Society
DORA	Defence of the Realm Act
ELFS	East London Federation of Suffragettes
FANY	First Aid Nursing Yeomanry
FWVRC	Friends' War Victims Relief Committee
GSVAD	General Service Voluntary Aid Detachment
ILP	Independent Labour Party
IWSA	International Woman Suffrage Alliance
MS	manuscript
NCF	No-Conscription Fellowship
NFWW	National Federation of Women Workers
NUWSS	National Union of Women's Suffrage Societies
NUWW	National Union of Women Workers
OTC	Officers' Training Corps
PHL	Peter H. Liddle (Keeper of the Liddle Collection)
QAIMNS	Queen Alexandra Imperial Military Nursing Service
QAIMNS (R)	Queen Alexandra Imperial Military Nursing Service (Reserve)
QMAAC	Queen Mary's Army Auxiliary Corps
RAMC	Royal Army Medical Corps
RFA	Royal Field Artillery
RFC	Royal Flying Corps
RNAS	Royal Naval Air Service
RRC	Royal Red Cross
SWH	Scottish Women's Hospitals
TFNS	Territorial Force Nursing Service
TS	typescript
UDC	Union of Democratic Control
VAD	Voluntary Aid Detachment
WAAC	Women's Army Auxiliary Corps
WILPF	Women's International League for Peace and Freedom
WLA	Women's Land Army
WNLSC	Women's National Land Service Corps

ABBREVIATIONS

WRAC	Women's Royal Army Corps
WRNS	Women's Royal Naval Service
WSPU	Women's Social and Political Union
WVR	Women's Volunteer Reserve

INTRODUCTION

The very idea that women produced writing about the First World War has often been received with some scepticism. Women, after all, *didn't* write about the war. They weren't in it. They didn't bear arms, only glimpsed the blood and muck of the battlefields from the shelter of the hospital, and thought plum puddings a Christmas treat rather than a military necessity. Their experience, their appearance and their language excluded them from the military zones. They wrote bad poems about second-rate ordeals because their hearts, minds and bodies were not there on the battlefields, but were screened from the intensity of suffering by the protective exigencies of duty and decorum.[1]

This book aims, implicitly, to open up the field of war writing. Where there is total war, the full range of experience, rather than seeing enemy action alone, may be construed as war experience. Christabel Pankhurst proclaimed that the work of five individuals was required in order to maintain a fully equipped soldier at the front.[2] Vera Brittain declared that she 'went to the war'[3] in much the same way as did her male contemporaries. Women such as Elsie Inglis, Mairi Chisholm and Elsie Knocker literally came under fire from the enemy, and metaphorically from the British military authorities. Ordinary working women struggled to feed and maintain their families on severely reduced incomes, and often in the face of accusations of drunkenness or unchastity by the local authorities. Women lost husbands, fathers, brothers, sons; children grew up without fathers. When millions of men are involved in armed combat, the full record of war experience could not possibly be limited to theirs alone.

This does not claim to be a ground-breaking book, but a work of consolidation. Points such as those made above have been developed and debated elsewhere by myself, Claire Tylee, Sandra Gilbert, Suzanne Raitt and Trudi Tate,[4] and by numerous other scholars of literature and history. This book aims to provide a large body of evidence in support of the argument that women wrote a great deal about the war, and that their writings are of interest from a number of perspectives. It is a reference book that might provide leads for those pondering the large questions: did the war change things for women? Were they better or worse off as a result of the war? Was the war a fulfilling or a debilitating experience? Was it responsible for their being given the vote? It should also provide information for those pursuing more detailed or localised studies on, for example, Hector Munro's Ambulance Corps, or the establishment of the Women's Police.

The war years brought together a series of upheavals, providing opportunities, restrictions, possibilities for better pay, poverty, liberation, death, the climax of the suffrage movement, Irish problems, international socialism, artistic experimentation, the Russian Revolution and organised pacifism. Many of these are reflected in the accounts that have been selected, along with, of course, the more mundane descriptions of managing war's upheavals with the minimum of personal and social disruption, or the poignant narratives of passive suffering. I have tried to include materials that reflect the range and complexity of women's responses to the war. The book is not comprehensive, but part of a continuing exploration by scholars of a field that is varied and, in places, still obscure.

The material selected is mostly, but not exclusively, by British women, and, in the case of the fiction and contemporary accounts, was written or published between 1914 and 1939. This is to give a sense of the war's immediacy, while not excluding accounts published in the late 1920s and 1930s, when a great deal of war material reached the public. Foreign language material is not included, neither is American, with one or two exceptions, such as when it relates to British organisation and propaganda, or involves the direct input of a British author (such as Rebecca West's drafting of Corinne Andrews' story). Where material has been translated during the war period and included in the British propaganda field, it has been included. My expertise does not extend to American literature in general, nor to drama nor poetry. A volume two or three times the size of this one would be required to document all such material, and other researchers may have already done this kind of work (as in the case of Catherine Reilly's bibliography: *English Poetry of the First World War*, London: Prior, 1978), or may have relevant work in process.

The range is best seen in the kind of writing included. The section on fiction includes the 'literature' of Virginia Woolf and Katherine Mansfield, the 'middle-brow' contributions of May Wedderburn Cannan and G.B. Stern, and the more popular works by Ruby M. Ayres, Berta Ruck and Brenda Girvin. This sits alongside contemporary accounts, some of which recount experiences of wartime activity or employment, or are direct propagandist appeals to women to play their part in the war effort, or are attempts by political writers such as Helena Swanwick and Catherine Marshall to combine feminist and pacifist ideals. Diaries, letters, autobiographies and archival materials extend, intensify and complicate the range of women's responses to war. A brief account of some women's magazines and journals guides the researcher towards further material, often written from an explicitly ideological position. The section on secondary materials provides accounts of recent work in literary, historical and cultural studies on women and war.

This is not intended as a full guide, but as a starting point for readers interested in this particular subject, or keen to seek out references to a related field. Other guides and bibliographies will supplement it. Some are listed in section I, 'Bibliographies and Reference Works', but it is worth drawing attention to Hager and Taylor's *The Novels of World War 1: An Annotated Bibliography* and Margaret Barrow's *Women 1870–1928* (I1; I16). The first will supplement the fiction list to include male and American writers; the second will give further details on archival sources. This volume, then, does not stand alone. Scholarship, although frequently written up in solitude, is rarely carried out without the help of librarians, archivists and colleagues, whether local or distant.

The theoretical interventions into English Studies over recent years have expanded its boundaries to the extent that, in itself, it can be described as an interdisciplinary subject. Women's Studies, in its institutionalised existence, has always had interdisciplinary ideals. The research undertaken for this volume was carried out in the spirit of those ideals. Inevitably, as a study of women writers, it is grounded in literary studies, but only a few of the writers listed would make their way on to English literature courses. Some might be more likely to find their way onto history courses. Whatever means of defending or expanding the disciplinary boundaries that institutions might develop, it remains the case that studies of this kind have benefited enormously from enquiring into new territory, and from developing new methodological criteria. It would be all too easy to dismiss Berta Ruck and Brenda Girvin as simply 'no good'. Analysis of their writings in terms of the ideologies encoded within a popular literary form, and then perhaps compared with other writings that employ a similar range of discourses or subject positions, provide various lines of enquiry that might contribute to a broad analysis of the representation and self-representation of women in this period. A great deal of the writing is concerned with managing change: the discourses employed in so doing frequently reveal assumptions about class, femininity, national identity and human progress that were under acute pressure during the international crisis.

My hope then, is that this book will encourage readers and researchers to compare varieties of form, voice, genre and experience. It is aimed towards the generally interested reader, of whom I have met many at talks, conferences and day schools I have attended over recent years. It will also, of course, be of use to researchers seeking to develop their holdings in this field, who might already have expertise in women's writing, war writing, popular writing or any other cultural or historical aspects of the First World War. Each entry is annotated to provide an indication of content (e.g. range of experience, attitude towards war), plot (in the case of fiction) and, where appropriate, style. I have not set out to provide critical evaluations lest my own values obscure the merits of particular writings. I am well aware, however, that objectivity might be aspired to, but is rarely achieved. There are occasional cross-references included in the annotations, and an index, which should help to trace further references to individuals or particular areas of First World War experience, whether to do with international espionage or the Ministry of Food.

The book is organised into two parts which deal with primary and secondary material, each divided into sub-sections:

Primary material
A   Fiction
B   Contemporary accounts
C   Diaries, letters and autobiographies
D   Journals
E   Archives.

Secondary material
F   Literary criticism
G   Social and cultural history
H   Biography
I   Bibliographies and reference works.

A   FICTION

The fiction is arranged alphabetically by author, and then chronologically where there is more than one work. A great deal of fiction that came out during and immediately after the war period was popular in form and concerned with managing feminine ideals; it often confined war work within a structure that was both reassuring and provided some level of fantasy. Frequently, the more threatening of war's challenges were held in check by the constraints of romantic fiction, and by the more dominant of the ideologies that provided Britain with its sense of nationhood. Thus the unworthy girl, in these stories, might demonstrate her poor judgement by befriending a German prisoner or spy (Ruck, Girvin; A113, A46, A47), and the good girl all too often wins the right man through a demonstration of pluck and good sense, often acting against the odds (driving a car through the rear of the battlefields; uncovering a spy ring set to destroy a munitions factory). Not all of the endings are unequivocally cheerful: Ruck's *The Years for Rachel* speaks to the anxiety of awaiting a loved one engaged on a dangerous mission (A112).

There is a fair number of spy stories, some faintly humorous, like Mrs Belloc Lowndes' *Good Old Anna*, or *Out of the War?* (A82, A85); others more sinister, such as Dorota Flatau's *Yellow English* (A44), or genuinely troubling, such as Jessie Rickard's *The Light Above the Crossroads* (A104) and Charlotte Mansfield's *The Dupe* (A89). Most popular fiction treats Germans as villains. There are texts, however, more 'middle-brow' in disposition, that are sympathetic to the firm friendships and love affairs that are thwarted by a seemingly arbitrary outbreak of hostilities: Margaret Skelton's *Below the Watchtowers* (A128), Alice Allen's *The Trap* (A3), G.B. Stern's *Children of No Man's Land* (A133). Others, although these are rare, deal overtly with the horrors of German invasion in a Belgian setting: for example, Annie Chartres' *Vae Victus* (A36) and Lilith Hope's *Behold and See!* (A60).

While the romantic fiction tends to restore the hero to the heroine, whether by unexpected valour combined with injury (Ruby Ayres, *Richard Chatterton*, Ethel M. Dell, *The Bars of Iron*; A8, A42) or a series of realisations (Berta Ruck, *In Another Girl's Shoes*; A111), other texts deal more thoughtfully with loss, bereavement and the need to find new structures in a world that has deprived a heroine, not only of her romantic hero, but of all the accompanying moral and psychological certainties. May Wedderburn Cannan, Ruth Holland, Sylvia Thompson and May Sinclair, among others, deal with this central dilemma in varying ways, but it becomes clear in all that a structuring narrative has been wrecked, and the female lead is left to fill the void, either successfully, by restructuring her life through the dignity of work and a second-best hero (Brittain, Cannan), or less satisfactorily, by floundering through a succession of cynically-motivated relationships (Thompson, Evadne Price).

War provides a context of crisis or adventure, in which outmoded conventions seem ripe for overthrow. Mrs Belloc Lowndes demonstrates the amorous excitement that can accompany a sense of liberation in *Lilla: A Part of Her Life* (A83); May Sinclair plays the misjudgements of the suffragette movement against the more acceptable sacrifices in the name of war in *The Tree of Heaven* (A123); Evadne Price demonstrates rather brutally the demolition of genteel, suburban feminine ideals in *'Not So Quiet'* (A129). The war provides opportunities for work, for travel, and for unchaperoned liaisons. It also provides excuses for plot devices such as amnesia, sudden death and self-discovery. In Evadne Price's *'Not So Quiet'* and Vera Brittain's *Honourable Estate* (A28), sexual self-discovery is part of the heroine's renegotiation of her subject identity. In Radclyffe Hall's *The Well of Loneliness* (A49) and Rose Allatini's *Despised and Rejected* (A1) the war precipitates discovery of homosexuality, and the 'freedoms' provided by the war are short-lived and problematic.

Virginia Woolf, for years, was considered anything but a war writer. Recent feminist criticism has altered the general critical view, and it can be illuminating to compare her oblique, allusive style with narratives that pursue in more overt narrative form issues that she develops through a network of images, allusions and symbols. Thus *Teddy, R.N.D.* (A94) might be compared with *Jacob's Room* (A151); the relationship between mother and daughter in *Mrs Dalloway* (A152) might bear comparison with similar relationships in *The Tree of Heaven* and *The Hounds of Spring* (A123, A139); the three-part structure of *To the Lighthouse* (A153) resembles similar structures in novels by Vera Brittain, Sylvia Thompson, Ruth Holland – which share a concern with a central house; and Woolf's allusive critique of patriarchal bellicosity is articulated clearly in Macaulay's *Non-Combatants and Others* and Mary Agnes Hamilton's *Dead Yesterday* (A86, A51).

B CONTEMPORARY ACCOUNTS

The written accounts in this section are non-fictional – at least in the formal sense – and published between 1914 and 1939. They focus clearly on the war, and on women's experiences in relation to mobilisation, armed conflict, employment, domestic life, etc. Many of the accounts are concerned with women's work during the war, whether paid or voluntary, whether inside or outside the home. Thus, while providing information, they often resemble narratives of progress, as the particular qualities of womanhood are increasingly valued by the war-dominated world. A great deal of interest lies in the ways in which authors sought to make sense of women's employment. Those writing with government backing, or from positions of authority within organisations, often made use of domestic imagery to soften women's entry into a mechanised and automated workforce. Some, on the other hand, were keen to emphasise the regimental aspects of work more conventionally associated with the feminine sphere as a way of granting it the authority of being of national importance. Some accounts will have been published primarily to raise funds: Kathleen Burke was known as the 'thousand-dollar-a-minute girl'; organisations such as the Scottish Women's Hospitals, and individuals such as the Two Women of Pervyse were wholly dependent upon voluntary contributions. 'The Two Women of Pervyse', as Elsie Knocker and Mairi Chisholm were known, provide an example of the extraordinary lengths to which women were prepared to go in order to make a meaningful contribution to the war effort. Their dressing station, right behind the fighting lines, attracted considerable attention (and a varied number of visitors) for the medical and human support provided there, and for the resourcefulness of those who staffed it. Elsie Inglis is another who orchestrated her way into the battle zones without waiting for an invitation. The establishment of the Scottish Women's Hospitals in France and Serbia ensured her a dedicated following. Flora Sandes also made her name in Serbia, as a result of joining the army there; thus she became known as the only British woman soldier.

There are numerous books enumerating the war's heroines. They are often women who, through fearlessness and force of character, transgressed conventional lines of decorum and persuaded military and governmental authorities, by example, that women *could* act efficiently in emergency situations. Other accounts are by more ordinary middle-class women, who were persuaded to overcome timidity or deference, or simply to follow a dormant spirit of adventure in order to play a largely anonymous, but deeply appreciated, part in the war. In the majority of cases it was middle- or upper-class women who broke with convention and volunteered for service overseas, in auxiliary organisations, or at overseer level in industry. Indeed, the language of recruitment makes it clear that 'ladies' were particularly required to set an example. One of the effects of this was that working-class women, in public discourse at least, continued to be characterised by their 'tawdry finery', their strangled accents and their tendency to squabble over hats. It was normally those writers committed to radical rather than temporary social change, such as Ada Nield Chew or Sylvia Pankhurst, who were prepared to recognise the nature of the sacrifices made by those who are less economically and socially privileged.

Of course, not all women were in favour of the war. The suffrage movement was split, with the Pankhursts turning their efforts towards recruitment, and the followers of Mrs Fawcett taking the philanthropic line by setting up workrooms and providing resources for Belgian refugees. Some former adherents of the NUWSS, such as Helena Swanwick and Catherine Marshall, turned towards anti-war organisations. Thus, alongside the militant call for women volunteers, there were equally sincere invocations to women to rethink their relationship to bellicosity. Some were made on maternalist grounds (e.g. Ellen Key's book, which was roundly dismissed by Rebecca West, B149); others were concerned with a structure of thought related to internationalism, to a possible union of nations, to a form of international socialism that asserted the importance of women's roles in active political, industrial and economic life. The Hague Peace Congress of 1915 provided a focal point for this debate.

Material in this section, then, sets out to inform, to provide propaganda on behalf of government and other auxiliary agencies, to educate as to, for example, more economic methods of food and fuel consumption, and to provide individual accounts of war experience. Some pieces are published in order to launch new organisations (such as the Fight for Right movement), others to stimulate debate around issues concerned with socialism, pacifism and, of course, the rights and qualities of women. The section includes biographies of notable women published before 1939 – such as Elsie Inglis and Florence Nightingale – when those women played a prominent part in the war.

C   DIARIES, LETTERS AND AUTOBIOGRAPHIES

This section is sub-divided into the forms named above. The autobiographies cover more of the life of the individual than war experience alone – thus the Baroness de T'Serclaes (Elsie Knocker) tells of the unhappy childhood and ill-advised marriage that forced her to train as nurse and cook and provided space to fuel her obsession with motorbikes, which left her peculiarly well-qualified to join Hector Munro's team in Flanders.

Material in sections A and B, 'Fiction' and 'Contemporary accounts', is more likely to be written by 'the daughters of educated men' than by working women. The same social class predominates here, but there *are* autobiographies, by, for example, Kathleen Dayus, Louise Jermy and Annie Kenney, that provide insights into working-class lives, ordinary and extraordinary. There are also accounts of women who, for reasons of marriage, remained in Germany as German subjects during the war (see Blücher and Pless), accounts of experience on the Russian and Serbian fronts and, closer to home, the autobiographies of, for example, Katherine Furse, Mary Agnes Hamilton, Lena Ashwell, Ottoline Morrell, provide accounts of the texture of political and literary life during and around the war.

The diaries and letters are similarly revealing. Enid Bagnold's *Diary Without Dates* and May Sinclair's *Journal of Impressions* are both well known by now. Sarah Macnaughtan's diary provides a fascinating account of her work in France and Belgium, and Haillie Eustace Miles reveals some interesting attitudes prevalent in wartime England. Katherine Mansfield's diaries and letters illuminate her own war experience, and reflect on those around her, including Woolf, Lawrence and her beloved bother, who died in the war. Woolf herself, notoriously oblique about the war, made that famous, and similarly oblique comment describing the 'preposterous masculine fiction' purveyed in the press, in a letter to Margaret Llewelyn Davies.

This is not the place for a theoretical interjection on autobiography, discourse, voice and plural or conflicting ideologies, but the material outlined in this section, particularly if read alongside that in the earlier sections, provides plenty of opportunities for enquiries of that kind.

D   JOURNALS

This is a brief guide to some of the journals and magazines that provided a commentary on the week-by-week or month-by-month events of the war. The penny weeklies, predictably, commented on domestic savings, knitting patterns and ways of managing the departure of husband, son, father or fiancé. The political journals, such as *The Vote*, *The Woman's Dreadnought* and *Jus Suffragii* provided commentary on suffrage activity, the various rifts and reorganisations that war engendered and, in the case of the last named, international peace news.

E   ARCHIVES

There are, of course, hundreds of archive collections all over the world that will contain papers, documents and manuscripts relating to the authors named in this volume. I have not attempted to provide an account that covers holdings of individual authors, and would refer readers to a directory of manuscript locations for information of that kind. Instead, I have taken the two major archives of First World War material in this country – the Imperial War Museum, London, and the Liddle Collection, Brotherton Library, Leeds – and have outlined what they have in the way of holdings on women's war experience. Both collections are large and continually expanding, and both are invaluable for gaining increasingly detailed and intricate insights into a range of women's war experiences that do not always find their way into print.

The Imperial War Museum, in addition to papers reflecting experiences as varied as those of nurses in Serbia, women signallers, a child in the East End, a governess in Russia and an MI5 secretary, holds the diaries of Florence Farmborough, Irene Rathbone and Mrs St Clair Stobart. The Liddle Collection is equally varied and expansive. It takes its name from the former Keeper, Dr Peter Liddle, who was largely responsible for building up and maintaining the archive.

The section itself provides a more detailed introduction to these archives, plus further brief comments on some other useful collections.

F, G, H, I   SECONDARY MATERIALS

This part is very heavily selected, largely because, in printed form, an account of this kind will rapidly go out of date. The availability of bibliographies in electronic format means that the researcher can easily find the more recently published material through the use of key search words.

The material that is included provides a guide to research on women in the First World War in the fields of literature, social and cultural history, and biography. A final section lists useful bibliographies and reference works. Biographies published before 1939 are listed in the Contemporary Accounts section (B). No attempt has been made to be exhaustive. There are bibliographies in existence on individual authors; this attempts to deal specifically with a focus on the First World War.

I am completing this bibliography on the eightieth anniversary of the Armistice. Two minutes of silence have been observed in order to commemorate those men who died in the war, and to reflect on its effect on our culture and history. I have no wish to underestimate the suffering of those men, nor the effect of their loss. I do wish, however, to invite consideration of the roles played by women in the conflict: consideration of their activities – domestic, political, professional, voluntary – and of their own reflections. In recent years the fiction of Pat Barker and Sebastian Faulks has done a great deal to bring the First World War alive to an audience approaching the end of the twentieth century. I hope that this volume will act as encouragement and aid to further detailed consideration, and extensive research.

NOTES

1 Simon Featherstone describes this argument in his *War Poetry* (London: Routledge, 1995), pp. 95–104.
2 Pankhurst, Christabel *The War* (London: The Women's Social and Political Union, 1914) (B110).
3 Brittain, Vera *Testament of Experience* (London: Victor Gollancz, 1959, reprinted Virago, 1979), p. 77 (C48).
4 See particularly Ouditt *Fighting Forces, Writing Women: Identity and Ideology in the First World War* (London: Routledge, 1994); Tylee *The Great War and Women's Consciousness* (Macmillan 1990); Gilbert and Gubar *No Man's Land: The Place of the Woman Writer in the Twentieth Century* (vol. II, New Haven CT and London: Yale University Press, 1989); Raitt and Tate (eds) *Women's Fiction and the Great War* (Oxford: Clarendon Press, 1997) (F72; F92; F34; F79).

Part I

PRIMARY SOURCES

A

FICTION

I   NOVELS

A1   Allatini, Rose (pseudonym A. T. Fitzroy) *Despised and Rejected*,
London: C.W. Daniel, 1918. Reprinted New York: Arno Press, 1975.

Centres on the story of Dennis Blackwood, musician, homosexual and pacifist, a
conscientious objector, despite the vigorous opposition of his more conservative
family. A parallel plot concerns Antoinette, a lesbian, whose suffering, in this militaristic context, is comparatively slight. Dennis falls in love with Alan, an Oxford-
educated mine-owner's son, and a socialist, who regularly meets a crowd of
'outsiders' in a basement café. Much of the substance of the novel is taken up with
'speeches' articulating the various standpoints of the individuals, marginalised for
their sexuality, their politics, their disability or their race. The homosexuality is
explained as one of the 'poor little deformities' in an evolutionary process, which is
heading towards 'the human soul complete in itself, perfectly balanced' (349).
Ultimately, the Christ image prevails: 'They're despised and rejected of their fellow
men today. What they suffer in a world not yet ready to admit their right to existence, their right to love, no normal person can realise' (348).

The novel was banned, and the publisher successfully prosecuted for sedition
under DORA. It is rare to find a novel that begins in a formally conservative way,
but goes on to reject so many social conventions so completely.

A2   Allen, Alice Maud (pseudonym Allen Havens) *Silhouette*, London:
Chapman & Dodd Ltd, 1923.

Written in a popular style, but with a political setting – the postwar 'Working
Women's Conference'. One of the reps, Miss Lee Howard, is, ideologically, a
'Labour Woman', but with the demeanour and background of a 'lady'. She supports
total disarmament, policed by an international inspectorate, and finds herself up
against, on the one hand, the spirit of entrepreneurial capitalism (represented by
Lord Fowell) and, on the other, a younger, more feisty, 'war-made' opponent, Pearl
Smith. The novel debates the appeal of war work, of marriage, the future of
Europe, the rhetorical appeal of the 'Mothers of the Race'. Ultimately, in a vote for
the post of International Secretary, Lee Howard gives way to Pearl Smith, feeling
that she has been beaten by her 'silhouette', the product of thirty years' training,
and that she belongs neither to the world of the past, nor of the present.

11

A3   Allen, Alice Maud (pseudonym Allen Havens) *The Trap,* London: Hogarth Press, 1931.

A novel in four parts (Prologue, The Eve, The War, Epilogue), that represents the war, and reactions to it from the perspectives of women, workers, artists, pacifists, fighters of a number of nationalities, political affiliations and generations. Has an almost Lukacsian range of characters, among whom Rachel Butterworth and Ian Fisher are central. The novel follows their relationship from prewar discussions on the relationship in Germany between militarism and Romanticism, through to Ian's death, following a meeting with his 'enemy' friend, Rudolf. The work of women involved in the IWSA and, later, the League of Nations, provides a backdrop to debates that circulate around the power of the ideology of war and an alternative, artistic, idealistic vision. Ends with a sense of loss and of the destructive force of brutish modernity.

A4   Andrews, Corinne *War Nurse: The True Story of a Woman Who Lived, Loved and Suffered on the Western Front,* New York: Cosmopolitan Book Corporation, 1930.

A first-person narrative, relating the experiences of an American woman who signs on as a voluntary nurse in France and falls in love with Waldron Hiller, an ambulance driver turned aviator. They have a sexual relationship, and spend some 'crazy' nights in Paris. They plan to marry, once Waldron can talk round his recalcitrant grandfather. She has to return home for an operation and hears that, meanwhile, Waldron has married someone else. The war ends, she travels a great deal and a few years later meets Waldron by chance in New York: they resume their relationship. The novel seems to be about the barbarism that war unleashes, and which is inescapable, no matter how tidy and Puritan one's upbringing might have been: 'finding myself in primitive conditions I just had to choose a man that went with them' (264).

The novel was ghosted by Rebecca West, in order to appear as a serial in New York's *Cosmopolitan* magazine, under West's name. She had her name removed when it was published in book form.

See Glendinning, *Rebecca West* (H15) for further details.

Ashton, Winifred *see* Dane, Clemence.

A5   Askew, Alice and Claude *Nurse!,* London: Hodder and Stoughton, 1916.

A story that sets a compassionate, wise and saintly girl (Elizabeth, who had recently inherited some money) against a materialistic, vain and shallow one, called Amy. When war is declared Elizabeth, who is already a trained nurse, goes out to Belgium to work in a field hospital. Among her patients is Cuthbert Herbert, who adores Amy, and whose uncle Elizabeth had nursed prior to the war. Cuthbert's uncle had warned him against girls like Amy, but still Cuthbert fails to comprehend Amy's basically faithless nature. The novel ends with Amy flitting with some of Elizabeth's money and Uncle Herbert returning from the (presumed) dead to identify Elizabeth as the nurse to whom he had left his fortune.

A6   Asquith, Cynthia *The Spring House*, London: Michael Joseph Ltd, 1936.

Opens May 1915. Miranda Grey, cradled in the grace and opulence of her family's home, is sitting out the war with her son, while her husband is in Canada. She has her portrait painted a few times and takes on a little nursing work, but the centre of the story concerns her relationship with another man, John (who ultimately gets killed), the effect on her and her older brother of a younger brother's death in battle, and the views and activities of various other family members and friends. Her husband dies, having (she discovers) only recently asked her for a divorce. The book is about the effect on her of the war, and her need, in the end, to face the future with her son, being sure of having been loved in the past.

A7   Atherton, Gertrude *The White Morning, A Novel of the Power of the German Women in Wartime*, New York: Frederick A. Stokes Co., 1918.

Not seen.

A8   Ayres, Ruby M. *Richard Chatterton, V. C.*, London: Hodder and Stoughton, 1915.

' "A laggard in love and a laggard in war; What did they give him his manhood for?" Richard Chatterton, the hero of Miss Ruby M. Ayres' delightful romance, began as both, but ended by being neither, and it is round this theme that the authoress has written her tale so charmingly and with such refreshing daintiness...' says the publisher's catalogue. Plot revolves around the relationship between the (initially feckless) Richard and the wealthy Sonia. Richard, having been rejected by Sonia, secretly heads off for France and receives the highest decoration for brave deeds. He returns, wounded, but accompanied by an attractive young nurse. Sonia in the meantime has taken up with his 'friend', Montague. The friend turns out to be a bounder, the nurse a peach, and the right pair eventually are reunited.

A9   Ayres, Ruby M. *The Long Lane to Happiness*, London: Hodder & Stoughton, 1915.

A direct sequel to the above (A8), whose loose ends take on new life, and tangle up to produce cause for jealousy and mistrust between the newly married Richard and Sonia. Montague is jealous. He plots to separate Richard and Sonia. Richard, however, tells no-one that he has been given only six months to live, and goes off, secretly, to have an operation, from which he recovers. War is a backdrop, rather than an active plot mechanism. Members of the supporting cast leave to fight and are reported killed. Sonia, still a 'girl', finds it impossible to take responsibility for her part in a future decision as to whether or not Richard should go back.

A10   Ayres, Ruby M. *'Invalided Out'*, London: Hodder & Stoughton, 1918.

A young Captain, invalided out of the army, goes as a paying guest to a family, and proposes to the daughter. However, he encounters her step-sister, Pauline, one evening (unwittingly) and hears how he has been entrapped by a scheming mother for the sake of his wealth – he is the heir to the local manor house. The Captain builds up a relationship with Pauline mainly around the household of her exiled sister, Julia, who has a young husband in the army. Pauline and the Captain ultimately marry. The novel, a popular romance, debates issues concerned with wealth, jealousy, pride and, of course, true love.

A11   Bagnold, Enid *The Happy Foreigner*, London: W. Heinemann, 1920. Reprinted London: Virago, 1987.

A love story, inspired by Bagnold's experience as an army driver, and set in the unpromising landscape of France, immediately following the Armistice. Contains a lot of documentary detail regarding the experience of driving under difficult conditions, but is mostly concerned with the heroine's growing self-reliance as she realises that the relationship cannot flourish, and must be ended by demobilisation.

A12   Barclay, Florence L. *My Heart's Right There*, London: G.P. Putnam's Sons, 1914.

A cottage home in England yields its willing man, Jim, leaving Polly and Tiny to manage bravely. Jim sends letters describing how he gave up his bread ration to a starving Belgian woman and child, but yet is not depressed by these things. He gets wounded and well looked after – the King and Queen visit the hospital, and he *knows* they feel for *him*. He returns home to convalesce. There are things he can't tell Polly about, and things he can – such as his faith, prayers and reverence for Field Marshal Roberts. Simple and patronising; would be quite at home in one of the women's penny weeklies.

A13   Benson, Stella *I Pose*, London: Macmillan, 1915.

The story of the Suffragette and the Gardener. Self-conscious authorial interjections, satirical in style; self-consciously naive and non-realist. No direct commentary on the war, although some reflection on suffrage practices which arguably contribute to the debate on the relationship between women and violence. For example: 'The gardener, of course, shared the views of all decent men on this subject. One may virtuously destroy life in a good cause, but to destroy property is a heinous crime, whatever its motive' (12).

A14   Benson, Stella *This Is The End*, London: Macmillan, 1917.

The story of Jay, a bus conductor in London, during the war. Offsets the material world of London, war work committees, raids, war news with a fantastical House by the Sea, and a Secret Friend.

A15   Benson, Stella *Living Alone*, London: Macmillan 1919.

A witch interrupts a committee meeting and disrupts its pompous sense of worthiness with magic. One of the more distinguished members, Lady Arabel Higgins, has a son, who, it transpires, is a wizard, on leave from the army. Descriptions of an air raid – from below, in a church crypt – and from above, as the English witch meets a German witch, and finds her spouting just the same nonsense as is written in the *Daily Mail*, but with the names of the countries transposed. The witch is charged with an offence against DORA: of possessing a flying machine (her broomstick). She heads off to America, 'the greater House of Living Alone'. Fantastical, whimsical narrative, satirising the complacency of some British attitudes, but not entirely without sympathy.

A16   Bentley, Phyllis *Cat-in-the-Manger*, London: Sidgwick & Jackson, 1923.

Love story in a postwar setting. Bertha, who is deeply affected by the death of her younger brother in Gallipoli, is looking for a husband. She finally marries William Henry Irwell, but only after some serious complications arising from Irwell's divorce, and from the attentions of Eustace Hollins, who, having been in the same regiment as brother Fred, is warmly welcomed by the family.

A17   Bentley, Phyllis *A Modern Tragedy*, London: Victor Gollancz, 1934.

Postwar, West Riding setting. Mostly concerned with industrial power, greed, fear, the hunger marches, but intercut with memories of war losses, particularly at Passchendaele.

A18   Black, Dorothy *Her Lonely Soldier*, London: Hodder & Stoughton, 1916.

Predictable love story drawing on the wartime popularity of 'Lonely Soldier' adverts in newspapers. Young Cicely is married to elderly James. She perches, flutters and strokes his hair while he 'protects' her. She returns a lost diary to a 'lonely soldier', meets him and they fall in love. James dies, leaving his blessing. The soldier is in a fierce battle, feared dead. Cicely meets a kindly Red Cross lady (the Duchess of Rushmere) who persuades her to become a volunteer. She does and, lo and behold, discovers the soldier in the amnesiacs' ward. He is cured, they marry and live happily ever after.

Blanco-White, Amber *see* Reeves, Amber.

A19   Borden, Mary *Sarah Gay*, London: W. Heinemann Ltd, 1931.

Meandering love story set in Paris in 1918. Sarah Howick is married to Lord Howick, a rich Viscount, twice her age. Life with him and their children bores her, however, and the war offers the chance of stimulating work with the Red Cross. She meets and falls in love with the feckless, ne'er-do-well John Gay, Captain of British Infantry. When she returns home to care for her ill daughter, John begins an affair. Sarah returns to Paris, finds out, bursts in on them, fires a gun and misses, faints, and is applauded by the whole of Paris. Her husband in the meantime has died. She and Johnnie marry, he works in the family banking business (the war has finished by this point) the girls are provided for, they all live happily in England. Seems to be exploring the nature of love and moral responsibility in the context of a changing world.

A20   Bottome, Phyllis *The Captive*, London: Chapman & Hall, 1915.

Not seen.

A21   Bottome, Phyllis *Secretly Armed*, London: Chapman & Hall Ltd, 1916.

Title comes from Rupert Brooke: 'Secretly armed against all death's endeavour.'

Tells, in humorous tones, the story of Major Winn Staines, who enters into a disastrous marriage which he manages to escape by going abroad for the sake of his health. There he finds true love and is happy. He finds out from his doctor that war is imminent, but that he has only two years to live. With this in view he says goodbye to his wife, joins his regiment and soon sets off for France. He dies an heroic death, in battle, leading his men.

A22   Bottome, Phyllis *A Servant of Reality*, London: Hodder & Stoughton, 1919.

The novel centres on the thoughts and feelings of Anthony Arden, a rising young surgeon, who had been a German prisoner for two years. His brother, Henry, is reluctant to listen to anything beyond the most superficial details, while his sister, Daphne, is full of tenderness and realises immediately that he has been deeply hurt. He develops a relationship with Kitty, which does not meet with approval. Mostly concerned with 'proper behaviour' in the context of the personal devastation inflicted by war.

A23   Bottome, Phyllis *Old Wine*, London: W. Collins Sons & Co. Ltd, 1926.

A novel set in Austria at the end of the war. It follows the experiences of an American journalist, Carol Hunter, who finds herself in a relief mission. Explores the relationships between capital, power, political interests, honour, vanity and business. The mood is one of intense cynicism and corruption, the fruits of an old empire.

A24   Brazil, Angela *A Patriotic Schoolgirl*, London and Glasgow: Blackie & Son, n.d. [1919].

Marjorie and Dona set off for boarding school, where Marjorie lands herself in quite a few scrapes, owing to her high-spirited patriotism. The acid-drop teacher turns out to be a lovable aunt of a poorly child (her sister had married beneath her); the temperamental school-chum is the German spy (*not* the teacher); there's a Red Cross Hospital nearby with a lovely nurse (a relative) and some gallant brotherly heroes, and the whole thing is rounded off with a cry of 'God Save the King!'

A25   Brazil, Angela *A Harum-Scarum Schoolgirl*, London & Glasgow, Blackie & Son, n.d. [1920].

An American girl, whose father is off to Paris on Embassy business, is dumped at the school and makes a firm friend of Loveday. There is a wartime setting, with references to WAACs and WRNs, and the new Head (the old one, heroine of a war-wedding, has gone off with her husband) develops a scheme to teach the girls land work. Lots of scrapes (mostly on the part of the undisciplined but well-meaning American girl), false accusations, surprise discoveries and in the end, the not-so-wealthy Loveday ends up with an inheritance that is enough to send her to agricultural college.

A26   Brazil, Angela *A Popular Schoolgirl*, London and Glasgow: Blackie & Son, 1920.

This story has an immediately postwar setting. Ingred is reunited with her father,

Mr Saxon, and her brothers Egbert and Athelsane, who have only just been demo-
bilised, and with her older sister Quenrede, who is a little disappointed: 'It's *too*
bad that just when I'm old enough all the jolly things are closed to women!' They
all have to face some readjustment, though, when their parents break the news that
they are not to return to their country estate, lent to the Red Cross during the war.
Their architect father has lost commissions, his investments are worthless – they
are the new poor. A change of status causes difficulties for Ingred at school, but the
good deal with it well, the bad, badly and, in the end, having made sacrifices and
pulled through as a family, all is restored.

A27   Brittain, Vera *The Dark Tide*, London: Grant Richards, 1923.

Brittain's first novel, dedicated to Winifred Holtby. It tells the story of Daphne
Lethbridge, who returns to Oxford after 'a war that had brought her neither
personal sorrow nor romantic adventures' (9), and her friendship with Virginia
Dennison, who is more clever, better focussed, and who, like Brittain herself, faced
the demands of nursing during the war. Daphne's more simple disposition leads her
into a foolish marriage. Her husband leaves her with a (literal) blow that delivers
her, prematurely, of a crippled child. Virginia helps her to come to terms with her
own values and her mistakes, a process which gives her the dignity to withstand
her husband's histrionics when he attempts to return to her. A novel about the
dignity of work (Daphne intends to be a writer, Virginia returns to nursing), which
is among the war's legacies to women.

A28   Brittain, Vera *Honourable Estate*, London: Victor Gollancz, 1936.

Large-scale novel covering two families across two generations. Ruth, who takes a
first from Oxford, serves with the VAD and does postwar service in Russia, fulfils
some of the feminist dreams of her mother-in-law Janet, whose aspirations were
thwarted, and who died lonely and in poverty in London's East End. Ruth marries
Janet's son, Denis, who always had sympathy with his mother's suffragette
projects. The final section concerns Ruth's own family and professional development. She has her twins immediately following preparations for the Great Strike
(thus depriving herself of transport necessary to bear her children safely and
thereby mirroring the experience of a former employee in her parents' well-to-do
household). There are lengthy comments on the need for mothers to interest themselves in politics, so that they might prevent their children being destroyed in
another war. Links (in political speeches delivered on lecture tours and in an election campaign) peace, the women's movement and the eradication of poverty. Very
optimistic, considering the growth of fascism in the late 1930s.

A29   Buckrose, J.E. (pseudonym of Annie Edith Jameson) *The Silent Legion*,
         London: Hodder & Stoughton, 1918.

A love story, set in spring 1917, based around the inhabitants of Chestnut Avenue,
and focussing on the Simpson family. Barbara returns from nursing to look after
her ailing mother, meets a soldier called Brooke, who wants her to marry him and
go to live in Canada. Barbara is reluctant to do this on account of her mother's
health, but her mother reassures her that her happiness elsewhere is more important
than her unhappiness at home. The narrative includes a war wedding, a war
baby (called Kitchener) and various comic episodes concerning blackouts and

misunderstandings, and charts a generally downwardly mobile trend as the war economy eats into the pockets of ordinary folk.

A30   Buckrose, J.E. (pseudonym of Annie Edith Jameson) *Marriage While You Wait*, London: Hodder & Stoughton, 1919.

Devoted to one of the more contentious social events of the hostilities: a war wedding. This tells the story of how it might be done, beginning with the meeting of the young couple and finishing with the conventional happy ending.

A31   Butts, Mary *Ashe of Rings*, Paris: Contract Editions, Three Mountain Press, n.d. [1925].

A strange tale of myth, magic, ritual and inheritance, set in a house called Rings, where Anthony Ashe, following the death of his son, needs an heir. The first part is set before the war; the second, twelve years later, in 1917, when Ashe's daughter, Vanna, exists in an environment tinged with violence and destruction, and peopled by Judy, a friend, and a Russian painter called Serge. Vanna is finally reconciled with her mother, who had been picked for breeding purposes, and discarded by her father: her intellect seemed to him unimpressive, her desires banal. The style is fragmented and allusive, representing a tapestry of knowledge, history, and family lore that Anthony Ashe instilled in his daughter.

A32   Cannan, Joanna Maxwell *High Table*, London: Ernest Benn, 1931.

An 'Oxford' novel. A character study of Theodore Fletcher who, in the years before the war achieves his ambition and becomes Warden of St Mary's College. The war provides Oxford with changes, an increasing military presence, and a young soldier whom Theodore believes to be his son from a brief, failed, early relationship. The differences between the young, vivacious Lennie, who marries his sweetheart Doreen, and the older, self-searching man who has begun to see his life as a series of failures, are explored. Joanna Cannan was the daughter of the Dean of Trinity College.

A33   Cannan, May Wedderburn *The Lonely Generation*, London: Hutchinson, 1934.

The story of Delphine, brought up by her father and his philosophising, artistic friends, until he dies and Delphine is sent to live with her more practical aunt. Becomes engaged to Bobbie, who goes to Sandhurst and to India, and goes off to fight on the outbreak of war. Delphine does VAD work until she hears of Bobbie's death. Recovering from near collapse, she takes a job, procured by an Oxford friend of her father's, at the Ministry of Information in Paris. A large section of the novel, however, is concerned with her postwar life. She feels that she 'belongs' to the war and to an England characterised by chivalry, endurance and honesty: prewar values. She doesn't fit into the 'dance mad' England of the 1920s, in which work is hard to find for gently bred women without university education, and is troubled by unwelcome advances from her over-confident and ill-bred boss. Finally, having suffered near-poverty, she turns again to her father's friend who finds her a job with a publisher. The novel ends with the possibility of her marrying an ex-soldier, similarly affected by the war, who shares her passion for

Housman's poetry. The novel is characterised by its chivalric, often romantic, phraseology particularly in the first part, and, on the other hand, by the detail of Delphine's financial difficulties, her impoverished living conditions, and the unpleasant nature of those with whom she works before being restored to moneyed gentility by Lucius Carey. It seems to be about a woman, determined to live independently and honestly, according to her own (outdated) values, but being unable to do so in the postwar world without some help from the established order. May Wedderburn Cannan was Joanna Cannan's sister.

A34   Castle, Agnes (Sweetman) and Egerton *The Hope of the House*, London: Cassell & Co., 1915.

The novel opens with 20-year-old David Owen being advised to sell Treowen, the family's Welsh country seat. He declines to do so, and sets himself up as a farmer instead, despite the sacrifices necessary. Ten years later, his younger brother Johnny is all set to marry the tousle-haired, free-spirited Peg, when he is killed in the war. Peggy, despite her own grief, is instrumental in uniting the rather dour David with Vivianne, a Belgian refugee, who has suffered a series of losses and betrayals. The novel is resolved, then, in favour of the house, rather than the most likeable characters.

A35   Cather, Willa *One of Ours*, London: Heinemann, 1923.

The story of a young American who leaves behind his rural setting in order to take part in this major European conflagration.

A36   Chartres, Annie (Vivanti) *Vae Victus*, London: Edward Arnold, 1917.

A novel about the horrific effects of violence and rape. Two Belgian women and a girl are in their home when it is suddenly overrun by brutal and drunken German officers. Chérie and Louise are raped; Mireille, Louise's daughter, witnesses the attack. They arrive in England, as refugees, and are housed with the Whitakers. Mireille is now deaf and dumb; Louise and Chérie are hardly cheerful company. Both women find that they are pregnant. Louise, with great difficulty, asks that her pregnancy be terminated; a compassionate doctor grants her wish. Chérie blanks out the meaning of the experience – but gives birth to her child. They return to Belgium. Louise's husband and Chérie's fiancé are found to be safe, but the latter leaves, cursing the child. Mireille's illness is cured when she offers the child a blessing that no-one else will give it.

A37   Conyers, Dorothea *The Scratch Pack*, London: Hutchinson & Co., 1916.

Combination of love story, spy story and fox-hunting story, set on the south coast of Ireland. The main participants are Gheena, Darby Dillon (who has been permanently injured in a polo accident) and an American, Basil Stafford. Gheena, initially, would like to marry Darby (who buys her father's horses) but, after she finds a store of petrol in a hidden cave, suspects Basil of being a spy, is captured by the Germans, escapes from them and unwittingly lures them into a trap, she finds that it is (the innocent) Basil that she cares for after all.

A38 Dane, Clemence (pseudonym of Winifred Ashton) *First the Blade*, London: Heinemann, 1918.

The story of an immature couple's immature love (hence the title, which comes from Mark iv. 28: 'First the blade, then the ear, after that the full corn in the ear'). Self-consciously set and narrated at some point during the war: 'The postman has gone by for the last time to-night – no letters – but the news was not so bad to-day – the Russians have taken prisoners – our front is quiet – we dare forget the war for an hour' (1). The war interrupts the love affair of the hero and heroine, which has already been disrupted by a serious disagreement. There is no conclusion, only a narrative interjection: 'They're not real people! They're not real troubles! Only marionettes that we have set a-jig-jigging up and down our mantelpiece to make us laugh o'nights and forget the unending war' (297). The absence of closure seems to mimic the unfinished war and the sense of forces beyond the control of author or narrator.

Dashwood E.E.M. *see* Delafield, E.M.

A39 Deane, Peter (pseudonym of Pamela Hinkson) *The Victors*, London: Constable, 1925.

First-person narrative, male perspective, the subject of which is Michael. Michael left school to fight in the war, but once that war is over, the world has no place for him. He tries to find a future for himself, but ends by committing suicide in a rented bed-sitting room. The tale is told with a grim energy, by one of Michael's friends, who, towards the end says: 'I thought if Siegfried Sassoon had been there, he could have written a poem perhaps on a world where there was only room for the old.'

See Hugh Cecil, *The Flower of Battle* (F21) for further information.

A40 Deane, Peter (pseudonym of Pamela Hinkson) *Harvest*, London: Hodder & Stoughton, 1927.

A tale set in postwar Germany and told, again, from a masculine perspective, with a grim, angry tone. The harvest is that of despair. The cruelties of peace for the women and children of occupied Germany are outlined – their hunger, humiliation, rape. A French soldier is in love with a German girl, but their relationship can have no future: 'He and she, children of today, were just pawns, helpless things against the will of nations.'

A41 Delafield, E.M. *The War-Workers*, London: Heinemann, 1918.

A satire of the cult of (upper class) personality and of the accompanying short-sighted devotion to work of the lady volunteer, who desires a combination of power, national importance and unquestioning deference from the 'girls' in her charge. Miss Charmian Vivian manages the Midland Supply Depot, with the devoted loyalty of a number of other helpers. She hogs all the responsibility, and the others think her 'wonderful', until, that is, the common-sensical perspective of Grace Jones, plus Miss Vivian's neglect of her father who suffers a stroke, tarnish her resplendent surface. Speaks to the need for moderation in war work, for a sensible attitude which accounts for all of women's responsibilities – which include those of the home and its residents. The norm is articulated by Charmian's mother, by Grace Jones and by a Staff Officer, John Trevellyan, who provides the romantic interest.

De La Pasture, Edmee Elizabeth *see* Delafield, E.M.

A42   Dell, Ethel M. *The Bars of Iron*, London: Putnam's, 1916.

A conventional love story, in which the war figures as a *deus ex machina* to reunite the central couple. Avery Denys, a young widow and mother's help, meets and eventually marries the tempestuous Piers, heir to the local manor. Only after the wedding does she realise that it was Piers who, six years earlier, had killed her drunken husband in a fight. When she finds out she finds it difficult to forgive and, in her grief and confusion, loses her baby. At the outbreak of war (more than three-quarters of the way through the novel), Piers sets off for France without telling Avery. She comes to her senses and forgives him; he is badly wounded, and rescued by the local doctor, his one-time rival. Eventually they are reunited, both having suffered and matured, and are presumed to live happily ever after.

A43   Diver, (Katherine Helen) Maud *Unconquered: A Romance*, London: John Murray, 1917.

A novel in which the gallant and aristocratic hero has to learn to distinguish the right girl from the wrong one. Sir Mark Forsyth is engaged to Miss Bel Alison. He goes off to fight and is reported missing, believed killed. In the meantime his mother and Sheila Melrose also go to Boulogne, and Bel, under the influence of Miss O'Neill (guilty of a 'wrong-headed zeal for the Suffrage and Home Rule'), begins to make speeches in favour of pacifism. Mark is rediscovered, lame and with no voice. The relationship with Bel is broken off, and Sheila, the gentle, kind one, takes her place.

A44   Flatau, Dorota *Yellow English*, London: Hutchinson & Co., 1918.

A German spy story. It opens in 1891, when Otto Friedrich Schultz, a self-made banker, marries the widowed and impecunious Lady Mary Cranleigh. He hires a German woman to 'instruct' their son, and personally ensures that he grows up learning to observe, to manipulate, to lie in order to get what he wants and to prey on the good will of others. He goes to Eton then Oxford, gets a job in the Foreign Office and marries. Lady Mary divorces her husband when she finds out. Her son, however, betrays the English and is hurled from a cliff by the wives of drowned sailors, whom he helped to kill, when his espionage is discovered. His son is also killed. The novel ends with an unpleasantly robust invocation to the people of England to show no mercy for his kind.

A45   Fulton, Mary *Grass of Parnassus*, London: Chapman & Hall, 1923.

A postwar setting to a novel that speaks to the restlessness that war engendered in some women, who were unassuaged by the banalities of wife-and-motherhood. Viola, a Catholic, has been married to Dick for some time, and the marriage now feels stale. He agrees that she might travel in Italy, taking their daughter and governess with her. When in Rome, she meets Nicola, a passionate man, who has returned from the war a champion of the poor, the noble 'grand heroes of the war', who are subject to a corrupt government. They fall in love, travel together, but ultimately he kills her in a passionate fit of jealousy. This is a thoughtful novel, with a great deal of detail. Unusual.

A46   Girvin, Brenda *Munition Mary*, London: Humphrey Milford, Oxford University Press, 1918.

The story of Mary, who uncovers a spy-ring centred on a munitions factory. Plot involves convincing the factory owner that women are good workers and, in any case, essential to the war effort; a romantic liaison between Mary and the factory owner's nephew; and an adventure element as Mary discovers the plans of the spy, Mrs Webb, who runs the canteen and is intent on sabotaging the reputation of women as workers, and on actually sabotaging the factory, by means of zeppelins and lights.

A47   Girvin, Brenda *Jenny Wren*, London: Humphrey Milford, Oxford University Press, 1920.

Jenny, the daughter of an Admiral, is a charming girl, but has the reputation of being something of a blabbermouth. This is put to the test when she gets a decoding job at the naval base and has to keep secrets. A childhood friend, Henry Corfield, now in charge of a fishing trawler (which is really a destroyer in disguise) is unsure that she's up to the job. To make matters worse, there *is* a spy, and Henry suspects Jenny. By elaborate means, involving fortune tellers and red ink, Jenny discovers the wrongdoer. The Armistice is signed, Jenny and Henry find renewed confidence in each other, and all ends happily.

A48   Hale, Beatrice Forbes-Robertson *The Nest-builder: A Novel*, New York: F.A. Stokes Co., 1916.

An English girl called Mary and an American artist, Stefan, meet on board a ship and marry all too rapidly. Mary is the nest-builder; Stefan uses art to escape the selfishness of his own nature. War setting.

A49   Hall, Radclyffe *The Well of Loneliness*, London: Jonathan Cape, 1928. Reprinted London: Virago, 1982.

A lesbian classic, famous for its trial in 1928, in which Virginia Woolf, among others, testified in favour of the author. It is the story of the 'invert' Stephen Gordon, who responds (just over half-way through the novel) to the call of war: 'England was calling her men into battle, her women to the bedsides of the wounded and dying, and between these two chivalrous, surging forces, she, Stephen, might well be crushed out of existence' (271). She joins an ambulance column, however, and 'finds herself' in a role that demands authority, courage, strength, is awarded the *croix de guerre* and receives three mentions in despatches. The period of self-fulfilment, though, is brief: 'Great wars will be followed by great discontents – the pruning knife has been laid to the tree, and the urge to grow throbs through its mutilated branches' (298). Comments on the postwar rejection of lesbian women: 'England had called them and they had come; for once, unabashed, they had faced the daylight. And now because they were not prepared to slink back and hide in their holes and corners, the very public whom they had served was the first to turn round and spit on them; to cry: "Away with this canker in our midst, this nest of unrighteousness and corruption!" ' (412). Interesting for contemporary notions of sexuality (derived from Krafft-Ebing, Karl Ulrichs, Edward Carpenter, amongst others), and for discourse of chivalry, combat and sacrifice.

A50   Hamilton, Cicely *William – An Englishman*, London: Skeffington, 1919.

A satire on extreme and blinkered adherence to causes. William, a socialist and pacifist, and Griselda, a militant suffragette, meet and marry immediately before the outbreak of war, and honeymoon in Belgium. War breaks out; they are captured and forced to witness the execution of Belgian hostages. Griselda is raped, injured, and finally dies; William escapes to Paris and ultimately joins up, having recognised that war is a 'Fact', and needing to seek revenge for the treatment of Griselda. He becomes a clerk in the army and is killed by a raid on his base. His is a small, unheroic, insignificant life, but tragic nonetheless. The tone of the novel shifts from irony in the first part to compassion in the second, with the sense of war's arbitrariness and the depth of human suffering, irrespective of the quality of the characters' self-reflection or analysis, feelingly portrayed. An interesting articulation of confusion and moral weakness. The novel won the Feminia Vie Heureuse prize in 1919.

A51   Hamilton, Mary Agnes *Dead Yesterday*, London: Duckworth, 1916.

A pacifist novel, in which the maternal figure of Aurelia Leonard occupies the moral high ground as a woman of internationalist socialist leanings, and her daughter's fiancé, Nigel Strode, represents the voice of the press: unthinking, sensationalist, imaginatively dull. Daphne Leonard is the confused human centre to the novel. She has to release herself from the blinding glow of romantic love, in order to see clearly how the war affects ordinary women, children and fighting soldiers. The novel dwells on the vacuousness of many of the ordinary public, the power of the Liberal press, and the lack of influence of the politically-informed, pacifist thinkers, who ultimately retreat to the country, shed illusions of romantic love and build on the strengths of maternal love and true friendship. Lots of local detail, a little too much earnest speech writing.

A52   Hamilton, Mary Agnes *Special Providence: A Tale of 1917*, London: George Allen & Unwin, 1930.

This novel centres on a court case, in which Harold, an English lieutenant, is accused of murdering Stephen, a pacifist, as the latter 'comforts' Jean, Harold's wife. The novel explores and debates the issues behind a seemingly cut-and-dried case. Flashbacks are used to develop the characters and their relationships, and to discuss the pacifist position. The subtlety of individual human emotions is presented against the crude responses of the public. Harold is acquitted of murder and realises the truth when Jean explains it to him. The absurdity of that one death in the context of the millions who died in battle is evoked.

A53   Harraden, Beatrice *Where Your Treasure Is*, London:
Hutchinson & Co., 1918.

The story of Tamar Scott, redoubtable business woman and collector of precious
stones, whose avarice is gradually softened and cured by the events surrounding
the war. She comes into contact with young people, she visits Belgium, she houses
refugees, and is by turns consoled and taunted by her desire for precious gems. It is
a study of greed and sacrifice, punctuated with examples of selfless war work,
youthful liveliness and mature self-sacrifice, and framed by a love story.

A54   Haverfield, E.L. *The Girls of St Olave's*, London & Glasgow:
Collins, 1919.

A school story, conducted in the discourse of playing the game, white feathers,
funk and pluck. Margaret Macdonald, a Scots girl, is the heroine. She arrives at the
school, lonely, bereaved and is horribly mocked. Later the school decides to decamp
for Scotland, following an air raid, and Margaret gradually comes into her own as
her basic decency and courage reveal themselves on her home territory.

A55   H.D. *Bid Me to Live*, New York: Grove Press, 1960.
Reprinted London: Virago, 1984.

Although this novel was not published until 1960, it was first written in 1927, and
reflects on the relationships between H.D. and Aldington, Cecil Gray, and D.H.
Lawrence. It explores the relationships between Julia and Rafe Ashton, and
Frederico, in the context of a war that 'will never end', where art, love and sex bid
the characters to live.

A56   Hinkson, Pamela *The Ladies' Road*, London: Victor Golancz, 1932.

The story of four children, Cynthia and Godfrey, Stella and David, and the changes
wrought in them by school, growing up, and, inevitably, war. Stella and David are
particularly close, and Stella is tortured with grief when David is killed. The beauty
of Ireland, offset by the horrors of its politics provides part of the setting. The
novel, which deals sensitively, and in some detail, with the emotions of those
women who are bereaved, and isolated in their grief, finishes with the Irish 'home'
of the family being burnt to the ground, thus eliminating the past, just as so many
young men have been obliterated.

A57   Holland, Ruth *The Lost Generation*, London: Victor Gollancz, 1932.

A novel of prewar bliss, wartime devastation and loss, postwar dislocation and
alienation. Jinnie and Eliot grew up together in the 'golden world' of Wales. Eliot is
killed in the war, leaving Jinnie rootless and restless. Her family disperses, Jinnie
marries, but her husband dies of a war wound. Even in Wales she no longer
belongs: 'She was feeling lost, a little anxious and bewildered, looking at a world,
stirred up and chaotic, in which new generations were already crowding up,
pushing her back into the past; the war generation was a back number' (273).

A58   Holme, Constance *The Trumpet in the Dust*, London: Mills & Boon, 1921. Reprinted London: World's Classics, 1933 and London: Ivor Nicholson & Watson, 1934, with 6 woodcuts by Clare Leighton.

One of a number of novels set in the Westmoreland area. This is set immediately after the war, and includes commentary on war weddings.

A59   Holtby, Winifred *The Crowded Street*, London: John Lane at the Bodley Head 1924. Reprinted London: Virago, 1981.

An evocative story, feelingly told, of what it is like to be passive, dependent, frightened of life. Muriel Hammond lives with her parents and sister in a small, prosperous northern town, where Edwardian conventions of female propriety prevail. The war shows other women undergoing life-transforming experiences: Delia (said to be partly modelled on Vera Brittain) loses her fiancé, but is sustained by her Cambridge education and desire to make a difference to the world; Connie, Muriel's sister, rebels, works on a bleak, severe farm, and dies, pregnant. Muriel helps her mother and grows increasingly depressed, until Delia upbraids her for her cowardly self-deprecation and her unwillingness to take responsibility for herself. Muriel agrees to go to live with Delia in London and help her in her work for the Twentieth Century Reform League. She turns down an offer of marriage in order to pursue the development of her own personality and an ideal of service. There are interesting contrasts between country and town: the country is stifling and repressive, not a place of succour. London is the seat of civilised values and opportunities for social progress. Includes an account of the Scarborough bombing, which Holtby witnessed.

A60   Hope, Lilith *Behold and See!*, London: Hurst & Blackett, 1917.

A story about motherhood, martyrdom, forgiveness and love. It is set, initially, in a Belgian convent. Namur has just fallen and the advancing German army is expected soon. Rather than evacuate, they decide to convert into a nursing home, but the German officers are every bit as brutal as their reputation suggests, and a number of nuns are raped or killed by them. Sister Rose finds she is pregnant, and is sent away with a number of others. Unusually, however, she decides to keep her child. She sees motherhood as a holy calling. The rest of the novel deals with her independent life in England, her secret, her own love for the child in the face of the repulsion felt by those who discover the truth. She is seen as an 'ecstatic martyr ... to be pitied, reverenced, but outside the pale of marriage' (234).

A61   Hunt, Violet *Their Lives*, London: Stanley Paul & Co., 1916.

Has an interesting preface by Miles Ignotus, who describes reading the novel while watching the gas shells bursting in Poperinghe, which he describes as 'just casual cruelty, quite systematic ... suddenly it occurred to me that Violet Hunt's characters were Prussians'. And he goes on the say that 'the selfishness of the Eighties – of the Victorian and Albert era – is the direct ancestor of ... Armageddon'. The novel is about three sisters: Christina, Virgilia and Orinthia, who are manipulative, possessive and vain in their operations on the 'battle-ground' that constitutes the marriage market in the prewar period.

A62   Hunt, Violet *The Last Ditch*, London: Stanley Paul & Co., 1918.

A novel that opens in America, 1915, with Laura Quinney (an Englishwoman married to an American) observing the Americans 'taking their summer pleasure', while her mother and sisters are 'wallowing in that civilian slough' in the UK. Written mostly in the form of letters. Reflects on the fact that Americans are profiting by the distress of the British, and on the manners and habits of the aristocracy, the denizens of the 'last ditch' of the title.

A63   Jacob, Naomi *'Honour Come Back –'*, London: Hutchinson, 1935.

The story of Michael, the son of a military father, who languishes in the shadow of his more sportsmanlike brother, who dies of pneumonia. The war sees Michael in a state of political and emotional confusion. He desires his father's approval, but can't bear to inflict pain. He joins up and goes out to France, but has a breakdown and deserts following the death of a friend. He goes to Italy and, in a postwar world, reconstructs an identity for himself based on love, comradeship and the seasonal demands of the land, rather than the patrician, military values that his father represents.

A64   Jameson, Storm *The Clash*, London: Heineman, 1922.

Elizabeth, the orphaned daughter of unhappy parents, marries Jamie, who is lame but decent. In the second part of the book, once war has broken out, an American arrives at Jamie's RFC base. He, Jess Cornish, puts the case to Jamie that America is a young nation, full of ambition and vigour. The old nation, Britain, is criticised for its past greed (imperialism), its entropy, its weakness, but is also seen as possessing dignity and being capable of regeneration.

A65   Jameson, Storm *The Pitiful Wife*, London: Constable & Co., 1923.

The story of the relationship between Jael and Richmond Drew. Jael suffers an unhappy childhood, and falls passionately and childishly in love with the local boy, Richmond. After four years, war is declared and Richmond joins up, but his experience of male comradeship ends tragically when his friend, Paul, is killed. He finds it difficult to recover from this. Jael tries to be near him, but has to care for their son, David. The pair are reunited after Jael brings David back to life and Richmond, gazing on his son, realises that the chances of finding beauty in the world are slim.

A66   Jameson, Storm *Three Kingdoms*, London: Constable and Co., 1926.

The story of Laurence Storm, a gifted student, who marries the wealthy Dysart Ford. Dysart joins up as war breaks out and Laurence has their son, whom she leaves with her mother-in-law while she attempts to make her way in an advertising agency. The novel is about the different circumstances that war enforces on the men who go and the women who stay.

A67   Jameson, Storm *Farewell to Youth*, London: Heineman, 1928.

Centres on the unstable relationship between Nat and Denny. Nat, a young man as war breaks out, joins up, providing the opportunity for jealous rivalry between his mother, Emily, and his wife. Nat enjoys being at the front but finds himself envious of Denny's other admirers, one of whom she falls for rather seriously. The novel explores relationships between men and women and between mother and son.

A68   Jameson, Storm *A Richer Dust*, London: Heineman, 1931.

Completes the story of Mary Hervy (see *The Lovely Ship* and *The Voyage Home* for earlier instalments), and is set around the Shipbuilding and Marine Engineering works where Mary becomes chair of the board of directors. A richly textured, realist novel dealing with personal and family relationships, gun-running, the building of aeroplanes, unions, strikes, 'clever' and 'modern' women, all in the context of the war. Ends on a note of uncertainty that undermines the idea of a dynastic continuum as Mary dies, and her grandson declines to take over the business.

A69   Jameson, Storm *That Was Yesterday*, London: Heinemann, 1932.

A fictionalised version of Jameson's experiences between 1913 and 1918.

A70   Jameson, Storm *Company Parade*, London: Cassell & Co., 1934.

The first in the *Mirror in Darkness* trilogy centring on Hervey Russell (grand-daughter of Mary Hervey). Set as the war ends, with Hervey's friends all dead or overseas, and her needing to take care of her baby son, while establishing a career in literary London.

A71   Joly, Mrs John Swift *Those-Dash-Amateurs*, London: John Long, 1918.

A bunch of rather ripping ladies are intent on war schemes. The latest wheeze is to get hold of a mansion, preferably in France, and equip it as a convalescent hospital. This they do with a great deal of self-conscious idiocy – it is clear that the professionals can't bear them, but that their hearts, 'throbbing with ecstacy', are probably in the right place.

A72   Jones, Miss E.B.C. *Quiet Interior*, London: Richard Cobden-Sanderson, 1920.

A discursive novel, centring on the relationship between two sisters, Claire and Pauline Norris, and set in London during the war. The Norris sisters, their friends, the Lincolns, and another friend, Clement, discuss life, death, immortality, the war. … Russell Lincoln is killed at Ypres (the news is conveyed in the middle of a party); Clement leaves to rejoin his regiment. Henrietta Lincoln is sure that 'The war's dished *us*' (61) and Claire, an 'urban Brontë', falls in love with Clement, while believing him to be attached to her sister.

A73   Jones, Miss E.B.C. *The Singing Captives*, London: R. Cobden-Sanderson, 1921.

A novel concerned with the impact of war and the postwar world on a well-to-do family. Caroline Peel's fiancé had been killed in 1917, and, in 1920, she reflects on the confusions of the period – 'trivial excitement, boredom, self-satisfaction, and sometimes the ravages of grief' (27). Her brother attempts to make his reputation as a poet, with little success. The family loses its money, through poor investments, which precipitates a period of decline, financially and socially, which is offset by friendship, sibling affection, work taking the place of leisure.

A74   Jones, Miss E.B.C. *The Wedgwood Medallion*, London: Chatto & Windus, 1922.

A novel about the educated classes and their family life: marriage, sibling loyalties, sibling rivalries. Enid Ash and Nicholas Watergate became engaged in 1915 and married before Nicholas went out to France. It was, however, a mistake, and the novel plays out the emotional tangles that ensue when Nicholas, his brothers and a friend, encounter three sisters in Cornwall. Stability, propriety and tradition are set against breakdown and pretence in a world struggling with the impact of war and modernity.

A75   Jones, Miss E.B.C. *Indigo Sandys*, London: Chatto & Windus, 1924.

Set in postwar Cambridge (references to Keynes and Strachey invoke an intellectual framework), with the sense that war has bequeathed a dangerous and unstable society. Henrietta, Claire and Pauline reappear, but the main character is Inigo Sandys, who just missed the war, but who ultimately commits suicide.

A76   Kaye-Smith, Sheila *Sussex Gorse: The Story of a Fight*, London: Nisbet & Co. Ltd, 1916.

Covers a large swathe of the nineteenth century and moves into the twentieth. Doesn't overtly refer to the war, but the structure, from 'The Beginning of the Fight' to 'The Victory', suggests an allusion to battle. Its narrative covers the story of a man's fight to subdue the land in Sussex: 'Out of a small obscure farm of barely sixty acres he had raised up the splendid dominion, and he had tamed the roughest, toughest, fiercest, cruellest piece of ground in Sussex, the beast of Boarzell' (461).

A77   Kaye-Smith, Sheila *Little England*, London: Nisbet, 1918. Reprinted London: Cassell & Co., 1923.

Not one of her better-known novels (e.g. *Sussex Gorse*, 1916; *Joanna Godden*, 1922), but one set again in the Sussex countryside, from where, in the words of one of the characters, 'You hear 'em pretty plain ... the guns in France' (4). It concerns two Sussex families and their relationships with each other. The war is registered as an antithesis to English rural life in terms of food shortages, its effect on agricultural life and letters from those at the Front. It is also used as the 'machinery' that sorts out the conventionally heroic from the wild and unpredictable. One young man is killed, heroically, leaving a young pregnant wife. Another, who has gypsy blood in him, is shot for desertion, having fallen in love with the 'wrong' girl. Ivy, the sister of the 'hero', goes to work on the trams in Hastings and ultimately marries a Canadian soldier and plans to emigrate with him in order to farm.

A78   Laing, Janet *Before the Wind*, London: J.M. Dent & Sons, 1918.

Seventeen-year-old Ann Charteris, following the deaths of her brother and both of her parents, bravely sets off for Scotland to act as a companion to Miss Caroline and Miss Emily Barton, a pair of eccentric ladies. Anne's contribution to the war effort is to persuade the elderly sisters to allow other wealthy folk to take up residence in Bartonsmuir, thus freeing their own servants for war work. The atmosphere of eccentricity and jolly japes is given colour and romance by jewel thieves, detective work and a wounded hero.

A79   Laing, Janet *Wintergreen*, London: Hodder & Stoughton, n.d. [1921].

Julia Glenferlie is fifty years old in 1919. Among other things, she survived the sinking of the *Lusitania* (1915). A terribly boring man whom she helped to keep alive on that occasion, James MacFarlane, writes to her four years later (he had lost his mind in the interim). She takes the opportunity to leave abruptly, change her name and relinquish the monotonous existence she had led hitherto. James MacFarlane, though (having died on his way to the train station to seek her out), leaves her a substantial inheritance. The novel is sub-titled 'A Tale of Reconstruction'.

A80   Lee, Mary *'It's a Great War!'*, London: Allen & Unwin, 1929.

An American nurse on the Western Front. Largely written in an impressionistic style, making full use of ellipses. 'It's a great war!' is a refrain, usually meant ironically: her experiences are frequently nightmarish. 'The French are dirty dogs' is another refrain that frequently alludes to sexual activity of which the narrator doesn't approve. Interesting, but at 575 pages, rather long.

A81   Lee, Vernon (pseudonym of Violet Paget) *Satan the Waster: A Philosophic War Trilogy with Notes and Introduction*, London: John Lane, The Bodley Head, 1920.

The drama consists of a Prologue, The Ballet of the Nations and an Epilogue. The central part was first composed in 1915, and is described by the author as 'merely such an extemporised shadow-play as a throng of passionate thoughts may cast up into the lucid spaces of one's mind: symbolical figures, grotesquely embodying what seems too multifold and fluctuating, also too unendurable, to be taken stock of' (Intro, vii). This suggests a form more abstract than realist, which is indeed the case. Broadly, the 'plot' is that Satan, the 'Waster of Human Virtue' is staging his latest dance of death, assisted by Delusion and Confusion, and accompanied by passions high and low in the orchestra of Patriotism. Pity and Indignation, Lady Idealism and Prince Adventure keep things going while Ballet Master Death, adored by the beautiful blind boy Heroism, dozes drunkenly. Unworkable as drama, although of interest as a set of ideas expressed in a form other than realism.

For the accompanying Introduction *see* B87.

A82   Lowndes, Mrs Belloc (Marie Adelaide [Belloc] Lowndes) *Good Old Anna*, London: Hutchinson, 1915.

A popular novel, set in a small cathedral town in the south of England. Anna has been the faithful servant of Mrs Otway for eighteen years, and is characterised by her large-hearted, small-minded activities. She unwittingly acts as a spy to a community of fellow Germans, by passing on 'gossip' she hears from her indiscreet mistress. The spy-ring takes advantage of her naivety and good nature, by requiring her to keep some parcels. Needless to say she has no idea what is in them and when her part in the plot is revealed, she, rather shockingly, hangs herself.

A83　　Lowndes, Mrs Belloc (Marie Adelaide [Belloc] Lowndes) *Lilla: A Part of Her Life*, London: Hutchinson & Co., 1916.

Lilla is married to Robert Singleton, twelve years her senior and an 'old campaigner' who had seen service in the South African war. When war breaks out they are living in the house of his rather domineering mother. A telegram arrives, however, to say that he has been reported killed. Lilla liberates herself from the family establishment and successfully takes over the management of a canteen in a munitions factory. The sighting of a zeppelin during a train journey forces her into the care of Dare Carteret, who works in Intelligence. They spend an exhilarating evening driving into London and witnessing the fires that result from the zep attack. Having fallen ecstatically in love with him, Lilla marries Dare. But soon afterwards, Robert returns. She is left not knowing what to do. She decides to go abroad, but is first received into the Roman Catholic faith. Dare, we hear, is drowned alongside Kitchener on a top secret mission.

A84　　Lowndes, Mrs Belloc (Marie Adelaide [Belloc] Lowndes) *The Red Cross Barge*, London: Smith, Elder & Co., 1916.

Set in France during the early weeks of the war, when the Germans advance on Paris, then rapidly retreat. A German Red Cross surgeon, Max Keller, falls in love with the daughter of a French doctor. Mlle Rouannes runs the Red Cross Barge, which serves as a hospital, and which she tries to keep secret from the German forces. Max, however, is civilised and courteous; he does what he can to help Mlle Rouannes's father (who dies), and is himself fatally wounded by an exploding shell. The Prussian soldiers are every bit as barbaric as contemporary propaganda will have them; the doctors, however, transcend this and manage to inspire some degree of compassion which, in true Red Cross style, crosses boundaries of nationalism.

A85　　Lowndes, Mrs Belloc (Marie Adelaide [Belloc] Lowndes) *Out of the War?*, London: Chapman & Hall Ltd, 1918.

An American, Betty Felbrigge, is married to a British naval officer, and goes to one of his childhood seaside haunts, supposedly to get away from the war for a while. While there she meets a rather odd officer, Captain Drake, who works in Intelligence, and who lets her into a few of his secrets – even allows her to help him out. Meanwhile, the sleepy coastal town is troubled by strange happenings and spy sightings. Betty becomes increasingly mesmerised by her Captain, and ultimately allows him to take her out to dinner. The next day her husband returns, flushed with success: he has captured an infamous German spy just off the nearby coast. And in his pocket was a receipt for a cosy dinner for two. ...

A86　　Macaulay, Rose *Non-Combatants and Others*, London: Hodder & Stoughton, 1916. Reprinted London: Methuen, 1986.

The story of Alix's rejection of her cynical, indifferent attitude to the war, in favour of a stance which is actively committed to peace. Her mother, Daphne Sandomir, is a peace worker and spends much of her time abroad (cf. Aurelia Leonard in

Hamilton *Dead Yesterday*). Alix initially dismisses this and elects to live, not with her well-to-do Aunt and family, but with the slightly lower-class members of the 'Violette' household in Clapham, where the 'Evening Thrill' is read avidly and the 'womanly' Evie has no qualms about interfering in Alix's relationship with Basil. Alix, however, discovers the suffering that her younger brother Paul went through in the trenches, and turns her attention away from romantic attachments to anti-war activity, through the agency of her mother (a member of a Society for Promoting Permanent Peace) and a friend of her brother's who is a vicar, a member of the UDC, and a reader of the *Cambridge Magazine*. Ultimately she attends a peace meeting, an episode notable for the large proportion of reported speeches, and the critical commentary from Alix's point of view. The novel is interesting for its politics, its style, its descriptions of wartime London and its rendition of the attitude of artistic, disillusioned young people.

A87   Macaulay, Rose *What Not: A Prophetic Comedy*, London: Constable & Co. Ltd, 1918.

A satire on government ministries, dedicated 'To Civil Servants I have Known'. The book opens with an 'Apology', saying that 'wars do not conduce to intelligence' and that the book offers a 'cure for this world-old ill'. It proposes a Ministry of Brains, to 'further social progress and avert another Great War'. Everybody has their brain quality certified (A – C3), and is advised to take a suitable partner with whom to bear children, accompanied by inducements or penalties according to the wisdom of their decision. The whole of this is held in place by a Mental Progress Act, and is bolstered by a 'Brains Week', a 'Government Mind Training Course', etc. This highly-polished administrative exercise, the project of the Minister himself, is rendered vulnerable when the Minister and Kitty Grammont fall in love: the Minister is 'unclassified'; Kitty is 'A'. The novel is wittily alert to the clichés of the day (a novel entitled *The Dangers of Dora* is suppressed – it's in a series along with *The Perils of Pauline* and *The Exploits of Elaine*), and is all too aware of the incompatibility between the pursuit of abstract principle and the murky complexities of human motivations. A compassionate and mocking novel.

A88   McDougall, Grace *The Golden Bowl*, London: Geoffrey Bles, 1926.

Begins as war ends. Marion and Humphrey, passionately in love, agree to go to Italy together, where they spend a wonderful couple of months until Humphrey dies suddenly, from the long-term effects of gas. Marion is desolate and, to add to her confusion, a man she had married during the war, and who had gone missing, reappears, gruff and unlovely. They buy a farm in Rhodesia, where Marion is utterly miserable. She has her son (Humphrey is the father) and leaves with him to make her living in Europe. Numerous plots intervene until Marion and her husband are reunited, having paid, in suffering, for their sins. A romantic novel, in which the war has blurred and muddled the conventional love-marriage-children sequence.

A89   Mansfield, Charlotte *The Dupe: A British and South African Story of the Years 1914 and 1915*, London: Simpkin, Marshall, Hamilton, Kent & Co. Ltd, 1917.

A detailed and intricate plot which opens in London, with Gladys Potts, an

American widow (34) discussing with her younger friend Dawn (25) whether or not to marry Otto, a German with British nationality. Gladys has a weakness: she likes to spend money and, following the death of her husband, she has little. The Germans are willing to exploit this and, before she knows it, Gladys is married and bound for South Africa, carrying a sealed packet and a series of instructions in German. She gradually realises that she is conveying a sabotage kit and can only extricate herself from the situation by using her wits, courage, and the help of her British friends. Includes a vivid account of the anti-German riots on Ascension Day in Durban, following the sinking of the *Lusitania*.

A90   Marchant, Bessie *A Girl Munition Worker: The Story of a Girl's Work During the Great War*, London: Blackie & Son Ltd, 1916.

The story of Deborah Lynch, an upper-class young lady, who does her bit in a munitions factory, setting new standards for production, and also stumbles across a German spy, planning to blow up the local cordite factory. His plan, however, is already being foiled by the young and uncertain Elsie Marsh, who misdirects the offensive zeppelin. A story pivoted on the 'fiery zeal and red-hot patriotism' of a girl whose father and brother are both at the front. Interesting sub-plots concerning social class, the dangers of working in munitions, gender and action (Deborah and her father *inadvertently* kill the spy when he falls under their taxi).

A91   Marchant, Bessie *A V.A.D. in Salonika*, London: Blackie & Sons, 1917.

Not seen.

A92   Marchant, Bessie *A Transport Girl in France: A Story of the Adventures of a WAAC*, London: Blackie & Son, 1919.

Gwen Lovell had been brought up in a well-to-do family but, following the death and financial demise of her parents, is left to her own devices. She finds work on a farm, but later goes one step further, by driving an army car in London, before finally achieving her ambition to get out to the Front. There are spies, inevitably; disguised curates, escaped German prisoners, unreliable girls, but Gwen is a magnificent driver and quite good at catching saboteurs too. Ultimately she and Captain Broome declare their mutual love as she rescues him from a burning wreck.

A93   Massie, Alice *Freda's Great Adventure*, London: Blackie & Son, 1917.

Children's story. Freda lives alone with her Great Aunt Anna. She meets some children next door and they decide to smuggle her with them to their home in Paris. They are found out, however, and Freda is taken care of by her Uncle Edgar in Paris. But before she can be sent back, war breaks out. Edgar joins up and it is agreed that Freda will stay with her friends after all. She manages, while looking for the dog, to disturb a German outpost at a remote cottage. She is rewarded for her valour and ultimately returns home, with no other wish than to 'be a comfort' to her Great Aunt.

A94   Moore, Edith Mary *Teddy, R.N.D.*, London: Hodder and Stoughton, 1917.

The story of a little boy, Teddy, who grows up with his brother and sister in the nursery, then goes on to public school and then to architectural college. About half-way through the novel, war breaks out and Teddy joins the Public Schools Battalion of the Royal Naval Division. His mother promises to be 'reasonable' as long as she is kept informed of what he is doing. She hides her fear of what may happen as well as he hides his knowledge of what *has* happened. We see him at the end, having transferred to the Royal Flying Corps, 'serene and assured ... winged mariner of new seas'. The book has tremendous confidence in his courage and innocence, and as much in his mother's courage and common sense. Interesting to compare with Woolf's *Jacob's Room* (A151).

A95   Neff, Wanda Fraiken *We Sing Diana*, London: Chapman & Hall, 1928.

Mostly American setting. Nora has been adopted, and is sent off to college near New York. When she and her friends go back in 1914, it is to hear of the war and attendant disruptions. They find it all rather boring and distant at first, but Nora becomes interested in its causes and in related debates on women's franchise and socialism. She is invited to join the staff as an instructor. She does so, gets her degree, cuts her hair off and comes to spend some time in England. She ultimately returns to her college, but to modernise it by removing the 'maternal' protection that smothers the girls, and takes the radical step of adopting a baby as a signal of her liberated attitude.

A96   Orr, Christine *The Glorious Thing*, London: Hodder & Stoughton, 1919.

Set in the third year of war. David Grant is at home in Scotland, recovering from a war wound. His WAAC sister Minnie comes up to join him when she can, but he spends most of his time negotiating relationships with the Sutherland sisters. They are a fairly boisterous lot, all trying to come to terms with the war, the need to work or contribute to the household, the fact that there seems no central ideology that will help them to make sense of their lives. The title comes from G.K. Chesterton: 'Life is a thing too glorious to be enjoyed.' It is about the difficulties of bereavement, dislocation and change that come with the war, but with reminders of childhood innocence and pleasures.

A97   Pennell, Elizabeth Robins *The Lovers*, London: Heinemann, 1917.

The story, in four sections, of two unnamed lovers, observed by a narrator who sees them from a neighbouring attic flat. The lovers initially live for love and art, and live in poverty. The man becomes involved in the Vorticist movement before war is declared. He dies at Loos, 'with nothing to distinguish him from the least worthy', although he has made an enormous sacrifice in compromising his allegiance to Love and Art. The third and fourth sections detail his letters, which concern his training, poor conditions, a mutiny and an increasing sense that he is losing his humanity. Becomes aware that although they 'love' each other, they no longer 'know' each other. Touching account of the developing chasm between home and Front; lots of detail; has sentiment without being sentimental.

A98   Penny, F.E. *Desire and Delight*, London: Chatto & Windus, 1919.

Nurse Mary is a VAD in Bangalore. The connotations of her name are exploited to the full: she is loved and admired, but no-one knows much about her past. It transpires that, immediately before the outbreak of war, she was summoned to India to marry a man she loved. He was called up, however, before the ceremony could take place. When he returned a year later, gaunt, haggard, deathly, they went through with the wedding, but Rosemary (her full name) could not bear it. They parted. She returned to nursing. After a further lapse of time (and back to the narrative present), we hear that her husband is to return. We also hear of his illness and suffering in Gallipoli, and of his subsequent cure and recovery. Rosemary forgives all and they are reunited. Desire and Delight is the name of their house.

A99   Rathbone, Irene *We That Were Young*, London: Chatto & Windus, 1932. Reprinted London: Virago, 1988.

A semi-autobiographical novel that follows the experiences of Joan, Pamela and Betty, all well-bred young ladies, who take on war work during the years 1914–18. The details of YMCA work, nursing and munitions work are vivid and convincing. Their world, their relationships with family, brothers and lovers, friends, the books they read and meetings they attend are all portrayed in detail. By the end of the novel (1928) their youth has gone, as have many of the young men they loved, but they look back on the war as something bound up with love, hate and youthfulness.

A100   Rathbone, Irene *They Call it Peace*, London: J.M. Dent & Sons, 1936.

Not seen.

A101   Reeves, Amber [Mrs Blanco White] *Give and Take*, London: Hurst and Blackett Ltd [1923].

A novel set at the Board of Reconciliation, which has been set up to develop agreements between government and labour employed on munitions work. The novel is conscious of the conditions under which munitions workers are operating – and of the machinations of the civil service. Mostly about trade, politics, ideals, administration and the minutiae of civil service life, which revolves mostly around masculine power play.

A102   Reynolds, Gertrude M. (Robins) (pseudonym Mrs Baillie-Reynolds) *The Lonely Stronghold*, London: Cassell, 1918.

The story of Olwen Innes, who, thinking herself orphaned and penniless, works in a bank. She soon discovers that she has been left a fortune and becomes increasingly rich and sad as the effects of war reach her: her new house is converted into a hospital. The novel charts her uncertain relationship with Ninian, who is wounded in the war, and is concerned with the winning and losing of money and property.

A103   Reynolds, Gertrude M. (Robins) (pseudonym Mrs Baillie-Reynolds)
            Also Ran, London: Hutchinson, 1920.

A trained Red Cross nurse, Jacynth Pennant, forms a mild attachment to one of her patients, Captain Monkland. They discover that they come from the same part of England. Captain Monkland, however, is well-to-do, while Jacynth's father is known as a drunk and a swindler. Jass is persuaded to marry Ranulf Warristoun as a means of redeeming her father's disgrace. She does so reluctantly and they go off to Brittany, where he has a castle that has been converted into a hospital. Against a complex tale of family feuds, vendettas and deathbed confessions, the two ultimately come to love each other. A tale concerned with class, breeding and trust.

A104   Rickard, Jessie Louisa (Moore) (pseudonym Mrs Victor Rickard)
            The Light Above the Crossroads, London: Constable & Co. Ltd, 1916.

Marcus Janover, the son of a British diplomat, has been educated in Germany. He, too, is destined for the diplomatic service, when his father dies, leaving him with a financial problem. War breaks out; he discovers that he and his best (German) friend are in love with the same (Irish) girl, and he is asked to become a spy, extracting military secrets for the use of the British. He feels he has no choice. The novel charts his moral dilemmas, which circulate around the effects of his work, and his love for both of his friends.

A105   Rickard, Jessie Louisa (Moore) (pseudonym Mrs Victor Rickard)
            The Fire of Green Boughs, London: Duckworth, 1918.

Sylvia Tracey has to find a way of living her life in war-torn Britain with no settled income. She can't bear the futility of official bureaucracy, and when the chance arises to take a house in Ireland, she accepts it. Her cousin, Dominic Royden, has returned wounded from Flanders and become a very popular preacher, and it is to him and to his friends that she turns when a dying German sailor appears at Kerry and Sylvia takes him in. She is arrested on suspicion of helping enemy forces.

A106   Rickard, Jessie Louisa (Moore) (pseudonym Mrs Victor Rickard)
            The House of Courage, London: Duckworth, 1919.

Prewar scenes bring together a group of friends at Castle Glenfield. The outbreak of war sees the men joining up, and the women seeking to employ themselves usefully. Scenes in a German prisoner of war camp, and in London, where the female protagonists are working. Concerned mostly with moral and emotional dilemmas; the nature of love; the effects of anxiety. Thoughtful in mood; romantic in structure and outcome.

A107   Robins, Elizabeth *The Messenger*, London: Hodder & Stoughton,
            1919.

Spy story. Miss Greta von Schwarzenberg is a governess at the McIntyres' house. She has an American friend to stay, whom she mysteriously silences when they meet some (German) friends of Greta's. When war breaks out Greta, with suspicious ease, secures the family a house on the Essex coast. Spirit lamps, stolen diamonds, transcripts of conversations, photographs all ultimately incriminate Greta, who turns out to be one of the most notorious spies in Europe.

A108   Ruck, Berta (Mrs Oliver Onions) *The Lad with Wings*, London:
              Hutchinson, 1915.

A young pilot and his girl, Gwenna, marry at war's outbreak, just before he has to
fly off for the sake of his country.

A109   Ruck, Berta (Mrs Oliver Onions) *The Girls at His Billet*, London:
              Hutchinson & Co., 1916.

Three sisters – Nancy, Evelyn and the narrator, Elizabeth ('Rattle'), live with their
aunt in uninspiring mud flats on the East Coast of England. Things liven up when
a military instruction camp is set up nearby and they are promised a billet: Frank
Lascelles. He's a little disappointing at first as a khaki specimen, but following
some girlish japes (spoof letter-writing, Nancy's secret elopement) and a zep raid,
Frank seems much more appealing to Rattle.

A110   Ruck, Berta (Mrs Oliver Onions) *The Bridge of Kisses*, London:
              Hutchinson & Co., 1917.

Joey Dale is a sensible, practical girl, who falls out with Lieutenant Dick Rowlands,
heading a group of sappers who are building a military-strength bridge, when he
locks up some troublesome children – among them Joey's younger brother. Joey, in
the meantime, is engaged to the effeminate Hilary Sykes. The plot eddies along
around children, families, friends, until Joey disengages herself from Hilary and is
betrothed to the manly Dick. The names are interesting.

A111   Ruck, Berta (Mrs Oliver Onions) *In Another Girl's Shoes*, London:
              Hodder & Stoughton, 1917.

First-person narrator, Rose Whitelands (well-educated, but poor), is sharing a
railway carriage with actress, Vera Vayne, who is on her way to meet the family of
her recently killed (and recently married) husband. Rose is heading to Wales, where
she is to be a nursery governess. Neither is looking forward to her destination.
Vera suggests, then suddenly imposes, a swap. Rose is a trifle incoherent, but the
charming Meredith family want to keep her. They take her off to Paris where, lo
and behold, George Meredith turns out to be alive, with a leg wound. The plot is
complicated by an RAMC officer, who wants to marry Rose, and Philippa,
charming and beautiful, who loves, but doesn't want to marry George.

A112   Ruck, Berta (Mrs Oliver Onions) *The Years for Rachel*, London: Hodder
              & Stoughton, 1918.

Gwen Brook has been engaged to Selby Henderson for about ten years. When war
breaks out she goes to work on the buses in London, where she meets Jack Owen,
a friend of her brother's. They have a whirlwind romance. A zep comes down over
London and Gwen hears that Jack 'strafed' it. She terminates her engagement to
Selby, but then Jack comes back to life and they marry. The novel ends, rather
more sombrely than the others, with Gwen holding her baby son and wondering if
she will ever see Jack again: he is being held prisoner by the Germans.

A113   Ruck, Berta (Mrs Oliver Onions) *The Land-Girl's Love Story*, London: Hodder & Stoughton, 1918.

A love story with agricultural work as the setting. Some of the material could have come straight from war propaganda (e.g. the recruitment rally at Trafalgar Square, the social mix of recruits – from the governing class to bare-headed factory girls, the high-spirits and camaraderie). Joan (the heroine) eventually falls in love with a wounded soldier, but only after he has taught her to shovel muck efficiently. She has brief competition from the flirtatious Muriel, who is seen speaking to a German prisoner. The prisoner sets fire to a barn full of recently harvested corn; Muriel gets her come-uppance by becoming engaged to a repulsive millionaire. The happy couples (Joan's friend, too, finds the right man) celebrate their unions along with the peace celebrations, congratulating themselves on having done their 'little bit to help'. Interesting in terms of how the conventions of popular romance are spliced into those of patriotic endeavour against the backdrop of the rural organic myth.

A114   Sackville-West, Vita *Challenge*, London: Collins, 1974.

A Foreword by Nigel Nicolson explains that this was written May 1918–November 1919 and published in New York, but withdrawn in Britain because of the scandal it might cause. It is about Vita and her lover, Violet Trefusis. Mrs Belloc Lowndes helped Lady Sackville to persuade Vita not to publish. There is no overt First World War content, but Julian (a male character, said to resemble Vita) shows all the instinct of the British military hero: 'Life … had come to him of its own accord and ordered him to take the choice of peace or war within its folded cloak' (72). It is set in the Greek Islands.

A115   Saunders, Margaret Baillie *The Belfry*, London: Hodder & Stoughton, 1914.

Lady Lucy Briarwell, a young woman with an older husband in an asylum, travels to Bruges, where she meets Constant Ysambert, a theological student and 'dramatic genius', who is seeking out the history of Flanders, its wars, invasions, culture and folklore. He writes a play, 'The Belfry', which culminates in the Flemish people requesting help from the Queen of Heaven to save them from invading forces. A light appears in the Belfry, illuminating the Madonna and Child: the battle stops, the enemy flies. Lucy plays the part of Mary. The novel is about the courage and spirit of ordinary Belgian people; it's also about Lucy and Ysambert, the morality of their relationship, the relationships between art and religion, and between marriage and love.

Billed as 'the most popular novel of gallant Belgium that has yet appeared' (publisher's catalogue, Autumn 1915).

A116   Saunders, Margaret Baillie *Captain the Curé*, London: Hodder & Stoughton, 1915.

Another 'Gallant Belgium' novel. Begins with the Prussians ransacking Louvain. Ottilie, the youngest daughter of the doctor, is caught up in it; the curé, Van Susterens, decides to give up the priesthood and join the army. Ottilie is later arrested as a German spy. Kapetein Van Susterens offers to marry her to give her a 'name' and a reputable position. They are described as 'two of Belgium's martyred ideals – the broken priest and the ruined girl' (205). The novel is concerned with the girl's struggle to survive: she chooses dishonour rather than death, and with the making of a saint. Van Susterens returns to the church.

A117   Sayers, Dorothy L. *Unnatural Death*, London: Ernest Benn Ltd, 1927.

Lord Peter Wimsey murder mystery. Set postwar with some interesting comments on the 'surplus two million' women, the effects of war on hunting and postwar taxes, price rises and unemployment. Sleuthing helps to calm Wimsey's postwar nerves and dispel his depression.

A118   Sayers, Dorothy L. *The Unpleasantness at the Bellona Club*, London: Ernest Benn Ltd, 1928.

Opens on Armistice night in the Bellona Club, as some friends have gathered to mark the death of Colonel Marchbanks' son, who was killed at Hill 60. Captain Fentiman (whose grandfather is later found dead in his chair at the Club) rails against the war and the way its survivors are treated: 'A man goes and fights for his country, gets his inside gassed out, and loses his job, and all they give him is the privilege of marching past the Cenotaph once a year and paying four shillings in the pound income-tax.' Another Lord Peter Wimsey murder mystery.

A119   Sedgwick, Anne Douglas (Mrs Basil de Sélincourt) *Adrienne Toner*, London: Edward Arnold, 1921.

An American woman, Adrienne Toner, appears on the London scene. She has unconventional views and spiritualist inclinations, can cure headaches, insomnia and other ills. She marries Barney Chadwick (a one-time connoisseur of post-impressionism and the Russian ballet): Barney's friends aren't sure about her. She makes something of a fool of herself, in conventional terms, but then the war gives her the space to redeem herself. She 'disappears' at one stage, and it turns out that she ran an ambulance unit in Salonika. She later appears in a Boulogne hospital and nurses Roger Oldmeadow (one of Barney's more sceptical friends) back to health. Her power to cure comes into its own and her ability to see through the artifice of social conventions is treated with sympathy.

A120   Sherwood, Margaret *The Worn Doorstep*, London: Hodder & Stoughton, 1917.

Written in the form of letters to her dead fiancé, this recounts the experiences of an American woman seeking a place to live in Oxfordshire, once her scholar-lover has been killed at the front. The opening pages are a frank exposition of grief, a little winsome in expression, but redolent of suffering. As the tale progresses, however, it becomes less plausible. The protagonist befriends a dog and a pony, adopts a kitten, persuades her socialist gardener to go off and fight, and magically helps a woman and baby find the baby's father, and a solitary Belgian refugee find her lover. The couple are married from her house and later she adopts an abandoned baby. An account of grief management, by turns touching and ridiculous, this includes, by displacement, the conventional markers of marriage and childcare.

A121   Sidgwick, Ethel *Jamesie*, London: Sidgwick & Jackson Ltd, 1918.

An epistolary novel, set between members of the English and French sides of a family. War is declared; men and women alike enlist or go off to help. Jamesie, a boy, is sent to Ireland to be out of it. He is drowned, however, when the ship returning him to his mother goes down. The humour and bustle of the preceding letters seems to be undercut by this needless loss.

A122   Sinclair, May *Tasker Jevons*, London: Hutchinson & Co., 1916.

The story of Tasker Jevons and Viola, narrated by 'Furny', one-time suitor of Viola and fellow journalist with Jevons. Concerns the relationships between the unrefined Jevons and Viola, from whose well-to-do family circle Jevons is excluded. Jevons and Viola marry; Jevons becomes increasingly successful as a journalist and begins a long-standing relationship with a car. The marriage does not run smoothly and as war is declared Jevons decides to go to Belgium to scout for wounded with his car (despite being an 'arrant coward'), rather than being a war correspondent – the more obvious course of action. Viola follows with Furny. The narrative takes them through a number of incidents in Belgium, most of which testify to Jevons' courage. Ultimately he rescues Viola's brother Reggie, is wounded, declines the last of the hospital's anaesthetic in favour of his brother-in-law, and has his right hand (his writing hand) amputated. He thus wins the love and admiration of Viola's family – and confesses to experiencing abject terror before arriving in Belgium.

A123   Sinclair, May *The Tree of Heaven*, London: Cassell, 1917.

A novel divided into three parts: 'Peace', 'The Vortex' and 'Victory', in which the first is set around the 1890s and the turn of the century, the second around 1910, and the third covers the war period. The setting involves a family with four children (Dorothy, Nicky, Michael and John) and various other relatives. The 'Tree of Heaven' is the tree in the Edenic garden of the large, protective, Englishman's-castle house. The basic characteristics of the children (and parents) are introduced in the first part, and developed in the second, which is the period of unrest shot through with suffrage battles (in which Dorothy is involved), moral experiments (Nicky's area) and artistic revolt (Michael's interest). The declaration of war, however, forces them all to reassess their values. Dorothy becomes an ambulance driver and realises that this, rather than suffragist militarism, is the true way forward; Nicky marries the gifted Ronnie, develops plans for a 'moving fortress' and is killed in battle; Michael discovers that his earlier resistance to war was one of the many 'subterfuges of funk' that he had been hiding behind, and experiences the 'ecstacy' of battle before being killed. The novel ends with the youngest son, John, going off to fight. The novel contains some interesting scenes referring to the suffrage movement and to the areas of artistic and moral/sexual experimentation preceding the war. Like the *Journal* (C15), it is interested in fear and in how fear is articulated and confronted. Unfortunately, though, this is not analysed in any great detail: patriotism, the recognition of the 'reality' of the war ultimately unites and harmonises the fragmentations and multiple visions engendered by the 'Vortex'.

A124   Sinclair, May *The Romantic*, London: W. Collins Sons & Co., 1920.

A novel that reflects Sinclair's growing interest in psychoanalysis. It is divided into two parts: the first set on a farm in England, the second in Belgium, where the main characters are part of a field ambulance corps. In the first part Charlotte and John meet while doing agricultural work. Their different attitudes to that work act as a register of their mental states. Charlotte sees the earth as soft, benevolent; John equates farming with fighting: 'Seeing the blade shine, and the long wounds coming in rows; hundreds of wounds, wet and shining' (32). Their relationship becomes increasingly fraught when, in Belgium, John insists on the 'romance' of the exercise but exhibits signs of cowardice, and Charlotte is 'wanting – wanting frightfully – to help' (67). John is ultimately shot in the act of deserting a wounded officer. Both Charlotte and John are then 'analysed' by the Commandant, who is also a psychoanalyst: Charlotte has to deal with her suppression of her sexual instincts; John suffered from some unexplained 'physical disability' that prevented him from 'liv[ing] a man's life' (244). The novel is interesting in that it departs from and critiques the romantic heroism that is appealed to elsewhere in Sinclair's writing.

A125   Sinclair, May *Anne Severn and the Fieldings*, London: Hutchinson & Co., n.d. [1922].

Following the death of her mother and her father's departure for India, Ann Severn stays with the Fieldings family, in which there are three boys: Eliot, Jerrold and Colin. Immediately before the war, Colin marries the fearless and manipulative Queenie, who persuades him to join up. He becomes permanently shell-shocked. Queenie refuses to return from her Ambulance Unit to care for him. Anne, who is in the same unit, goes to Colin's aid, and is asked, at Queenie's request, not to return. But it costs her: 'To be safe from the chance of sudden violent death was to be only half-alive' (105). Anne has been in love with Jerrold all along. The war, coming in the middle of the novel, disrupts and confuses the central relationships, but Anne and Jerrold are finally united, following a lot of pain and misunderstanding.

A126   Sinclair, May *The Rector of Wyck*, London: Hutchinson & Co., 1925.

The novel opens in 1882, when Matty Fenwick watches her sister preparing for her marriage with the clever Philip Attwater, and her cousin marries a dull curate. Then she, unexpectedly, falls in love with a curate – the Rector of Wyck – and most of the novel tells of them, their children, their lives. The war enters towards the end and separates them in their reasonable, rural patriotism, from the sophisticated urban pacifism of the Attwaters. Their renegade son, Derek, returns from Australia to fight – and is killed, heroically.

A127   Sinclair, May *Far End*, London: Hutchinson, 1926.

There are two couples: Hilda and Christopher, who is a writer; Christopher's sister Cecily and Maurice. For a brief time before the war they live together at Far End, a country house with a special character. When war comes both men join up. Maurice is killed and Cecily dies, as if in sympathy. Christopher is invalided home and in April 1918 they have a child although Hilda, as if mirroring the military situation, nearly dies. After the war they leave the house and Christopher sets about writing a stream-of-consciousness novel, which is a great success. But the marriage comes under strain. They are haunted by the loss of Cecily and Maurice;

they have another child, who is sickly and demanding; Christopher has affairs. As a last resort they decide to go back to Far End, and this restores them to their former equilibrium and understanding. A novel in which the postwar years provide the scenes of conflict, as far as the marriage is concerned, and in which the English countryside has a healing, restorative force.

A128   Skelton, Margaret *Below the Watchtowers*, London: Leonard Parsons, 1926.

A novel set in 'Gunton' (Woolwich) in the years before and during the war. Valentine and Isabel Day arrive in Gunton as children, from Germany, and are brought up there by their aunt Lucy. War breaks out on the day that Isabel was due to be married to a German doctor. Valentine goes off to fight, believing this to be a war to end wars. There are comments on the sentimentality of the Liberal press, on the shift in emphasis from suffragism to militarism (Isabel had been a suffrage worker), and scenes of racial violence as the premises of all and any foreigners are attacked and looted. The novel weaves into the relationship between brother, sister and German friend, ideas concerning poverty, socialism, suffering and lost youth. It is searching in tone, and depicts many perspectives on the war. Isabel and her fiancé meet again; Valentine, however, dies.

A129   Smith, Helen Zenna (Evadne Price) *'Not So Quiet'... Stepdaughters of War*, London: A.E. Marriott, 1930. Reprinted with Introduction by Barbara Hardy, London: Virago, 1988.

Hardy's Introduction explains that this was originally commissioned as a spoof of the Remarque classic, but that the author refused to write such a book. Instead she produces the story of an ambulance driver's experience of war, based on a factual account, very much in sympathy with and structurally similar to Remarque's novel. It is a denunciation of armchair patriotism. The tone is often railing, malcontent, determined not to spare the reader any of the grotesque details of the agonised deaths and mutilations of the soldiers. Nor does it underplay the mental torture suffered by the 'gently-bred' recruits, haunted by processions of wounded, brutally disfigured men and alienated from the drawing-room patriots at home. Its outlook, however, is pacifist with hints of feminism: 'Women will be the ones to stop war' (55). It documents the loss of happiness and youth of the war generation and is interesting as a piece of genuinely popular writing with a specifically gendered viewpoint: comments on class, sexuality and women in authority contrast sharply with the 'official' line laid out by the propaganda, and, in a setting that surely owes something to girls school stories, there are revealing comments on lesbianism, hero-worship and female camaraderie.

A130   Smith, Helen Zenna (Evadne Price) *Women of the Aftermath*, London: John Long, 1931.

Sequel to *'Not So Quiet...'*. Begins in 1918 with Nellie married to Roy, who is blind, impotent and bitter. She meets a former lover and leaves her husband who then kills himself. The rest charts her gradual decline, which is accompanied by comments on women's postwar attitudes (they refuse to go back to their uneventful prewar lives, think themselves as competent as men, are unsentimental about khaki, etc.). Exemplifies a bitter, hard-headed, lonely independence on the part of women, some of whom, like Nell, have been taught no skills and therefore have difficulty in earning their living. Ends with Nell having duped a silly young rich boy into buying her an aeroplane and her taking a purgative flight – 'I am clean again, clean as a little child' (235). Sensationalist, lacking the structure and political drive of its forerunner.

A131   Smith, Helen Zenna (Evadne Price) *Shadow Women*, London: John Long, 1932.

The last in the sequence. Nell has an air crash and is left destitute, with a large scar on her face. She marries again, is rapidly widowed and uses money she is left to open a home for down and outs. She marries a third time and extends the project. The story loses its drive almost completely, but it shows something of the 'land fit for heroes to live in'. Very heavy on Great British Hypocrisy, without painting the heroine as an angel; the war has relieved her of any such innocence.

A132   Stern, G[ladys] B[ronwyn] *A Marrying Man*, London: Nisbet & Co., 1918.

Gareth Temple struggles with 'an inversion of leadership' in two marriages. He longs to write. He becomes a publisher's reader. His second wife, Patricia, joins an ambulance corps when war breaks out – all of his friends, in fact, appear to be involved in war work of some kind. He isn't, and is now too old to be a soldier. He writes a novel, but its 'morbid and self-analytic hero' is not admired. His wife publishes a book recording her impressions of ambulance work: it sells over twenty-thousand copies. There is a great deal of discussion about publishing in wartime: the morality of it, the dearth of paper, labour and transport facilities, the ubiquitous Red Cross nurse in the penny serials 'with an adjustable face that can remind each and every wounded officer on the ward of his girl at home' (296), and the relationship between the chaos of activity and the order of words. Gareth is ultimately killed by a random bomb in London. The newspaper reports casualties as 'insignificant'.

A133   Stern, G[ladys] B[ronwyn] *Children of No Man's Land*, London: Gerald Duckworth & Co., 1919.

A novel about the complexities inherent in identity and culture at a moment of historical crisis. Richard and Deb are the children of a Christian mother and a father whose own father was German Jewish. When Richard nears the age at which he could join up, he finds that he was born in Germany and has German nationality. This provides him with a confusing puzzle and a suspicion of 'natural' loyalties, further complicated by discussions with a Zionist friend, which evoke the aspect of his identity that is Jewish. Deb is similarly exercised by the disparities between 'old' and 'new' moralities. 'What guidance is there, moral or religious or traditional?' (277) is the question. A novel that deals with complex ideas to do with national, religious, cultural and political identity – and implicitly with gendered identity too.

A134   Sutherland, Joan *Wings of the Morning*, London:
Hodder & Stoughton, 1919.

A portrait painter with a past, Milton Collingwood, returns to England to see family after years spent in America and Europe. War breaks out. He is over-age by now, but joins an Ambulance Unit. A tale of love and war, home front and war front, in which the past makes its claims on the present.

A135   Swan, Annie S. *Letters to a War Bride*, London: Hodder & Stoughton,
1915.

A series of letters from a kindly and experienced family friend, to a 'little war bride' who has just set up home with her soldier husband. The earlier section is taken up with tasty and nutritious meals dominated by the stockpot; later we move to the finer details of housekeeping (O-Cedar mops and Bissel carpet sweepers). Brian, the husband, in the meantime leaves for France and the war bride has to keep herself busy and cheerful finding, furnishing and equipping a house ready for his return. Many more details concern servants (how many, of what age, how much free time to allow them), the housekeeping regime and budget. Tone very much like that of the women's magazines: cheerful, helpful, patronising.

A136   Swan, Annie S. *The Woman's Part*, London: Hodder & Stoughton,
1916. Reprinted Bath: Lythway Press, 1972.

The story of war experiences and relationships centring on two families: the Ogilvys and the Maitlands. Includes a German spy (a Fräulein, who manages to keep bombs hidden under her bed), a war wedding, the redemption of a ne'er-do-well by war service, VAD workers, a lame but wise child, and the restoration of sight to a blinded war hero when he hears of his wife's pregnancy.

A137   Talbot, Ethel *The Warringtons in War-Time*, London: Thomas Nelson
& Sons Ltd, n.d.

The Warrington family pull themselves together and do the only things possible in wartime. Aunt Sophie is a tower of strength on numberless committees, Dr Warrington gives the best of his professional skills and Jane forgoes the opportunity to take the university entrance exam in order to take care of the family and help where she can. Belgian refugees, wounded and killed soldiers, VADs, volunteers of every kind populate a story that focuses on a romance between Jane and Jon, lover of all things beautiful, who loses his sight in battle.

A138   Thompson, Sylvia *The Rough Crossing*, Oxford: Basil Blackwell, 1921.

The crossing in question is that from childhood to adulthood, and it coincides with the duration of the war. Elizabeth and her mother are on their own. Elizabeth is a tad unconventional and goes through a number of schools in a rough-and-tumble way. The war is an accompaniment, which sometimes rises to the surface and sometimes remains hidden, but its dynamics shape the novel.

A139   Thompson, Sylvia *The Hounds of Spring*, London: Heinemann, 1926.

A panoramic novel, covering the lives of a family from before the outbreak of war to some years after. Centres on Zina, an intellectually lazy young woman who cares for art and music and who loves Colin passionately. Zina's brother John is killed in the war; Colin is reported missing, presumed dead. Zina finds there is now no meaning to her life and drifts into marriage with the oafish George. Colin, we discover, had been taken prisoner and suffered from memory loss owing to shell-shock. A couple of years after the war he returns to England, and he and Zina meet. She wants him to 'take her away' from her husband and child, for neither of whom she feels any passion. Ultimately she decides for herself to leave George. A story about the destruction of ideals, about the uselessness of female life when it is structured only around romantic love, and when the object of that love dies. The novel finishes with Zina's younger sister Wendy, Oxford-educated, thinking about the best way in which to 'make for decency and beauty and peace' (339). Colin is the moral and intellectual centre of the novel; his reconstructive zeal, however, is more or less lost on the morally irresponsible Zina.

A140   Thompson, Sylvia *Chariot Wheels*, London: William Heinemann, 1929.

A novel in which the war appears as snapshots of the past: a suffragette governess becomes a WAAC; a mother cries when she sees her young son in uniform; a girl visits a wounded soldier. The postwar generation is described as having 'a vitiated palate', as opposed to the 'brave and liberal' beliefs of the previous generation.

A141   Tynan, Katharine *The Web of Fraulein*, London: Hodder & Stoughton, n.d. [1916].

Set in the 1870s in a literary environment of famous writers, this is the story of a German Fräulein who works her way into the Allanson household and flatters and relieves Mrs Allanson until she finds her indispensable. She takes over all the household arrangements and Mrs Allanson will deal with no-one but her. She works her way into the psyche of young Mr Francis until he too refuses to leave her – until she dies. A mysterious and manipulative character. The publisher's catalogue describes her as: 'an embodiment of the German spirit as it is revealing itself today' (publisher's catalogue, Spring 1916).

> *War Nurse: The True Story of a Woman Who Lived, Loved, and Suffered on the Western Front*, New York: Cosmopolitan Book Corp., 1930. *See* Andrews, Corinne (A4).

A142   Ward, Mrs Humphry *'Missing'*, London: Collins, 1917.

The story of young, pretty Nelly, her soldier-husband George, her wicked sister Bridget and the rich aristocrat Sir William Farrell, who would certainly marry Nelly if George were to be found dead rather than missing. Bridget plots the marriage of the two and conceals the whereabouts of the dangerously ill George (who dies), but is found out, leaving Nelly to come to her own mature and independent decisions about doing war work and rejecting the comfort and coddling by her self-interested sister and the utterly charming Farrells.

A143   Ward, Mrs Humphry *The War and Elizabeth*, London: W. Collins Sons & Co. Ltd, 1918.

There is a Foreword stating 'This book was finished in April 1918, and represents the mood of a supremely critical moment in the War.' This is a conversion, or a campaign narrative. Elizabeth, thirtyish, a Greek scholar, who has to earn her own income, converts the Squire, a feckless aristocrat, to the cause of war. Elizabeth is engaged as the Squire's secretary: he is a collector of Greek artefacts. He has taken no note of the local War Agricultural Committee and shown no interest in adapting his land or his practices to help the cause, which as Spring 1918 approaches, becomes increasingly desperate. Elizabeth is both a sound scholar and a patriot. She gains first his intellectual sympathy, then gradually takes over the running of the estate, looks after his children (Desmond, the favourite son, dies under a statue of the winged victory, with 'England' on his lips) and ultimately puts the entire estate to war work. The twists and turns in the plot are provided by various marriage plots and by the fact that the children are jealous of Elizabeth's efficiency and unique power over their father, and fearful that her plan is to marry him and take over entirely.

A144   Ward, Mrs Humphry *Harvest*, Collins Sons & Co., 1920.

A novel set towards the end of the war, and which culminates in the Armistice period. Rachel Henderson, a farmer, fully up to date with modern farming methods, goes into business with her friend, Janet Leighton. Captain Ellesborough, who is in command of a Forestry Corps nearby, falls in love with her. Rachel, however, has 'a past'; she was married and divorced in Canada, and her former (drunken, violent) husband, Roger Delane, appears on the scene and blackmails her. His threats are then augmented by another man, who threatens to reveal her as an adulteress – a sin of which she is innocent. After some heart-searching and a full confession to Janet, Rachel decides to tell all to George Ellesborough (whom she loves passionately) in the form of a letter on Armistice Day. They arrange to meet; he is not put off; they embrace for a moment and then Roger Delane shoots her through the window, and kills her. The narrator explains this as a violent, human act, by one who is not redeemable (Delane later shoots himself), but the combination of romance, tragedy and war in the plot, the novel's title and the symbolic resonance of the Armistice provide some interesting interpretative puzzles in this, the last of Mary Ward's novels.

A145   West, Rebecca *The Return of the Soldier*, London: Nisbet, 1918.
             Reprinted with introduction by Victoria Glendinning, London: Virago,
             1980.

Chris Baldry comes back to his exquisitely maintained country home unable to recognise his wife and remembering his cousin Jenny only as a childhood playmate. His heart lies with Margaret, his first love, now dowdy and worn and living in a nearby suburb. Chris is shell-shocked and living in the past. The women who surround him have to decide whether, and how, to cure him. It is decided that the memory of his dead child may restore him – sufficiently to send him back to the war 'every inch a soldier'. This, West's first novel, displays her interest in psycho-analysis.

West, Rebecca *War Nurse. See* Andrews, Corinne (A4).

A146   Wharton, Edith *The Marne*, New York: D. Appleton & Co., 1918.

The story of Troy Belknap, an American boy, who loses his heart to France in 1914, when his friend and companion is killed on the Marne. Too young to fight, he returns with his mother to America, only to make his way back to France as an ambulance worker when he reaches the age of eighteen. He is eventually wounded in battle, although officially still too young to fight. The novel is concerned with the varying attitudes of American supporters – some superficial, some desperately concerned to help – and with the determination of this young man to commit himself to the cause.

A147   Wharton, Edith *A Son at the Front*, London: Macmillan, and New
York: Charles Scribner's Sons, 1923.

Set among the American community in Paris during the war. Principally concerns the relationship between a father (Campton, a painter) and his son, George. Centres on the moral dilemmas that occur when Campton's desire to protect his son comes into conflict with his growing belief in the justice of the cause, and is further complicated by jealousy of his son's wealthy stepfather, unease at his son's shallow – and already married – girlfriend, and a growing sense that 'his vision of the boy was never quite in focus' (394; US edn). The novel increasingly concerns the distance between those who fight and the noncombatants – from the point of view of the latter. George is an empty centre: no-one really knows him, but they nevertheless project their desires onto him. He is ultimately killed and Campton, the artist, is left with the task of creating a suitable monument to him.

A148   Whipple, Dorothy *Greenbanks*, London: John Murray, 1932.

'Greenbanks' is a house, presided over by Louisa Ashton. The novel is mostly concerned with the occupants of the house and with the wartime activities of the members of the local village – 'The spoon of war stirred the contents of the provincial pan very thoroughly' (204).

A149   Wilson, Romer (Florence Roma Muir Wilson O'Brien) *If All These
Young Men*, London: Methuen, 1919.

Set in the Spring of 1918, when there was a very real possibility that the Allies might lose the war, this novel narrates the thoughts and emotions of a group of young people who are not directly involved in the fighting, but who experience the tensions of battle in the mental and affective landscapes of their lives. The 'charm' of intellectual urban life is played off against the richly satisfying beauty of the countryside, which seems to embody all that England stands for. Josephine Miller, Sebastian Hunt and the Sharpe sisters ply between the two, frustrated, unsure, suffering the tumult of a world in upheaval.

A150   Wilson, Theodora Wilson *The Last Weapon: A Vision*, London:
C.W. Daniel, 1916.

An allegory, from the Christian viewpoint, in which there is a battle between Fear and Love. A weapon, called Hellite, is invented, which destroys everything within range. It is put forward as a peace-making power – the Last Weapon. The inventor, however, threatens to offer the weapon to the enemy. In the meantime, a group of Pilgrims, led by a child, try to persuade people of the merits of peace, but 'the Sons of Fear dogged their footsteps and stirred up the great ones of the earth – aye and some of the poorest – to crush them to silence' (69). They are successful in some cases (including that of Lady Power, whose son is at the Front). The piece ends in stalemate, the final words being those of Christ: 'I have offered they My Last Weapon for more than nineteen hundred years. If they still refuse it, I have no other!'

Theodora Wilson Wilson was a Quaker who edited and financed the Christian revolutionary journal, the *New Crusader*.

A151   Woolf, Virginia *Jacob's Room*, London: Hogarth, 1922. Reprinted London: Granada, 1976.

The story of Jacob Flanders, as seen, impressionistically, through the eyes of an unnamed narrator, who is female and older than Jacob. He is seen growing up, at school, at Cambridge, and beginning his professional life while living in London among friends. We catch glimpses of his relationships, his travels, his conversations. The novel ends with his quick, arbitrary death in the First World War, for which his life seems a particular form of masculine training.

A152   Woolf, Virginia *Mrs Dalloway*, London: Hogarth, 1925. Reprinted London: Granada, 1976.

Mrs Dalloway, wife of a Conservative MP, is to give a party. The novel follows her and her thoughts throughout the day as she makes her preparations and thinks back through her relationships with friends, her husband, her daughter and Doris Kilman. At the party she hears of the suicide of Septimus Warren Smith, a soldier who has survived the war, but was deeply shell-shocked. His story parallels that of Clarissa: his relatively impoverished upbringing, romantic idea of England, love for a fellow officer who is killed, and subsequent brutish handling by the medical profession form a narrative of masculinity tragically manipulated by the exigencies of war. His death is narrated through Clarissa's consciousness. This provides a stark contrast between the glitter and triviality of 'simply life' at a party, and the desperate consequences of an ideological system that punishes men who fail to live up to the militaristic ideals of masculinity. Issues of class, gender and nationality are brought into question, and Clarissa's daughter, Elizabeth, is seen as the one who might contribute to a more balanced postwar reconstruction.

A153   Woolf, Virginia *To the Lighthouse*, London: Hogarth, 1927. Reprinted Harmondsworth: Penguin, 1974.

This novel is divided into three parts, which cover the prewar period, the war itself and the postwar period. The second part is the shortest and the most allusive. It shows us the deterioration of the Ramsay family's holiday house in language that suggests the violence and arbitrariness of the war, and presents material details concerning the family members in square brackets. Thus we hear of the death of Mrs Ramsay, hitherto the heroine of the novel – a gracious and serene maternal figure who cannot, it seems, survive into the postwar world. Andrew Ramsay is killed in the war; Prue dies in childbirth. The certainties and optimism of the

Victorian and Edwardian periods are smashed in a chaotic vision of the world's meaninglessness and fragmentation. It is the artist, Lily Briscoe, who, in the novel's third section, is left to make some sense of recent happenings. She does so through observation, sympathy, desire and design, liberated from the constraints of Mrs Ramsay's conviction that she must marry, free to express her own vision.

A154   Woolf, Virginia *The Years*, London: Hogarth, 1937. Reprinted London: Granada, 1977.

A novel that follows the Pargiter family from the 1880s to the 1930s. Only one brief section directly relates to the war: the chapter entitled '1917' follows the conversations of family members on a night when there is an air raid. The war plays a part in seeing out the nineteenth century and, for all its violence and tragedy, in creating the possibility of living differently. Not all, however, are willing to make use of those possibilities as the radicalism of youth transmutes into conservatism in a later age.

A155   Young, Florence Ethel Mills *Beatrice Ashleigh*, London: Hodder & Stoughton, 1918.

Beatrice Ashleigh has been brought up by her father to have similar interests to her brother, and not to have her intellect curtailed by common prejudice against women. She's not that interested, though, and becomes attracted to Frederick Hurst. But he has a secret: while serving in India he became entangled with a married woman. Beatrice's brother informs her of this, and she cannot forgive Fred. Her father dies, and she is forced to live with her reverend uncle. When war breaks out, she catches the 'spirit of restless energy' and attends ambulance lectures. She hears from a curate cousin that Fred has been badly hurt: his face has mostly been destroyed. She goes to him and forgives everything, having realised that she really loved him all along.

II   SHORT FICTION

A156   Barclay, Florence L. *In Hoc Vince: the Story of A Red Cross Flag*, London: G.P. Putnam's Sons, 1915.

Originally printed as a contribution to King Albert's Book, this story tells the tale of a soldier who, at the request of a nurse, makes a Red Cross flag from a sheet and bloody bandages, and flies it above a shelter in a war-wrecked town. Attention is drawn to the significance of the blood-stained cross, to the Calvary of self-sacrifice that must logically lead to the triumph of resurrection.

A157   Bellerby, Frances *Come to an End And Other Stories*, London: Methuen, 1939.

A volume of mostly postwar stories, some of which deal with the remembered experience of war.

A158   Boas, Mrs F. S. [Boas, Henrietta O'Brien] *Comrades-in-Arms*, London: Wells Gardner, Darton & Co. Ltd, 1915.

Sequence of short stories about the war. Begins with a first-person narrative of a less successful brother, who effectively gives up his life for his more dashing brother, Jack. Mostly about comradeship, small-town, local, sentimental values.

A159   Borden, Mary *The Forbidden Zone*, London: Heinemann, 1929.

A collection of sketches, 'fragments of a great confusion' (Preface), written from the point of view of a nurse in the 'Forbidden Zone' – the strip of land immediately behind the firing lines. Mostly written in a deadpan tone: Belgium is 'mud with a broken fragment of a nation lolling in it' (4); there are no men, only body parts; as far as she is concerned 'Everything is arrranged. It is arranged that men should be broken and that they should be mended' (117). Combines a haunted sense of the absurdity and pathos of nursing the wounded in Belgium, but occasionally spills over into melodramatic phraseology. Borden was born in Chicago and settled in England; she was a prominent literary figure before the war. She received decorations from the British and the French for her work running a mobile hospital unit attached to the French Army.

A160   Buckrose, J.E. (pseudonym of Annie Edith Jameson) *War-Time in Our Street, The Story of Some Companies Behind the Firing Line*, London and New York: Hodder & Stoughton, 1917.

Vignettes, testifying to the courage and stamina of the women left behind. 'Our Lad' speaks to the generosity of a woman in giving hospitality to a pair of shabby grubby women, seeking 'their lad'. 'The Spy' is about a suspected spy who turns out to be one too old to volunteer and who dyes his hair to look younger. 'War Economy' refers to those who take the weekly papers' advice on 'How to Make Mock Goose with a Vegetable Marrow and a Mutton Bone'. Cheerful, up-beat fables of hope, honour, love and making the best of things with full community spirit.

A161   Butts, Mary *Speed the Plough and Other Stories*, London: Chapman & Hall Ltd, 1923.

Volume of short stories, some of which refer, albeit obliquely, to the war. The title story deals more centrally with war issues: a soldier wakes up in hospital, obsessed with rich, luxurious fabrics and the image of woman that goes with them. He works on a farm, but hankers after 'civilisation': wealth, fine clothes, city pleasures – war.

A162   Canfield, Dorothy *Home Fires in France*, London: Constable, 1919.

Series of sketches from the point of view of an American woman in occupied France. Many comments on American generosity and on the experience of seeing the war-wounded, the prisoners, of witnessing their despair and the terror of ordinary people when the Germans come in and wreck their lives.

A163   Castle, Agnes *Little House in Wartime*, London: Constable, 1915.

The Foreword quotes from Brooke's 'The Soldier' and introduces the book as 'the true record of the everyday life of an average family. ... We trust our pages may add a little mirth more to the gallant spirit abroad.' Consists of sketches of local life in a Surrey village – taking in Belgian refugees, the local Red Cross movement, the garden, the flowers, etc. The tone is both sentimental and religious; intended as an antidote to the horrors of war.

A164   Hall, Radclyffe *Miss Ogilvy finds Herself*, London: Heinemann, 1934.

The title story is the one that deals most clearly with the war. Similarly to Stephen Gordon in *The Well of Loneliness*, Miss Ogilvy responds to England's call to arms and distinguishes herself as a courageous and cool-headed ambulance commandant. Unwanted, after the war, she retreats to a remote part of the country, where she 'finds herself' in a fantasy of true love, as an ancient Briton. Involves a modulation of style from realist reportage to the rhythmic language of fantasy as 'Miss Ogilvy' undergoes the shift in identity from 'she' to 'he'. An 'Author's Forenote' describes its relation to *The Well* in terms of the 'noble and selfless work done by hundreds of sexually inverted women during the Great War'.
    Another story in the volume, 'Fräulein Schwarz', also refers to the war. Documents the reactions of a range of rather dull boarders in the Fräulein's house: men who join up, women who take on office work, all of whom turn on Fräulein Schwarz with 'the look of the hunter who corners his prey, watchful, alert with a sense of power' (164).

A165   Holtby, Winifred *Sentence of Life: Selected Short Stories of Winifred Holtby*, eds Paul Berry and Marion Shaw. London: Virago, 1999.

Forthcoming volume of Holtby's short stories.

A166   Lane, Mrs John *War Phases According to Maria*, London: John Lane 1917.

Satirical sketches, narrated in the voice of Maria, who is a mature woman, described in publicity material as 'serene, self-satisfied and suburbanly sophisticated'. A good-humoured war book, that exemplifies a very British tolerance towards a pompous and rather frivolous character. Illustrated by A.H. Fish.

A167   Mansfield, Katherine *The Stories of Katherine Mansfield*, ed. Antony Alpers. Auckland, Melbourne, Oxford: Oxford University Press, 1984.

Few of her stories refer directly to the war, but see 'The Fly' (first published in *The Doves' Nest*) and 'An Indiscreet Journey', 'Spring Pictures', 'Late at Night', 'Two Tuppeny Ones Please' (all published in *Something Childish*) for oblique, but intense renditions of civilian experience.

A168   Ruck, Berta (Mrs Oliver Onions) *Khaki and Kisses*, London: Hutchinson, 1915.

A series of patriotic sketches. A once-decadent girl agrees to marry the wounded soldier she had flirtatiously dismissed in prewar times; an English girl refuses to return to Germany with her husband who is from that country; an estranged couple are re-united over the birth of a baby boy on the day war is declared; a military censor reads about out how much he is loved; war weddings, white feathers, VADs, deaths of heroes, shirkers, cockneys, grannies all do the right thing in the end.

A169   Sharp, Evelyn *The War of All the Ages*, London: Sidgwick & Jackson, 1915.

A collection of short sketches and stories that depict the effect of war on the poor. Many of them take a cliché or phrase and defamiliarise it by applying it to another context. The first story, for example, 'The Casualty' takes a group of young boys playing at being wounded, who are interrupted by a mere girl who, in their estimation, cannot know what a casualty is. She then tells them that there is a 'casualty' at home: the baby, for want of food, owing to wartime unemployment, has died. Most are in sympathy with those suffering from economic deprivations, those in league with suffrage activity, and those who understand the broader social and economic hardships engendered by war.

A170   Woolf, Virginia *The Complete Shorter Fiction of Virginia Woolf*, ed. Susan Dick, London: Hogarth, 1985.

Few overt references to the war, but see 'The Mark on the Wall', 'A Society' (both first printed in *Monday or Tuesday*, London: Hogarth, 1921) and 'Mrs Dalloway in Bond Street' (first published in *Dial*, 1923; reprinted in *Mrs Dalloway's Party*, ed. Stella McNichol, London: Hogarth, 1973).

B CONTEMPORARY ACCOUNTS

I CONTEMPORARY BOOKS AND ARTICLES

B1   Addams, Jane, Emily G. Balch and Alice Hamilton *Women at the Hague*, New York: Macmillan 1915.

An account of the Hague Congress of 1915 by three American delegates, outlining the case for peace, the success of the congress itself, and commenting on the destructive comments in the press.

B2   Adler, N. 'Women's Industry After the War', *Contemporary Review* 108, (July–December 1915): 780–88.

A paper prepared for the National Union of Women Workers, which looks at opportunities for women and children, speculates on the effect on commercial activities of the cessation of hostilities, and comments on the likely way forward in retaining and rewarding domestic servants. Recommends, if improved labour conditions are to be secured after the war, better training for the young; a wider scheme of scholarships and grants; increase of trades to which the minimum wage shall apply; limitation on hours worked; development of language teaching.

B3   Aldridge, Olive *The Retreat from Serbia through Montenegro and Albania*, London: Minerva Publishing Co., 1916.

In July 1915 the author went to Serbia as a member of the 3rd Serbian Relief Unit, where she ran a dispensary at Vitanovatz, 30 miles from Mrs Stobart's field hospital at Kragujevatz. Begins with observations of local life, customs, religious practices, etc., but when the fighting began in earnest, she had to return to Kragujevatz to help with the many wounded. The order came to retreat, and this is what they did, along with the Serbian people. Colourful scenes of people camping out, roasting animals on makeshift fires, trekking across mountainous, wooded land, witnessing scenes of tragedy by the roadside, crossing frozen, slippery land until, seven weeks later, they reached the coast and boarded a ship. The book is dedicated to the Serbian people.

B4   Alec-Tweedie, Mrs *Women and Soldiers*, London: John Lane, The Bodley Head, 1918.

Articulates the 'topsy-turvey' theory: 'the world has discovered women, and women have found themselves. And a new world has been created' (2). Sprightly account concerned to praise the best efforts of the 'right sort' of women, to condemn 'slackers' and conscientious objectors, to encourage the adoption of uniform for women wherever possible, and to make a stand for a Women's Battalion to go out, if necessary, and fight. Combines advocacy of gendered equality (equal pay, education and prestige), class prejudice (to the typewriter girl the word 'moderation' is unknown) and inflexible patriotism (exterminate cats and dogs, ban chocolates and nighties for the sake of the economy) in the name of good, female sense.

B5   Allen, Mary S. *The Pioneer Policewoman*, ed. Julie Helen Heyneman. London: Chatto & Windus, 1925.

An account of the work of Margaret Damer Dawson and Mary S. Allen in establishing a women's police service. Dawson worked with Belgian refugees and perceived a need for a body of trained women in uniform to organise the arrivals at London stations to places of hospitality. Many of those attracted to the 'force' had been militant suffragettes, which gave them a certain kind of experience. Story of early hostilities, gradual acceptance, financial support from the government and the contract with the Ministry of Munitions. 'The protection of women by women' was their principle; much emphasis on the successes of the female qualities of humour, tact and conciliatory friendliness in potentially inflammatory situations.

B6   Andrews, Irene Osgood and M.A. Hobbs *The Economic Effects of the War upon Women and Children in Great Britain*, New York: Oxford University Press, 1918.

A detailed study that is sympathetic to women workers. Begins with the estimate that three to five workers are necessary to keep a soldier at the front completely equipped. Discusses early dislocation of women in industry and their gradual influx into most trades, and provides accounts of the increase in employment of women, organised efforts to recruit women, the sources of additional women workers, trades unions, munitions legislation and welfare. Notes a general increase in women's health resulting from higher pay and concludes that, although home life may have suffered, the general 'personality' of factory women was transformed by confidence, independence and interest in impersonal issues.

B7   Anon 'On the Fringe of the War', *Blackwood's Magazine* 200, (October 1916): 478–88.

An account of a doctor's wife in Central Persia. They are told to leave their village as international hostility mounts up, and have to make a difficult journey, over land, on mules, in order to join the British community in the Gulf.

B8   Anon *WAAC: The Woman's Story of the War*, London: T. Werner Laurie Ltd, 1930.

The story of a clergyman's daughter's experiences in France. She soon loses her innocence, falls deeply in love, and becomes involved with spying, as well as with hospital work, ambulance driving, etc. When her lover dies, she finds he has left her a considerable sum of money. The account details her close relationship with her father, her poor relationship with her mother, and various attitudes to her brothers, one of whom does not acquit himself well. More willing to discuss matters concerning sexuality than a number of other similar accounts.

B9   Atherton, Gertrude *The Living Present: The Work of French Women in War Time*, London: John Murray, 1917.

Account of women's work in France – society women turned voluntary hospital workers, munition workers, etc. Includes an account of the work of Madame Waddington, the wife of an American diplomat, who opened a sewing workroom in Paris for those with no other form of income.

B10   Baerami *A Call to Women or Woman's Part in the Great World Conflict*, Letchworth: Garden City Press, 1915.

Not seen.

B11   Balfour, Lady F. *Dr. Elsie Inglis*, London: British Periodicals Ltd, 1920.

A short book, with no footnotes or other supporting information, in a series designed to inspire 'Young Citizens'. Concentrates on the major events in Inglis's life: early travel and education, medical training in Edinburgh, experience at the London Hospital for Women, suffrage experience and then, at the outbreak of war, her efforts to set up the SWH, in particular the units that went to Serbia. Concentrates on her skills in management, delegation, judging character, her ability to conquer opposition (the memorable phrase 'My good lady, go home and sit still' was addressed to her), her love for the Serbians, devotion to duty and personal self-sacrifice.

B12   Barber, Margaret H. *A British Nurse in Bolshevik Russia April 1916 – December 1919*, London: A.C. Fifield, 1920.

The Preface to this unusual account comments that it is offered to remove the prejudices and fear with which Russian events are customarily viewed. Barber went out to Van, Armenia, with Harold Buxton's Armenian Relief Fund. She stayed when the unit left, tending peasants and POWs on the steppe, by the Urals. Her descriptions of Russia focus on the social conditions – the poverty and hunger, the shortage of bread. In Petrograd the begging by the poor is met with kindness by the Red Guards. She is generally complimentary towards Bolshevik thought and organisation, viewing their political and civic programme with approval.

B13   Barton, E.M. and Marguerite Cody *Eve in Khaki: The Story of the Women's Army at Home and Abroad*, London: Nelson, 1918.

Divided into two parts covering WAAC service in Britain and in France. Describes early work by the Women's Legion and the development of women's war service as army cooks, clerks, telegraphists, telephonists, etc. until the Women's Army Auxiliary Corps came into existence in June 1917. Then details personnel, training, conditions, types of work. A narrative of progress, charting the modern woman's growth in efficiency and discipline, and her strong, capable, balanced outlook, which has 'placed her side by side with man, as fellow-worker, comrade and fellow-citizen' (197).

B14   Beauchamp, Pat *Fanny Goes to War*, London, John Murray, 1919.

An Introduction by Major-General H.N. Thompson praises the powers of endurance and 'spirit of cheerfulness' that characterised FANY members. The account outlines the formation of the First Aid Nursing Yeomanry in 1910, with the stipulation that members must be able to ride bareback. They wore rather distinctive uniforms. The services of the organisation were rejected by the British War Office and accepted by the Belgian Army. Beauchamp describes experiences of being under fire, of distributing medical supplies in the trenches, of being bombed by a zep, of a friend witnessing a British soldier kill a wounded German who had assaulted a nurse –'It is thus that our brave soldiers avenge us from these brutes' (84). She joins a motor convoy and, ultimately, has an accident that results in a severe leg injury. She was awarded the *Croix de Guerre* and Silver Star.

See also Fanny Went to War (C 40) and the Liddle Collection (E240).

B15   Begbie, Harold *The Queen's Net: True Stories of all Sorts and Conditions of Women Saved from the War Flood of Suffering Privation and Despair by the Queen's Work for Women Fund*, London: Hodder & Stoughton, 1915.

A collection of brief lives, rescued from despair and decay, designed to celebrate the work done by the Queen's Work for Women Fund. The narrator leads us down numerous grubby alleys to dark and comfortless rooms, where women, variously spirited, serene or depressed, tell their stories in a variety of accents, from the grateful once well-educated opera singer, who was beaten and deserted with her small child, to an ageing ex-'detective', who has 'the soul of a ferret, and the cold passion of a cat'. The mood is generally sentimental and patronising. The penultimate chapter describes the operation and maintenance of the workrooms; the last chapter is in praise of the Queen.

B16   Bell, Julian *We Did Not Fight: 1914–1918 Experiences of War Resisters*, London: Cobden-Sanderson, 1935.

A collection of essays which includes a poem by Siegfried Sassoon and accounts by (e.g.) Norman Angell, David Garnett, Stephen Hobhouse, Bertrand Russell and Adrian Stephen. Accounts by women include that of Lella Secor Florence, whose 'The Ford Peace Ship and After' recounts her experiences as a journalist on the Ford Peace Ship, and Mrs Sheehy Skeffington, who tells of her husband's war years as an Irishman, nationalist, socialist, feminist and anti-clerical, before he was illegally killed by the British military.

B17   Bevan, Sophie K. *The Home and the War*, London: John Murray, 1918.

The 'home' in question is a sixteenth-century mansion with a massive country estate, to which the author decides to return in order to practise patriotic economy and efficiency. She follows the line of argument that sees war as a purifying force: 'To those who have eyes to see, it has been a resurrection of the national grit and character. We were rapidly becoming too soft, too flabby, too fond of the insidious gospel of comfort' (52). She reduces her staff, to allow them to enlist, and holds forth on keeping goats, making hayricks, running a dairy, the benefits of tomatoes, farming rabbits, hares, fish, deer, etc.

B18   Billington, Mary Frances *The Red Cross in War: Woman's Part in the Relief of Suffering*, London: Hodder & Stoughton, 1914.

A brief history of women in military nursing, from Florence Nightingale to QAIMNS to the Red Cross, written from the perspective of someone who has thought through the nursing implications of recent wars. Discusses the role of experienced, talented and unusual women in setting up women's military nursing organisations. Very much a 'gentle sex' approach, but one that insists on the nobility of the service. Mentions Violetta Thurstan and Millicent, Duchess of Sutherland among others, and provides a detailed breakdown of who ran which hospital.

B19   Billington, Mary Frances *The Roll-Call of Serving Women. A Record of Women's Work for Combatants and Sufferers in the Great War*, London: The Religious Tract Society, 1915.

An account of women's part in the first year of the war, with reference to Dr Munro's ambulance corps, women's welfare work on the home front, the good work of the aristocracy, women's work in France, and the contribution of particularly heroic nurses (Violetta Thurstan is mentioned). The account ends thus: 'For we cannot but believe that great good will come out of this devouring and devastating war' (221).

B20   Blackburn, D. *The Martyr Nurse*, London: The Ridd Masson Co., 1915.

This account of Edith Cavell's life provides details of her work for the poor of Hoxton, before she left England, and comments on the difficulty of the position she held as a Protestant in a Catholic nurses' training institution in Belgium. Contends that Cavell's own honesty provided the prosecution with the evidence needed to find her guilty, and retails the account of the appeals and pleas that she should not die. Also reprints the story of the British chaplain, who spoke to her last, and to whom she said the famous words: 'I realise that patriotism is not enough. I must have no hatred or bitterness towards anyone.' Includes details of the execution, of the international condemnation that it provoked, and considers the effect of the occasion on history.

B21   Bowser, Thekla *The Story of British V.A.D. Work in the Great War*, London: A. Melrose, 1917.

An enthusiastic account of the foundation and organisation of the VAD, convinced that class barriers have disintegrated and that 'a common chord of love and tenderness' (16) binds all who have been 'allowed to participate in this great work of patiotism' (19). All tasks, lofty and lowly are 'performed in humbleness of spirit and true gratitude by those who are denied the greater honour of joining the King's fighting forces' (35). Chivalric discourse dominates, in a cosy kind of way. There is nothing critical nor controversial here; no quarrels nor disagreements, only enthusiasm and devotion to duty. Everyone is cheery, the soldiers' hearts are warmed and the girls thrill with pride at the privilege of it all.

B22   British Committee of the Women's International Congress *Towards Permanent Peace: A Record of the Women's International Congress*, London: British Committee, WIC, 1915.

Contains an account of the mission of the congress envoys to the governments of Europe and the USA.

B23   Brittain, Vera *Halcyon, Or the Future of Monogamy*, London: Kegan Paul, Trench, Trubner & Co. Ltd, 1929.

A satire on early twentieth-century sexual attitudes. Contains references to the war and a brief section on hypocritical treatment of the mothers of 'war babies'.

B24   Brittain, Vera 'Why I Stand for Peace' in *Let Us Honour Peace*, London: Cobden-Sanderson, 1937.

Concentrates discussion on the responsibilities of motherhood, noting that militarised societies attach little economic value to mothers, while encouraging their maternal functions. Appeals to women to organise and educate themselves in order to prevent another war. Comments on the disparity between military expenditure and expenditure on maternity services. Focuses on conventional, educated women, saying that if they make no protest, 'what can we expect of the poor, the overworked, the under-nourished?' (62).

B25   Brittain, Vera and Winifred Holtby *Testament of a Generation: The Journalism of Vera Brittain and Winifred Holtby*, eds Paul Berry and Alan Bishop, London: Virago, 1985.

A selection of journalism by Brittain and Holtby, divided into sections on feminism, politics and writing, and preceded by an introduction and an account of their friendship. The articles were written after the First World War, but include many reflections on the war itself, and the war period.

B26   Bryant, Louise *Six Red Months in Russia. An Observer's Account of Russia Before and During the Proletarian Dictatorship*, London: Heinemann, 1919.

A sympathetic account of the Russian Revolution by an American war correspondent. As well as describing her own journey and experiences, she offers an explanation of the new political organisation and the constitutional changes. Aims to be clear and informative. Makes a heroine of Katherine Breshkovsky – 'Babushka'; describes Kerensky and the Revolutionary Tribunals. Visits the Women's Battalion of Death, and makes the point that women in Russia have always fought in the army. Ends thus: 'I wanted to go back and offer my life for the revolution.'

B27   Burke, Kathleen *The White Road to Verdun*, London: Hodder & Stoughton, 1916.

A book in praise of 'Mother France': her soldiers (the 'poilus'), her General ('No one could have been more gracious and kind than General Pétain, and in his presence one realised the strength and power of France') and her cities. Verdun is described as 'A white city of desolation, scorched and battered, yet the brightest jewel in the crown of France's glory.' Burke was known as a successful fundraiser.

B28   Buxton, Charles Roden (ed.) *Towards a Lasting Settlement*, London: George Allen & Unwin, Ltd, 1915.

Essays exploring the possibility of a lasting settlement in the context of a common European policy. Contributions by G. Lowes Dickinson, J.A. Hobson, H.N. Brailsford, Philip Snowden, among others, plus Irene Cooper Willis, who draws on 'The Parallel of the Great French War', A. Maude Royden, whose essay 'War and the Woman's Movement' takes on the physical force argument, and Vernon Lee, who argues in 'The Democratic Principle and International Relations' that consistency, responsibility, reciprocity and self-determination, rather than submission and dogma, should accompany democracy.

B29   Byron, M. *The Red Cross of Comfort*, London: Hodder & Stoughton, 1914.

A compilation, intended to comfort those suffering from the sorrows of the war. Publisher's blurb: 'The devotional character of "The Red Cross of Comfort" will endear it to those who are in need of such a companion, whilst the beautiful extracts which it contains will carry comfort to the sad heart.'

B30   Byron, M. *May Byron's 'How-to-Save' Cookery Book: A War-Time Cookery Book*, London: Hodder & Stoughton, 1915.

One in a series of cookery books, this one emphasising the 'close and thrifty times' in which it is produced. Advertised as being 'just plain common-sense right through. It shows what food is absolutely needful, and how to economise in it; how to prepare dishes which shall be cheap and nice instead of cheap and nasty; how to use up your odds and ends without using up yourself in the process.' Mood of unremitting cheerfulness.

B31   Cable, Boyd *Doing Their Bit: War Work at Home*, London: Hodder & Stoughton, 1916.

Account by a popular writer, written to boost morale with tales of excellent work on the home front. Chapter on 'The Women' singing the praises of their 'tractable and obedient' attitude in the munitions factories.

B32   Caine, Hall *Our Girls: Their Work for the War*, London: Hutchinson, 1916.

A propagandist piece, published for Christmas 1916, applauding the role of women in munitions factories, and geared towards encouraging recruitment. Written in a style rich with allusions to exotic lands: 'The scene reminds us of the human tide outside the gate of an Eastern city' (11); 'feeling as we felt when we walked, in Oriental slippers, into the Mosque of Omar on the site of the Temple of Solomon, we pass into a far more impressive and tremendous scene' (27). Tends to be deeply patronising, while claiming to celebrate the power and capabilities of the woman worker. Style is worthy of analysis, in the context of political and ideological expediencies.

B33   Campbell, Phyllis *Back of the Front,* London: George Newnes, 1915.

An account of a British worker for the French Red Cross, making use of the full panoply of chivalric discourse ('behold! the soul was a pure white light of knightly splendour' (25)), myths and visions (sightings of Joan of Arc), atrocity stories ('the child's body fell one way and its little golden dusty head another' (29)). An introduction claims that it is all true; evidence to the contrary suggests that its sources came from the Bryce report of German atrocities.

See Buitenhuis (F15).

B34   Carr, Kent *Women Who Dared: Heroines of the Great War*, London: S.W. Partridge, 1920.

Accounts of the war experiences of notable women. Includes The Queen of the Belgians, Nurse Cavell, The Women of the Hector Munro Field Ambulance Corps, The Women of Pervyse, Miss Macnaughtan, Lady Paget, Dr Elsie Inglis, Mrs St Clair Stobart, Mrs Percy Dearmer, Miss Violetta Thurstan.

B35   *Nurse Cavell: The Story of her Life and Martyrdom,* London: C. Arthur Pearson, 1915.

Brief (36pp.), first-person account of Edith Cavell's life and death. No indication of the identity of the author. Gives an account of her life, training, work in Belgium before the war, and her aid to Allied soldiers trying to escape. The narrative concentrates on the unfairness of her trial, and provides an Appendix which contains the official correspondence regarding her case. A personal testimony that centres on Cavell's quiet courage.

B36   Celarie, Henriette *Slaves of the Huns: The Experiences of Two Girls of Lille*, London: Cassell, 1918.

This account, translated from the French by M.C. ffoulkes, is prefaced by a publisher's note indicating the desirability of informing the British public of the consequences of German occupation. The note adds that this appears all the more necessary as there is evidence that 'English girls are willing to be on terms of amity with enemy prisoners'. There are two stories, that of Yvonne and that of Marie. Yvonne describes how her house in Lille was visited in the middle of the night (along with others), and young girls and women were told that they were to be taken away to work on the land. The 'real' reason for deporting them, she thinks, is to break down morale. They are indeed taken off and made to do agricultural work, treated fairly harshly, suffer threats of rape and other violence, but are returned unharmed. Marie, at twenty, is a little younger, and describes similar events.

B37   Chew, Ada Nield '"Womanly" Work', *The Common Cause* vi, 306, (February 1915): 724.

Brief but powerful (if faintly sentimental) article about work done in Manchester to relieve conditions of working-class mothers. 'I realised afresh that the working class wife and mother is a heroine all the time.' Useful corrective to glorifying tales of middle-class female endeavour.

B38   Churchill, Jennie (Lady Randolph) (ed.) *Women's Work in War Time*,
London: C. Arthur Pearson, 1916.

This account covers women's war work on the part of the belligerent countries –
including Germany and Austria – and of the USA and the colonies (i.e. Canada and
Australia). Concentrates on the *differences* between women's skills and is
concerned to dispel ideas about 'women's limitations'. Makes the cautionary point
that work is easily available to untrained women in the present abnormal conditions, but that after the war, without training, organisation and proper pay
structures, the situation is unlikely to continue: 'This is said by way of warning
against hilarious optimism over the position of the woman worker' (158).

B39   Cole, G.D.H. *Labour in War Time*, London: G. Bell & Sons, 1915.

Written by the economist and socialist who was to become the husband of
Margaret Postgate Cole. An account of the manner in which the war has affected
labour, and of the industrial problems to which it has given rise. Includes a chapter
on women and the war, which refers to women's unemployment, the Queen's Work
for Women Fund, the effect of women's labour on standard wage rates, the
regrading of some jobs, and the 'menace' provided by women to trades union standards and conditions.

B40   Cole, G.D.H. *Trade Unionism and Munitions,*Oxford: The Clarendon
Press, Humphrey Milford, 1923.

States in the Preface that his perspective is that of an adviser to the Amalgamated
Society of Engineers. Gives an account of trades union developments in the context
of dilution, the Munitions Acts, Military Service, the regulation of wages and the
restoration of prewar practices, saying that 'Munitions policy was anything but
coherent: it was a series of fits and starts, improvisations and expedients.' Mentions
that the importation of 'coloured labour' was the alternative to employing women
in munitions, and speaks to the 'failures' of the employment of women in industry,
largely as a result of the employers' reluctance to alter conditions to suit a different
kind of employee.

B41   Cosens, M. *Lloyd George's Munitions Girls*, London:
Hutchinson & Co., 1917.

An account by one who worked in a 'shell-shop', which begins: 'OH! I wanted –
wanted more than anything else in the world to become a "Miss Tommy Atkins"
in Lloyd George's army of Shell-Workers.' She tells how the recruitment lady tried
to put her off with tales of hard, heavy work, and obdurate foremen, but she is not
to be dissuaded. She thinks her workmates 'vulgar little hussies' at first – they fight
over hats and talk in cockney slang and have names like 'Mybel', 'I-ngel' and
'Muvver'. She makes it clear that the divisions between classes are absolute (lady
volunteers are called 'Miows'), but that they manage to work alongside each other
in a reasonably tolerant way.

B42   Coulson, Major Thomas *Mata Hari: Courtesan and Spy*, London:
Hutchinson & Co., 1930.

Tells the tale (with barely disguised distaste) of Mata Hari's fabricated past, her failed marriage and history as a courtesan, before relating incidents from her life as a spy, and her death. She is compared unfavourably with Louise de Bettignies. Tells of her attractions (although 'her bust was pendulous and ugly' (33)), and of her seduction technique. The following should give an idea of the prose style: 'In the voluptuous abandon of the semi-privacy, before a group of selected guests, reclining in luxurious ease after copious sacramental libations, and surrounded by her worshippers, Mata Hari invokes the image of her youth' (31).

B43   Coulson, Major Thomas *Queen of Spies: Louise de Bettignies*, London: Constable, 1935.

The story, told with a relish for a good yarn, of Louise de Bettignies who, under the name of Alice Dubois, became a spy for the Allies. She, who was seen as 'a shadowy mythical creature endowed with magical powers of invisibility' (47), worked from Lille, and risked capture, survived interrogations, and engineered miraculous escapes until ultimately she was caught and imprisoned. She died in jail. This account sees her as a heroine who sacrificed everything.

B44   Cowen, Hettie Broadbent *What is War? – & Two Other Essays*, London: The Cursitor Publishing Co., n.d. [1919].

A polemic (written while the war was still in progress) against conscientious objectors and other 'slackers', extolling 'the moral courage to fearlessly pursue [sic] the right in causes great and small whatever the consequences to oneself may be'. The other essays are entitled 'What is Freedom?' and 'Why Might is Right'. The answer to the first is: organise victory, then freedom will flourish through the strength of the power to serve; and to the second: 'When the imperfections of human nature are entirely eliminated we may not need armed forces. Until then they must be kept as strong and efficient servants of right.'

B45   Daggett, Mrs Mabel Potter *Women Wanted: The Story Written in Blood Red Letters on the Horizon of the Great War*, London: Hodder & Stoughton, 1918. New York: Doran, 1918.

The writer is an American suffragist and journalist, working for the *Pictorial Review*, who asks to be sent to Europe to cover the work done by women in the war. The narrative is carried forward by her self-characterisation as a suffragist and therefore a subversive (luckily she has letters of introduction to the British aristocracy, which ensure her permission to come ashore) and by the replacement of male labour by female – in the USA as well as in Europe. The refrain 'Women Wanted! Women Wanted!' is repeated rather too often and the book ends on a point made in dubious taste: 'For the ultimate programme toward which the Modern Woman Movement today is moving is no less than Paradise Regained! It may even, I think, have been worth this war to be there' (299).

B46   Davies, Ellen Chivers *A Farmer in Serbia*, London: Methuen, 1916.

Rather dreary account of the 'nursing' (not agricultural!) experiences of the 2nd Farmers' Unit in Serbia. They seem to have little work to do, nothing heroic to achieve. They retreat in response to the Austro-Hungarian advance, are invaded and ultimately deported back to England. Local customs, experience of living under siege, etc.

B47   Davies, Ellen Chivers *Ward Tales*, London: John Lane, 1920.

Tales from a military hospital by a VAD nurse. Attempts to reflect the humorous and comic side of events.

B48   Davies, Margaret Llewelyn, A. Honora Enfield, Lilian Harris *Co-operation versus Capitalism*, Hampstead Women's Co-operative Guild, 1919.

A proposal that the policy of the Co-operative Movement should adjust, in the light of developments in industry that have taken place as a result of the war, in order to secure international co-operative trade and control over raw materials. Concerned about the consolidation of capitalist interests as a result of war profits, business federations, and the links between business and government.

B49   Dent, Olive *A VAD in France*, London: Grant Richards Ltd, 1917.

Of the 'making the best of it' genre. Very sprightly in tone, determined to be 'a Kitchener nurse' (15). Trained and then went to France in summer 1915. Received a chilly welcome from the nursing professionals, but has sufficient confidence not to be 'overwhelmed with or impressed by, our manifold shortcomings' (29).Thrives on common sense, adaptability, the gratitude of the 'boys'. The arrival of the convoy, the preparations for Christmas, the documentation of 'types', and the organisation of The Concert structure the narrative.

B50   Douglas-Pennant, Violet *Under the Search-Light: A Record of a Great Scandal*, London: George Allen & Unwin, 1922.

An effort to make public the 'true facts' surrounding her dismissal from the Women's Royal Air Force. She understands that 'serious' information was supplied to Lady Rhondda by a 'total stranger' and that, although it wasn't investigated, that information provided the reason for her dismissal. She is looking to have her name cleared and for the authorities to admit to a mistake. This is a lengthy account (463pp.), including tales of her early experiences – problems getting material for uniforms, poor co-operation, being the object of attack by unreasonable women with a history of insubordination – and hints of intrigue and intimidation involving Dame Katharine Furse.

B51   Drake, Barbara *Women in the Engineering Trades*, Trade Union Series no. 3, London: Fabian Research Department and George Allen & Unwin Ltd, 1917.

A report by a Joint Committee of the Fabian Research Department and the Fabian Women's Group, which explores the history of women in the engineering trades (Birmingham shops had employed women since the 1860s), and which outlines the complex situation regarding sweated labour, the reorganisation of machinery (which reduced the number of skilled workers needed), dilution of labour, the point of view of the unions, the Munitions of War Act and the work of Mary Macarthur to increase women's organisation and representative power. A series of recommendations and alternative recommendations concludes the report, and they refer to rates of pay, provision against unemployment, protection from occupational injury, women in trades unions, equal pay for equal work, control of welfare by workers, etc.

B52   Drake, Barbara *Women in Trade Unions*, Trade Union Series no. 6, London: Fabian Research Department, 1920.

This is a broader version of the study that resulted in the report of women in the engineering trades. The first part provides a general history of the women's trades union movement, from the eighteenth century until 1918, with a section on the war. This outlines the employment of women following the initial disarray, and spends some time on the issues arising from munitions work. Difficulties were less marked in industries where women were not normally employed. The general conclusion is that in occupations where organisation has been strong, war conditions provided a rise in wages for women. But in the bulk of depressed women's industries, the rise in wages was nothing like equivalent to the increased cost of living. Part II provides a survey of women's organisations; Part III outlines the problems faced by women in trades unions and the obstacles to organisation that they encounter.

B53   Drucker, Amy J. 'A Cockney's Harvesting', *The Englishwoman* 20, 8, (April 1916): 13–21.

First-person account by 'a cockney born and bred' (although this is not registered in the prose style), who describes the hard, but nevertheless enjoyable work on a farm in Suffolk. Lots of detail concerning the nature of the work (hoeing, gleaning, shocking, etc.), which is physically arduous and often tedious. The conclusion is that there is nothing 'infra dig.' about women doing that kind of work, that the outdoor life is 'a splendid cure for brainfag', but that the wages are insufficient for any labourer, male or female, to live on, and are unattractive to women seeking war work when there are easier and better-paid jobs available.

B54   Fawcett, Mrs Henry (Millicent) 'War and Reconstruction: Women and their Use of the Vote', *The English Review* 26, (Jan–June 1918): 260–66.

Sketches the history of the suffrage movement, but her general point is that the political weight conferred by the vote will enable women to proceed with their work more efficiently. The next goals are equality of opportunity and equality before the law.

B55   Finzi, Kate John *Eighteen Months in the War Zone*, London: Cassell & Co., 1916.

An account by a VAD probationer of Boulogne's transformation into a hospital base. Pays particular attention to 'No.— Stationary Hospital' – the horrors, the vermin, the wounds. Repeats some of the so-called German atrocities, and gives an account of German soldiers being found chained to their machine guns. Is critical of some of the society ladies, who are trailed by press-men and appear in the weekly journals, and feels pity for 'those at home whose activities have not yet had occasion to be called into play'. She sets up a canteen.

B56   Fitzroy, Yvonne *With the Scottish Nurse in Roumania*, London: John Murray, 1918.

Accompanied Dr Elsie Inglis to Archangel in August 1916. Describes the difficult journey, preparing the hospital, receiving the first wounded from the Russian Front, having to retreat alongside refugees, troops, transport. Describes the panic that besets people as they hear that the Bulgars are coming. A hospital is set up at Braila, then, following futher retreat, at Galatz. Describes the confused national identity of those at Galatz – of Greek birth, but having been Turkish subjects for many years, with interests in Constantinople and Asia Minor. Conditions are poor – no beds, just straw, freezing winds, snow and ice. The tone is predominantly cheerful, and there is much about the routines that keep them sane. Includes photographs and map.

B57   Fitzwilliam, D.C.L. *A Nursing Manual for Nurses and Nursing Orderlies*, London: Hodder & Stoughton, 1914.

An instruction manual, mainly for Red Cross nurses. The assumption is that nurses in the field will be male.

Florence, Mary Sargant and C.K. Ogden *Militarism Versus Feminism*, London: Allen & Unwin, 1915. Reprinted eds Margaret Kamester and Jo Vellacott, London: Virago, 1987. *See* Ogden, C.K.

B58   Foxwell, A.K. *Munition Lasses: Six Months as Principal Overlooker in Danger Buildings*, London: Hodder & Stoughton, 1917.

A.K. Foxwell (MA, D.Litt.) is a university woman who takes a job at Woolwich Arsenal inspecting matters of health and safety, and reporting to the manager. The book was written in order to offer an insight into conditions. Praises the Lady Supervisor, gives general accounts of the danger buildings, filling shops, canteens, hostels, etc.

B59   Gardner, Alice *Our Outlook as Changed by the War: A Paper Read in Newnham College on Sunday 25th October 1914*, Cambridge: W. Heffer & Sons Ltd, 1914.

A measured account of the present (unknown and unknowable) situation in the *long* perspective of time, and in the context of an understanding of diverse cultures. Comments on the unsettling and resettling of proportion, on the elemental nature of man, and, on the subject of 'business as usual', refers to the students of Liège, who carried on with their exams during the bombardment of the town, and went out to fight when they had finished.

B60   Gell, Hon. Mrs E.M. *The War and the Objects of the Mother's Union. A Course of Model Addresses*, London: Wells Gardner, 1916.

Not seen.

B61 George, Gertrude A. *Eight Months with the Women's Royal Air Force*, London: Heath Cranton Ltd, 1921.

A nicely produced book, large format, with illustrations on every facing page, accompanying written sketches of, for example, 'Signing on', 'The Fortune Teller', 'Coal Fatigue', etc. The mood is somewhat wistful, the detail imprecise; the author performs mainly auxiliary tasks (cleaning, sign-writing, drill) but ultimately is 'prouder of [her] connection with the Force than of any artistic success [she has] ever had'.

B62 George, Samuel *Women's World-Wide Work with War OR Preparing for the Great International Peace*, London: The Power-Book Co., 1915.

The author wants to set about organising women into a Peace Army, and securing their full emancipation with the help of Christian love and an appeal to the individual. Foresees a new world: 'This is not A.D. 1915', he says, 'but W.E.1' – by which he means Women's Era 1. Thinks the campaign for the vote a wild goose chase, and has designed an emblem for a banner, a motto, and has written an International Hymn.

B63 Got, A. *The Case of Miss Cavell, From the Unpublished Documents of the Trial*, London: Hodder & Stoughton, 1920.

Not seen.

B64 Gould, Gerald 'Women War Novelists', *The Common Cause* x, 477, (May 31 1918): 77–78.

Raises questions concerning the nature of war writing and its value, suggesting that a novel can be 'about' the war by either taking the life of an individual and measuring the impact of the war on that life, or by taking a wider 'panoramic' vision. Proceeds with the assumption that the function of novels is to 'harmonise the sorrow of the world'. Refers to Mrs Humphry Ward, Sinclair's *The Tree of Heaven*, Hamilton's *Dead Yesterday*, Benson's *This is the End*, Stern's *A Marrying Man*, Dane's *First the Blade* and Delafield's *The War-Workers*. Neither belittles nor admires these books: is still waiting for this war's *War and Peace* to emerge.

B65 Gould, Gerald 'Psychoanalytical Novels', *The Common Cause* x, 480, (June 21, 1918): 114–15.

A review of Rebecca West's *The Return of the Soldier*, alongside J.D. Beresford's *God's Counterpoint*, in the context of popular interest in psychoanalysis. Admires the novel's artistry, its 'imaginative perceptions', its 'revelation of tender and intimate emotion'.

B66 Greig, G.A. *Women's Work on the Land*, London: Jarrold & Sons, 1916.

Low-key pamphlet written principally to convince farmers that it is necessary to employ women as land workers and that they can do the work, given appropriate conditions.

B67   Greville, F.E. (Countess of Warwick) *A Woman and the War*, London:
Chapman & Hall, 1916.

Daisy Warwick, once the mistress of King Edward VII (when he was Prince of
Wales), became a socialist in 1895 and an ardent advocate of greater freedoms for
women. These essays, on a variety of wartime subjects, represent a forthright articulation of her point of view. Among her convictions is that the children of the rural
poor should not be employed on the land until they have finished their schooling.
If any children should be required to bear part of the national burden, those who
attend the élite public schools should do so: at least they will have the chance to
complete their education at a later period.

B68   Grey, Maria G. *The Physical Force Objection to Women's Suffrage*,
London: Central Society for Women's Suffrage, 1901.

Admittedly well outside the limits of the 1914–18 period, but crucial to the development of the suffragist pacifist argument. Argues against the (anti-suffragist) doctrine
that political privileges should be conceded only to those who have brute force
enough to extort them on the grounds that (a) this argument runs counter to the
system of justice developed over generations of moral and intellectual reflection; (b)
that it is in any case not true: social order is maintained through agencies other than
brute force; (c) that suffrage granted on the ability to fight alone would disenfranchise
those men awarded exemption for whatever reason; and (d) that women should not
lose the 'privileges' granted to the 'gentler sex' by becoming full citizens, but should be
able to earn a proper respect based on shared responsibility and equality.

B69   Haldane, Elizabeth S. *The British Nurse in Peace and War*, London:
Murray, 1923.

A history, written from the point of view of a trained army nurse. The first section
concentrates on the more distant past, gives an account of the influence of Florence
Nightingale and the movement towards a proper system of registration. Part II, on
the nurse in war, gives a brief recap of the Queen Alexandra Imperial Nursing
Service (QAIMNS), the Territorial Army Nursing Service and the VAD, before
noting that army nurses were recalled to duty in August 1914, just as soldiers were,
and describing the gradual organisation of hospitals, clearing stations, ambulance
trains and hospital ships. Describes the necessity for volunteers, the need to expand
in 1916, and again in 1917, and the fact that nurses were still required as war
ended, to move into Belgium and Germany, to treat returned prisoners, and to cope
with the influenza epidemic.

B70   Hallowes, Mrs F.S. *Mothers of Men and Militarism*, London: Headley
Brothers, n.d. [1916].

Aims to help the 'mothers of men' to think, to work for a better way than war to
resolve disputes, to work for a Concert of Europe, to refuse to bear the burdens of
war in uncomplaining silence, to help to make and preserve peace. She appeals to
the symbolic figure of the mother as life-giver and life-preserver, and argues that
militarism is the enemy of women, who must do something to undermine its
power. Provides a list of national and international societies of women, of which
the International Woman Suffrage Alliance (IWSA) stands at the head.

B71   Hamilton, Cicely *Senlis*, London: W. Collins Sons & Co., 1917.

An account of the German occupation and burning of Senlis in September 1914. Notes particularly the brutal treatment of civilians by the invading Germans, the execution of the Mayor, and the role the event played in hardening the heart of France and the rest of the Allies towards their enemy. A consideration of the nature of modern warfare, in which all, civilians and soldiers alike, are required to be combatants.

See William – An Englishman (A50).

B72   Hamilton, Mary Agnes *Mary Macarthur: A Biographical Sketch*, London: Leonard Parsons, 1924.

This portrait, written in lively and admiring tones, covers Mary Macarthur's life from the time of her becoming chair of the Ayr branch of the Shop Assistant's Union, to her premature death in 1921. Macarthur became secretary, and later president of the Women's Trade Union League, founded the National Federation of Women Workers, launched the weekly journal *The Woman Worker*, and was active in securing proper representation for the thousands of unorganised women workers during the war. She was also largely responsible for running the Queen's Work for Women Fund. She remained concerned to see justice for men and women, in the future, as well as in the crisis years of the war. Her gifts were her ability to move a crowd with her impassioned eloquence, her ability to appeal to individuals (she had many dealings with Lloyd George over the pay and conditions of munitions workers), and an intelligence that was, at its worst, overly simple, but, at its best, acute in seeing to the heart of complex problems. Macarthur married the Labour MP Will Anderson, with whom she had a daughter during the war years, but he died during the influenza epidemic in 1919. She died in 1921.

B73   Hamilton, Lady Peggy *Three Years or the Duration: The Memoirs of a Munition Worker, 1914–1918*, London: Peter Owen, 1978.

An account of her experiences as a munitions worker at Woolwich Arsenal. Begins very much lacking in confidence (despite her elevated social background), doing unskilled work. In 1917 she moved to the barely completed Government Rolling Mills at Southampton Water, doing skilled work. Worked in Birmingham, alongside working-class women, and describes initiation rites, rivalries, wrestling matches. A thoughtful account, taking into consideration the fears of male workers, the poverty of many women, and the effect of redundancies as war draws to a close.

See Ursula Birnstingl, Liddle Collection (E249).

B74   Harraden, Beatrice *Our Warrior Women: A Story and an Appeal*, London: Witherby & Co., 1916.

Not seen.

B75   Heron-Maxwell, Beatrice *Through a Woman's Eyes*, London: Andrew Melrose, 1917.

A series of short essays on topical issues such as 'Bread-Winning Women', 'Women and Jealousy', 'Women and the Money-Sense', 'War the Leveller', 'Women and the Truth' – the last in praise of Edith Cavell. Mostly in favour of women's new opportunities, but conscious that poor judgement can set bad examples. Mellifluent and 'wise'.

B76   Hill, William Thomson *The Martyrdom of Nurse Cavell: The Life Story of the Victim of Germany's Most Barbarous Crime*, London: Hutchinson, 1915.

Brief (55pp.), biographical account of Edith Cavell. Quotes from an article to the *Nursing Mirror* in which she documents the invasion of Belgium by the Germans; speculates on the spies set up to watch her, and dramatises an account of her arrest. Mentions that there were suspicions concerning the fairness of her trial – her advocate was Austrian by birth – gives an account of the appeals, her last words, the execution. Draws attention to the fact that the event (which became generally known on Trafalgar Day) spurred further recruitment.

B77   Hobhouse, Mrs H. *'I Appeal Unto Caesar': The Case of the Conscientious Objector*, London: Allen & Unwin, 1917.

Includes an Introduction by Professor Gilbert Murray, and notes by the Earl of Selbourne, Lord Parmoor, Lord Hugh Cecil, MP, and Lord Henry Bentinck, MP. A pamphlet arguing for the release from prison of conscientious objectors, whose objection is genuine, but who have, nevertheless, served repeated prison sentences, often including elements of torture. Part I sets out the argument that those who refuse to do non-combatant service are being true to their convictions in refusing to equip the nation for the better prosecution of the war. Part II records the occupations of some of the imprisoned conscientious objectors and cites examples of the good character and high moral principles of some (e.g. the Quaker Maurice Rowntree, the Eton and Oxford-educated East End worker Stephen Hobhouse). Part III documents some of the appalling prison conditions. Most conscientious objectors were sentenced to periods of hard labour. Jo Vellacott's work on Bertrand Russell indicates that he, Russell, wrote most of this pamphlet.

See Vellacott *Bertrand Russell* (G67).

B78   Hockin, Olive *Two Girls on the Land. War-time on a Dartmoor Farm*, London: Arnold, 1918.

First-person narrative covering a year's experience doing heavy agricultural work on a farm in 'slow-moving' Devon. The narrator, who calls herself 'Sammy' arrives with 'an unbounded confidence in [her] own ability to do any mortal thing [she] wished to do' (8), but is very slowly re-educated as to the practical and physical hardships of the labouring life. She is a 'lady', not a member of an organisation, and (initally at least) rather patronising to the 'maester', who is in turn entirely sceptical about her ability to do the work. The account takes us through the seasons. 'Sammy' is accompanied by 'Jimmy', another female labourer. There are interesting comments on the 'superhuman' work required of the labourer's wife, luxuriant descriptions of the countryside, a sustained commentary on man's capacity to 'rid[e] roughshod through Nature' and renditions of the farmers' inability to comprehend the facts of the war. The narrative ends with the 'defeat' of the female labourers. The utterly exhausting work, the weather, the hardships, however, enable 'Sammy' to take a different, almost reverential view of the dynamics and economics of labourers' lives, and to voice the hope that after the war 'the country will spend on wages and homes for the living the millions it has been forced to spend on work-houses and homes for the dying' (157).

B79   Holtby, Winifred *Women and a Changing Civilisation*, London: John Lane, The Bodley Head Ltd, 1934.

A wide-ranging study that covers primitive and 'classical' civilisations, the Middle Ages, the Renaissance, and pauses on Mary Wollstonecraft before heading towards the present day. Debates basic questions about motherhood, education, labour, political emancipation, etc. Not much that directly impinges on the war, although the major debates refer to it. Also gives evidence of what is happening in Fascist Germany.

B80   Hutchins, B.L. *Women in Modern Industry*, London: G. Bell & Sons, Ltd, 1915. Reprinted New York and London: Garland Publishing Inc, 1980.

The first part of this study relates to the prewar period, and was undertaken before August 1914. It was intended as an account of the effects of the industrial revolution – in its broadest sense – on women. The last section refers to the early effects of the war and describes the initial dislocation of industry, the effects of unemployment, the sudden demand for skilled labour, and speaks to the need for training to a good general standard at school in order to develop the potential for better workers.

B81   Hutchins, B.L. *Conflicting Ideals of Woman's Work*, London: Thomas Murby & Co. Ltd, 1917.

An interesting, thoughtfully-argued book that, while it doesn't have overt war content, provides a vital context to the debates surrounding women and work. Provides an historical outline of women and work, considering the ideals of the patriarchal family, the role of women in social life, the distinctions to be made between 'individualist feminists' and those concerned to curtail the 'freedom' of the employer to exploit the weaker class of worker. She considers single women, married women who work and the social care of children. Has a wide range of literary references.

B82   Jenssen, Baroness Carla (pseudonym) *I Spy! Sensational Disclosures of a British Secret Service Agent*, London: Jarrolds, n.d. [1930].

An account of a woman's postwar spying adventures – with references to wartime intelligence too. Sensational indeed.

B83   Jesse, F.T. *The Sword of Deborah: First-hand Impressions of the British Women's Army in France*, London: Heinemann, 1919.

An appreciative and thoughtful account of women's war work in France. Begins with confessions of prejudices against women in uniform and a general sense of confusion about the differences between FANYs, WAACs, VADs and GSVADs, that the book gradually unravels. Takes the form, mostly, of descriptions of her visits to particular convoys or camps, and an outline of the work they do, how they are ranked, whether or not they are paid, and includes a defence of WAACs against charges that they were not successful and continually got pregnant.

B84   Key, Ellen *War, Peace and the Future: A Consideration of Nationalism and Internationalism, and of the Relation of Women to War*, translation Hildegard Norberg, London: G.P. Putnam & Sons, 1916.

A Swedish woman's view of the relationship between women and war, which emphasises the importance of education as a means of undermining the more brutal competitive instincts that lead to war. She sees this as a specifically maternal role, and hopes (like Mrs St Clair Stobart) that nursing experience may persuade women to become active, political pacifists. She is concerned with political reorganisation on local and international levels. Recognises, however, that maternity in itself does not make women pacifists, and spends some time railing against the Pankhurst school of militancy, and the female versions of militarism visible particularly in the women's auxiliary army services. Can only understand the latter as ex-militant suffragettes: those who 'found acts of violence a worthy means of furthering women's rights' (199). 'How can we then expect that "this man-made world" will be regenerated through woman's vote, if woman, by her personal share in the war, sanctions those means of settling national misunderstandings that she has claimed to wish to combat with her vote?' (200). Caught in the contradiction of assuming that women will be naturally opposed to war (because they are child-bearers), but acknowledging that they may be just as war-mongering as anyone else. Spends some time describing the Hague Peace Conference.

B85   Ladoux, G. *Marthe Richard the Skylark*, London: Cassell & Co., 1932.

Marthe Richard was a double agent who served both France and Germany during 1916–17, in Spain. Captain Ladoux organised the Telegraphic Censorship Service in Paris, and had contact with this highly intelligent woman, known as a skilled aviator and fluent speaker of German. She was sent to Spain to make contact with the Germans – immediately after her husband had been killed by them. This is an exciting tale of the escapades and challenges faced by a woman who surrounds herself with intrigue and mystery.

B86   La Motte, Ellen N. *The Backwash of War: The Human Wreckage of the Battlefield as Witnessed by an American Hospital Nurse*, London: G.P. Putnam's Sons, 1919.

Sketches of life in a military hospital. Begins with the predicament of a deserter who tries to shoot himself, bungles it, has to be rushed, on jolting roads, to hospital to be nursed back to health, so that he can be stood up against a wall and shot. Sustains a heavy and bitter ironic tone, outlining the ugly, ignoble deaths of soldiers who are decorated with tricolours and words conferring heroism. General moral seems to be that 'There is a dirty sediment at the bottom of most souls' (105) – and that this, the other side of heroism, is what the backwash of war reveals. Sold well on initial publication in 1916; suppressed in the summer of 1918, as the content was considered undesirable.

B87   Lee, Vernon (pseudonym of Violet Paget) *Satan the Waster:*
A Philosophic War Trilogy with Notes and Introduction, London and
New York: John Lane, The Bodley Head, 1920.

Vernon Lee's Introduction to this abstract drama is a substantial essay on the ethics
of war. Her own position is that of an outsider, one who has not been conditioned
by the common experiences and mental and moral habits of the ordinary British
people. She outlines two different kinds of suffering: the direct result of wounds,
terror, exile and bereavement, and the more abstract, impersonal grief at war in
itself, and says that although the latter 'cannot be mentioned in the same breath as
that of those who have *been in the war*, there would remain to prove that suffering
really helps to the forming of clearer opinions and more equitable judgements
about whatever has caused that suffering' (ix). She speaks of the 'spiritual mechanism of errors and myths' that has prolonged the war, the 'logic of the emotions
which is more cogent, more irrefutable than the logic of facts', the nature of delusion, the human instinct for meeting demands for sacrifice believing that sacrifice
to be meritorious, and the general feeling of those who suffer the most that 'The
aim must have been worth the means when the means have been such as these'
(xxxi). Her final comments are on the many-dimensional nature of reality, the
inadequacy of our intellectual and moral habits to respond to the full complexity
of the situation, and the consequent, monumental waste of human virtue and
endeavour. Aspects of her line of thought are to be found in Mary Hamilton's
Dead Yesterday (A51) and Rose Allatini's *Despised and Rejected* (A1). She was
acquainted with Ottoline Morrell, attended Bertrand Russell's pacifist lectures, and
is mentioned in Mary Agnes Hamilton's *Remembering My Good Friends* (C65).

For commentary on the drama, *see* A81.

B88   Leeds, H. *Edith Cavell*, London: Jarrold & Sons, 1915.

Includes biographical sketch, the diplomatic correspondence, and tributes from
Norfolk (Cavell was born near Norwich).

B89   *Let Us Honour Peace*, with Forward by Canon H.R.L. Sheppard,
London: Cobden-Sanderson, 1937.

The essays in this volume were written in the context of the Spanish Civil War and
the rise of fascism that was to culminate in the Second World War, but many of its
contributors had experience of the First World War and were drawing on that to
make their declarations. Contributors include Canon Dick Sheppard, founder of
the Peace Pledge Union, who wrote the Preface; Rose Macaulay, who debates the
survival potential of civilised behaviour in a barbarian world; Captain Philip
Mumford; L.B. Pekin; Canon C.E. Raven, who was a chaplain in France, 1917–18;
Vera Brittain, who describes a point of conversion at a point in the winter of
1917–18, when she was nursing the first mustard gas cases; J.D. Beresford; Dr E.
Graham Howe; Gerald Heard; Elizabeth Thorneycroft; and R.H. Ward. All are
seeking to open up definitions of pacifism to a broader moral and political
philosophy that might lead to 'a wiser, saner, more human social order'.

B90   Lind-af-Hageby, L. *Be Peacemakers. An Appeal to Women of the Twentieth Century to Remove the Causes of War*, London: The A.K. Press, 1924.

An appeal to women to cease to support war by one who was involved in the organisation of hospitals for wounded soldiers. Predicts the 'total' nature of wars to come and, in a series of arguments resembling those in *Militarism versus Feminism* (B108), exhorts women to break the spell of the past, as the bellicose ideals that maintain it keep women in subjection and dependency. Would like women to abstain from every action that supports war and to teach children that war is incompatible with civilisation, and that compassion, sympathy and reconciliation are more worthy ideals than those fostered by military games.

B91   Littlefair, Mary *An English Girl's Adventures in Hostile Germany*, London: John Long, 1915.

A first-person narrative of a girl who, with her family, is caught in Germany when war is unexpectedly declared. The brothers and sisters meet and then travel on to meet their parents in Nauheim. The narrative centres on the problems in travelling, having to pretend not to be English, the helpfulness (or otherwise) of fellow travellers. Descriptive rather than reflective.

B92   Lloyd, Gladys *An Englishwoman's Adventures in the German Lines*, London: C. Arthur Pearson, 1914.

The story of a woman journalist, who is on holiday in Belgium when war breaks out, and finds, all of a sudden, that the only trains that are running are troop trains. She remains undaunted by the invading Uhlans, whom she describes as 'a frightful bore', and, as she speaks German, she acts as a translator between the army and the village residents. She is eventually arrested, as a 'spy', and sent to Germany for questioning. She is searched frequently, but, to her relief, the conventional proprieties are observed: 'I do confess that, though no spy, I have a diary about the war concealed in my hair. Thank goodness they have not found that yet' (114). Ultimately she is set free, and takes lots of trains and a boat back home. It's all a bit of a jaunt, really; some of the Germans are quite kindly, and none really frightening to this plucky Britisher.

B93   [McDougall, Grace] *Nursing Adventures: A F.A.N.Y. in France*, London: William Heinemann, 1917.

Published anonymously, but the details suggest it was written by Grace Ashley-Smith, who ran the FANY, and who was also known as Grace McDougall. First part set in Flanders; scenes of working under shell fire, loading the wounded onto stretchers. In Antwerp Mrs St Clair Stobart apparently asks for help in getting away, but the evacuation scenes are dreadful and the author decides to stay at a convent where they need an English speaker. A 'Miss Sinclair' (presumably the novelist May Sinclair) appears, with a car, and agrees to take her and some wounded away: she returns alone, however, on hearing that a wounded English officer had been left in Ghent. The second part is set in France. The author has organised a motor ambulance, paid for it by selling stock, watched it being built and sailed off with it, with no promise of work. Begins at Calais, equips a hospital, moves around northern France, sets up a canteen. Is keen to promote the versatility of the FANYs, and to show that the war 'has proved to men that women can share men's dangers and privations and hardships and yet remain women' (78).

B94   Mack, Louise (pseudonym L. Creed) *A Woman's Experiences in the Great War*, London: Fisher Unwin, 1915.

Account of an Australian woman travelling in England and Belgium. She was the only Englishwoman to stay in Antwerp during the German occupation, and the only Englishwoman to enter Brussels while the Germans were actually in possession.

B95   McLaren, Barbara *Women of the War*, London: Hodder & Stoughton, 1917.

A series of portraits of women involved in war work of various kinds. Some are exceptional women (such as Elsie Inglis, Drs Garrett Anderson and Flora Murray, Mrs St Clair Stobart), others are taken as representatives of 'types', whether land-workers, welders, canteen managers or army drivers. Includes photographs. Profits derived from the sale of the book were to go to the Joint War Committee of the British Red Cross Society and the Order of St John.

B96   McLaren, Eva Shaw *A History of the Scottish Women's Hospitals*, London: Hodder & Stoughton, 1919.

Dedicated to Elsie Inglis, this history of the SWH is divided into sections on Calais, Royaumont, Serbia, 'Our Chief' (i.e. Dr Inglis), Russia and Roumania, continued work in Serbia (Ostrovo, Vranja), the Girton and Newnham unit (Troyes and Salonika). In each section there is a detailed account of the work done, illustrated by extracts from letters and photographs.

B97   McLaren, Eva Shaw *Elsie Inglis: The Woman with the Torch*, London: Society for Promoting Christian Knowledge, 1920.

This biography, which consciously follows that of Lady Balfour (B11), is written by Inglis's sister and provides new material, including extracts from an unpublished novel, entitled 'The Story of a Modern Woman' and written 1904–14. Goes through her parents' history, Inglis's childhood in India, Australia and Edinburgh, her early medical experiences, and uses parts of her novel to characterise her fearlessness, loneliness, inner strength and love of children. Outlines the establishment of the SWH – and notes that they were not the first in the field: that of Drs Murray and Anderson was very quickly established in Paris. Spends some time discussing the problems in Serbia and Russia that Inglis encountered and finishes with her death, and some tributes.

B98   Macnaughtan, Sarah *My War Experiences in Two Continents*, ed. Mrs Lionel Salmon, London: John Murray, 1919.

An account drawn from Sarah Macnaughtan's diaries, and edited by her niece, Mrs Elizabeth Salmon. The John Murray archive has correspondence relating to the book. Sarah Macnaughtan went to Antwerp with Mrs St Clair Stobart in September 1914, as head of the orderlies in an Ambulance Unit that was accepted by the Belgian Red Cross. She describes the poor organisation of medical facilities in the early stages of the war: 'There are not half enough nurses or doctors out here. In one hospital there are 400 beds and only two trained nurses' (13). Joins Hector Munro's convoy of 'oddly-dressed ladies' in October, when forced to evacuate Antwerp. Makes comments concerning the differences between women and men: 'I suppose women will always try to protect life because they know what it costs to produce it, and men will always try to protect property because it is what they themselves produce' (31). Makes a number of sceptical comments on the nature of women and war work: 'communal life is a mistake. I wonder if Christ got bored with it' (91); 'volunteer corps – especially women – are heroically bent on being uncomfortable' (94). Opened a soup kitchen in Adinkerke before leaving Belgium in May 1915 to lecture in England at munitions factories (to 'arouse slackers'). In October 1915 heads for Russia with Mrs Wynne and an Ambulance Unit, and spends much time waiting for work. Becomes increasingly ill, until returns in April to May 1916. Dies July 1916. Acerbic tone; combination of maverick and deeply conventional comments.

B99   Mansfield, Katherine *Novels and Novelists*, ed. J. Middleton Murray, London: Constable & Co. Ltd, 1930.

Collection of Mansfield's reviews for the *Atheneum*. Includes a number of pieces relating to the war, such as Romer Wilson's *If All These Young Men*, Stella Benson's *Living Alone*, G.B. Stern's *Children of No Man's Land*, Sarah Macnaughtan's *My War Experiences in Two Continents*, Rose Macaulay's *What Not*, and Mansfield's famous review of Woolf's *Night and Day*.

B100   Marshall, Catherine 'Women and War' 1915. Published in Margaret Kamester and Jo Vellacot (eds), *Militarism Versus Feminism: Writings on Women and War* London: Virago, 1987.

Brings together women's maternal training ('the destruction of life and the breaking up of homes is the undoing of women's work as life-givers' (40)) and the politically organised women's movement to argue that the political expression of women's motive-power is the hope for a non-militarist future.

B101   Marshall, Catherine 'The Future of Women in Politics' in *Labour Year Book*, 1916. Reprinted in *Militarism Versus Feminism*, eds Margaret Kamester and Jo Vellacott, London: Virago 1987.

Argues that militarism (that is, the desire to dominate through the exercise of power by force) permeates all levels of social and political struggle; that it is not peculiar to militarists (i.e. that trades unionists, socialists and suffragists have all made use of its discourse), but that women's future in politics is dependent on the discrediting of militarism. Argues that the common motherhood of women cuts across national and class barriers – thus they are disposed to act internationally – but that they need the vote if their qualities are to be called on to prevent the surrender to militarism.

B102   Martin-Nicholson, Sister *My Experiences on Three Fronts*, London: George Allen & Unwin Ltd, 1916.

A rather melodramatic introduction sets the scene: it is 2 August 1914, she is on a river trip, when a sudden storm with attendant lightening 'strik[es] a centuries-old oak, rending it to its stout heart' (18). She, a trained nurse, foresees it all. She dons her mackintosh, arranges her tarpaulin, and rows off. By 9 August she is in Belgium, the only nurse in a convent full of wounded men and German soldiers, whom she fends off with fiery patriotism. Like Violetta Thurstan, she is forced out to Denmark, and arranges to go on to Russia. Provides many local details and travel details, until she is ordered home, to find that she has lost all her money (no explanations). From there she goes out to France and provides tales of dying Tommies: 'Do these little tales harrow you, reader?' (266) Ends with a speech in praise of Tommy Atkins.

B103   Matthews, Caroline *Experiences of a Woman Doctor in Serbia*, London: Mills & Boon, 1916.

The account (first-person narrative) of a woman doctor who volunteered to go out to Serbia at her own expense and with her own equipment. Goes first to Malta and then on to Serbia and stays, alone, with the sick and wounded when the able-bodied evacuate the small town. 'Life was worth living in those days – when the wounded poured in, the sick, the frozen and the dying. I was glad I stayed!' (72). Soon after the Germans arrive she is charged with espionage and is taken, apparently to face the death penalty, overland on an extremely uncomfortable journey, to Belgrade. Is ultimately released. Adopts an adventurous, heroic tone, chivalric in places, responding to 'the call of the wild', and adamant about remaining in her (rather masculine) uniform.

B104   Meynell, Violet *Alice Meynell: A Memoir*, London: Jonathan Cape, 1929.

A rather sentimental account by Viola Meynell of her mother's upbringing, marriage, love for children and writing. Describes her parents' meeting, the literary environment in which Alice Meynell moved (Charles Dickens admired her, Ruskin and Meredith were part of her circle, she was elected to the Academic Committee of the Royal Society of Literature in 1914), the way she divided her time between town and country. The war provided her most intense poetry writing period: her son, Francis (known for being a conscientious objector) first published her poems.

B105   Mitton, G.E. (ed.) *The Cellar-House of Pervyse: A Tale of Uncommon Things from the Journals of The Baroness T'Serclaes and Mairi Chisholm*, London: A & C Black Ltd, 1916.

The story, told by G.E. Mitton, of the two women who were initially members of Hector Munro's ambulance corps (along with May Sinclair and Sarah Macnaughtan, among others), and who set up, independently, a *poste de secours* in a cellar, right near the fighting lines. From here they administered immediate first aid, and provided hot soup and warm drinks to the soldiers. They were frequently under fire, but their 'battered house, to nearly all of [the soldiers] for the moment represented "home"' (159). They were granted the Order of Leopold II. Being independent, however, they had to find ways of raising funds: publishing this book was one of them.

B106   Murray, Flora *Women as Army Surgeons: The History of the Women's Hospital Corps in Paris, Wimereux and Endell Street, Sept 1914–October 1919*, London: Hodder & Stoughton, 1920.

A Preface by Beatrice Harraden celebrates the work of Dr Flora Murray and Dr Louisa Garrett Anderson (daughter of Elizabeth) as having 'opened the doors to further fields of opportunity for women physicians and surgeons'. The two suffragists founded the Women's Hospital Corps, had it accepted by the French Red Cross, opened a hospital in Paris, expanded and opened a unit under the RAMC at Wimereux before opening a military hospital in London's Endell St. The account details the medical and surgical work carried out by the women, documents the general astonishment that women could be surgeons, and the odd meeting between a former policeman and a doctor, formerly a suffragette: roles were now considerably altered. Comments on prewar suffrage work and on an early demand for equal pay: the insistence that women military surgeons be paid and taxed at the same rate as male military surgeons.

B107   Navarro, A. de *The Scottish Women's Hospital at the French Abbey of Royaumont*, London: George Allen & Unwin Ltd, 1917.

The author is a Red Cross worker in France, who was initially moved to write a history of the Abbey of St Louis, but found a diversion in the presence there of the Scottish Women's Hospital unit, and so resolved to write the story of both. The first half is thus a history of the Abbey – its origin and construction, St Louis's crusades and canonisation, war, civil war, revolution and its effects. The second half concerns the hospital. It is a detailed and verbally rich narrative account of the conversion of the Abbey into a hospital, its inspections – unsuccessful and successful – Cicely Hamilton's entertainments, the arrival of the wounded, the X-ray machine, the work required to keep the place running efficiently. Thoughtful and detailed, the tone is one of admiration, and manages to avoid the conventional, clichéd language of praise that so often characterises accounts of this kind.

B108   Ogden, C.K. and Mary Sargant Florence *Militarism versus Feminism: An Enquiry and a Policy Demonstrating that Militarism Involves the Subjection of Women*, London: Allen & Unwin, 1915. Reprinted in *Militarism Versus Feminism* eds Magaret Kamester and Jo Vellacott, London: Virago 1987.

The basic argument is that war has kept women in subjection because they are required to provide the soldiers needed in battle. They are not seen as needing education in order to fulfil this role, and their voice in national affairs is not required because they have no understanding of war and its needs. 'And so war, which the influence of women alone might have prevented, was used as the main argument against enfranchisement' (1987: 57). Cites numerous examples from other cultures to show that 'the open parade of physical violence' (83) has been the undoing of women, that capitalistic competition is influenced by military ideals, that the teaching of history is dominated by lists of battles and names of warriors and that the sporting ethic of English public schools mimics warfare. It is up to the 'silent half of humanity', then, to seek out a 'real bond of unity for the redemption and regeneration of the civilised world' (62). Not a practical, political manual, but a moral treatise. Leaves the reader with little sense of what can be done, but with many arguments linking militarism with the subjection of women, and with the optimistic sense that women's engagement in politics may provide a release from military priorities.

B109   Onions, Maude *A Woman At War: Being Experiences of an Army Signaller in France in 1917–1919*, London: C.W. Daniel & Co., 1929. (Previously printed privately, 1928.)

Dedicated to 'Every Woman (irrespective of nationality or creed) who hates war and loves peace'. Written in the form of brief chapters outlining war's horrors, soldiers' dislocation, military blunders, etc., in which the narrator adopts the position of a naive patriot only to be informed by the experienced soldiers of the true crimes of the war and its debilitating effect on moral standards. Consistently attacks the 'holy war' argument: 'Lassie, if this war can be justified from the teachings of Christ, we must look for something else to put the world right' (21). Unsubtle in its anti-war rhetoric.

B110   Pankhurst, Christabel *The War*, London: The Women's Social and Political Union, 1914.

The text of a speech delivered at the London Opera House, 8 September 1914. Articulates her support for the war, saying that the suffrage fight has always been for the good of the country, and, in a fight between brutality and freedom, the support of women can be counted on. Pledges that, if women are needed in the fighting lines, they will be there, but maintains that their absence should not be seen as an index of their inequality.

B111   Pankhurst, Christabel *America and the War: A Speech Delivered at Carnegie Hall, New York, October 24th 1914*, London: The Women's Social and Political Union, 1914.

Maintains that Britain is involved in a fight for democracy: Germany refused arbitration and had planned to divide and conquer separately the Allied nations. Suggests that America is next as far as Germany is concerned, so Britain is effectively fighting for the USA. Argues that Germany is a male nation and thus invites American women to join in the campaign that will ultimately guarantee the peace of the world. This 20-page pamphlet includes a question and answer session.

B112   Pankhurst, Christabel *International Militancy: A Speech Delivered at Carnegie Hall, New York, January 13th 1915*, London: The Women's Social and Political Union, 1915.

Argues, mostly on the basis of the abstract principles of honour and liberty, that German rule is the enemy of freedom, and that the Germans are trying to engineer a rift between Britain and America. The 24-page publication includes improvised comments, questions from the audience and her answers. She has to argue against a minority that believes Britain to be responsible for the war.

B113   Pankhurst, Christabel *No Peace without Victory*, London: The Women's
Social and Political Union, 1917.

Not seen.

B114   Pankhurst, Sylvia *The Home Front*, London: Hutchinson & Co., 1932.

Long and extremely detailed account of her activities during the war, covering the
years 1914–16. Mostly concerns her dedicated and energetic work with the women
of the East End, who suffered greatly from poverty and deprivation in the face of
changing employment patterns, rising prices and inadequate separation allowances.
The events take place in the context of her suffragism, socialism and pacifism, and
her editorship of the paper of the East London Federation of Suffragettes, the
Dreadnought. She details her many projects, such as cost-price restaurants, the
founding of day care centres, the provision of free milk for babies and the development of a toy factory. The tone tends to be sentimental in places, but she is aware
of her single-minded, often maverick efforts to change governmental attitudes
towards those she represented.

B115   Peel, Mrs C.S. *'Daily Mail' War Recipes*, London: Constable & Co.,
1918.

By the woman who was co-director of the women's service in the Ministry of Food.
Contains down-to-earth recipes for, for example, mayonnaise without oil (using
unsweetened condensed milk and cornflour), and has an entire section on 'meatless
dishes', in which lentils loom large.

B116   Peel, Mrs C.S. *A Year in Public Life*, Constable & Co., 1919.

Mrs Peel and Mrs Pember Reeves were co-directors of women's service at the
Ministry of Food. Their work, for which they were answerable to the Food
Controller (Lord Davenport, Lord Rhondda and Mr Clynes, in succession), mostly
involved providing information, delivering talks and demonstrations and setting up
experimental or travelling kitchens, either to advise women on preparing food
under war restrictions, or to oversee the provision of cooked food in canteens for
those whose work did not permit them the time or the facilities to cook for themselves. Expresses genuine admiration for the way in which working-class women
keep things going and concludes that economies should be taking place among the
wealthier classes. Set up the National Kitchens (Dr Marion Phillips and Mary
Macarthur were involved in this) for the sale of cooked food, in order to save food,
fuel and labour, and to improve health. Visits to France (to Renault and Citroen
works, for example) provided ideas on how to improve the organisation and culi-
nary standards of lunch clubs and canteens.

B117   Peel, Mrs C.S. *How We Lived Then, 1914–1918: A Sketch of Social
and Domestic Life in England During the War*, London: John Lane, The
Bodley Head, 1929.

Remarkably detailed account of home front experience, which comments on the
changing nature of the domestic budget, shifts in food prices and eating habits, the
Lusitania riots, alcohol problems, war myths, zeppelin raids and women's work. Is
sensitive towards class differences and notes the 'twaddle' about 'our marvellous

women', saying that women have always worked hard and that pain and danger to life are commonplaces of female existence. Appendices outline the costs of running a household, and a large number of photographs illustrate the book. A very useful source.

B118   Protheroe, E. *Edith Cavell: Nurse and Martyr*, London: The Epworth Press, 1928.

This depicts the same events as accounts written earlier, but with greater concern for narrative. Thus a 'story' is made of the attempts of representatives from neutral governments (USA and Spain) to intercede in her favour.

B119   Redier, A. *The Story of Louise de Bettignies*, London: Hutchinson & Co., 1926.

The life and work of the spy, Louise de Bettignies, who, spirited, aristocratic, but poor, had been about to take the veil when war broke out and she was persuaded to take on this dangerous work. Her lieutenant, Marie-Léonie Vanhoutte (known as Charlotte), is the chief information source of this book. We are introduced to the 'world of people' who 'lived, worked and suffered around Louise de Bettignies' (51); we are told of the courage and special character of Louise, the dangers she faced, the close escapes, and of her unhappy fate – her death in prison.

B120   Royden, Agnes Maude *The Great Adventure: The Way to Peace*, London: Headly Bros, 1914.

Written from a Christian standpoint (she was a member of the Fellowship of Reconciliation), this pursues the argument that, rather than entering the war, 'We might have taken the great risk, accepted the great adventure – disarmed.' Argues that the weak are *never* safe if force is the basis of international relations, and that 'heresies' cannot be exterminated by killing 'heretics': militarism is a 'heresy' and it has been established in Britain. Paints peace as an adventure, a romance – rather than drab 'neutrality'.

B121   Royden, Agnes Maude 'Morals and Militarism', *The Common Cause* vii, 316, (April 1915): 46–47.

A bold and forceful article focussing on 'war babies' and their treatment. Royden points out that the glorification and sentimentality surrounding the birth of illegitimate children (particularly boys) is first, inevitably short-lived, and second, inextricable from the principles of militarism. If women are seen merely as the potential breeders of men and men are urged 'to forgo no opportunity of paternity', the social and moral consequences will be disastrous. Appeals for a long-term and a moral perspective on the question.

B122   Rudkin, M.S. *Inside Dover, 1914–1918: A Woman's Impressions*, London: Elliot Stock, 1933.

Her introduction says that the scenes and conversations are 'real' and that she hopes 'it may be regarded as a plea for the outlawry of war'. This is an account by a curate's wife of the war years in Dover. Dover, of course, sees the early waves of wounded soldiers, hordes of Belgian refugees, the Queen of Belgium dashing over to get her children into English schools, then dashing back. Rudkin also describes details of their reactions to a bomb landing near them, details of war news, and of local attitudes towards it, and of the ways in which Dover adapts to the influx of military and auxiliary organisations (her husband, for example, tries to tempt the soldiers into 'temperance teas' as a way of keeping them out of trouble). Very conversational, lots of descriptive local colour, no sense of having a particular axe to grind.

B123   Salmond, Lady A. Monica *Bright Armour: Memories of Four Years of War*, London: Faber & Faber, 1935.

The sister of Julian and Billy Grenfell, daughter of Lord and Lady Desborough, she is very much on the aristocratic side of voluntary nursing. She worked first in the London Hospital, where the dusting and sweeping seemed very tiring, then moved on to a Red Cross hospital in Wimereux, where the work was more absorbing, and friends were close at hand, notably the daughter of Millicent, Duchess of Sutherland. The family home was turned into a rest home for war nurses. Her brothers were killed in May and July 1915 – she managed to see Julian soon after he had written 'Into Battle'. A reserved account, with little personal reflection, but a strong sense of the duty and sacrifices performed by the so-called 'idle rich'.

B124   Sandes, Flora *An English Woman Sergeant in the Serbian Army*, London: Hodder & Stoughton, 1916.

An account of how Flora Sandes, a nurse with the Serbian Red Cross, joined the army when all medical services had to retreat. It seems a fairly informal business: evenings are spent sitting round the fire discussing the war; days are spent waiting for orders, trying to improvise some food, or retreating pursued by Bulgarians, the journeys cold and uncomfortable. There is a lot of descriptive local colour, details of horse rides, meeting locals who don't know what to make of her. She is made a Corporal, and later promoted to Sergeant. Being able to speak French and German is an advantage. The account ends with them having got as far as Corfu, having rested, eaten and been provided with new uniforms. Sandes goes on leave – but intends to rejoin them later.

See her autobiography (C87).

B125   Sanger, Sophy 'Health of Munition Workers', *Women's Industrial News* xxi, 78, (July 1917): 12–18.

Article on the Health of Munition Workers Committee's Interim Report on 'Industrial Efficiency and Fatigue'. Makes the point that long hours and poor conditions are no guarantee of high output; that workers faced with these conditions are likely to take occasional days off in order to forestall the onset of fatigue-induced illness, that there is no system of monitoring output, hours, lost time and sickness in order to provide data that might help with the solutions to some industrial problems. Generally critical of the management of women's involvement in the industry.

B126   Sarolea, C. *The Murder of Nurse Cavell*, London: George Allen
& Unwin, 1915.

A 'hate' book, that reads the execution as 'entirely a gratuitous crime of German
vendetta' (47), which 'deprives the onlooker of all powers of speech, and beyond
which human perversity cannot reach'. Has chapter titles such as 'Hunnish
Imbecility', 'German Knavery' and 'Are the German People Responsible?', to
which his unequivocal answer is 'yes'.

B127   Skeffington, Hannah Sheehy *British Militarism as I Have Known It*,
New York: Donnelly Press, 1917. Reprinted Tralee: The Kerryman Ltd,
1946.

The text of this pamphlet is that of a lecture delivered by the author in the USA,
1916–17, following the death of her husband. Publication was initially banned in
the UK. Francis Sheehy Skeffington was an anti-militarist and Sinn Feiner.
Following the Easter Rising, he was arrested and not charged. He witnessed a
murder by a British officer, was used by the military as a hostage, and was
executed by a firing squad, without a trial. The officer in charge was a Captain
Colthurst. This account describes the events in 1916 and Hannah Sheehy
Skeffington's subsequent attempts to find them out and to achieve some kind of
justice. The account speaks to the force of the military, its power to commit atrocities without being subject to normal laws, and the impotence of those who try to
reveal what is happening.

B128   Smith, L.N. *Four Years Out of Life*, London: Philip Allan, 1931.

Documents her prewar life of tennis parties, garden parties, weddings and dances –
the calm prosperity of middle-class existence. Becomes a voluntary nurse out of a
need to help, but is rapidly made to feel unhappy about the level of exploitation
and absence of any professional standing that is the lot of the auxiliary. Comments
on loss of individuality (which she resents), her hatred of women in authority, the
girls' school atmosphere, the discomfort, the horrors of nursing the sick and
wounded in France, and the increasing sense of alienation from those at home.

B129   Smith, Rosamund 'Women and Munition Work', *Women's Industrial
News xx*, 73, (April 1916): 14–20.

Article outlining the early successes and failures of the introduction of female
labour into the engineering industry. Comments on wages, lengths of shifts, rest
periods, welfare, housing, training, the particular roles played by 'educated
women', union membership. Hopes that their success in this work will reward
women by 'greater freedom that wider avenues of employment will bring them'.
Terse, factual account, in favour of women's entry into munitions factories, but not
at the expense of their health and wellbeing.

B130   Snowden, Mrs Philip *A Political Pilgrim in Europe*, London:
Cassell & Co., 1921.

Primarily concerned with the reconstruction period, this tells of Ethel Snowden's
journeys in Europe in an effort to restore good feeling between nations. She states
clearly that she believes war to be alien to the spirit and teaching of Christianity,

and that now 'the Imperialists of Europe are poisoning the world'. She had been involved with the working-class Women's Peace Crusade during the war, attended the International Congress of Women at Zurich in the company of Jane Addams, Helena Swanwick, Catherine Marshall, Isabella Ford and others, and was acquainted with the socialists Margaret Bondfield, Sophy Sanger, Arthur Henderson, Jim Middleton and Will Henderson.

B131   Spaull, H. *Women Peace-Makers*, London: Harrap, 1924.

Accounts of the achievements of seven women, focussing on their work during the war and then for the League of Nations. Henni Forchhammer founded the Danish National Council of Women and was the first woman to address the League of Nations conference in 1920. Rachel Crowdy, friend and colleague of Dame Katharine Furse, managed the VAD units in France and was chosen to carry out the League's Article 23: the Campaign for Social Betterment. Karen Jeppe looked after children of the Armenian massacres and set up a League of Nations home for children who had escaped from captivity. Fru Kjelsburg was the first woman elected to the Norwegian legislature and the first woman delegate to the International Labour Organisation conference. Marie Curie discovered radium and served on the League Committee of Intellectual Co-operation. Mrs Coombe Tennant, whose son was killed in the war, was on the executive committee of the NUWSS and attended the Third Assembly of the League of Nations. Dame Edith Lyttelton looked after Belgian refugees, took charge of the Women's Land Army and was invited to the Fourth Assembly of the League of Nations.

B132   Spearing, E.M. *From Cambridge to Camiers Under the Red Cross*, Cambridge: Heffer & Sons, 1917.

An account of a woman who was researching into Elizabethan dramas at Newnham at the outbreak of war, and who started an auxiliary hospital for wounded Belgian refugees. She later served as a VAD in a military hospital at Camiers, where she was living, rather precariously, under canvas. Takes the form of a series of sketches rather than a continuous narrative, and includes comments on 'types' of soldiers, the experience of night duty, the arrival of convoys of wounded in the Battle of the Somme, and general accounts of the harmonious relations between professionals and auxiliaries, and between nurses and soldiers.

B133   Spurgeon, Caroline F.E. *The Training of the Combatant*, London: J.M. Dent & Sons Ltd, 1916.

An address delivered for the Fight for Right Movement, whose founder was Sir Francis Younghusband, and whose vice presidents included Robert Bridges, John Buchan, Thomas Hardy and Jane Harrison. The aim of the movement was to sustain the spirit of the nation, resist premature peace and fight to a decisive victory. The address sets out the war as a battle of ideals, in which England stands for freedom of spirit and of the individual mind. The maintenance of these freedoms depends on each citizen taking on the responsibilities of a combatant and submitting to sacrifice, discipline and self-denial, and using nervous energy to understand the economy better, rather than indulging in unconstructive, irresponsible criticism.

B134   Stobart, Mrs St Clair *The Flaming Sword in Serbia and Elsewhere*, London: Hodder & Stoughton, 1916.

A long book, packed with illustrations of women's ability to act appropriately and professionally under war conditions. Stobart set up dispensaries all over Serbia and nursed the Serbian wounded and those suffering from typhus. Worked with Mabel Dearmer, who was among those who died from typhus. Praises the courage and character of the Serbians, of whom she thinks highly. Of equal interest are the Preface and the Conclusion. The Preface (preceded by a painting of her as 'The Lady of the Black Horse', by George Rankin) speaks to the need for women's involvement in belligerent situations, for 'woman' defends not only individual lives, but must, now, defend the abstract life of humankind. 'Militarism is maleness run riot' (vii) and requires female influence to undermine it. Concludes: 'Nature, in her beneficence, generally arranges that side by side with the poisonous plant, the anti-dote shall grow, and thus, side by side with the growth of militarism, has also grown the woman's movement' (316).

B135   Stone, Gilbert (ed.) *Women War Workers*, London: George G. Harrap & Co., 1917.

First-person accounts of work done by women during the war. Includes chapters on munitions work, land work, 'A Postwoman's Perambulations', banking, bus conductors (apparently mostly ex-servant girls), delivery women, VADs, Concerts at the Front, welfare work (in factories etc), plus chapters on women in Paris during the German advance, war organisations for women and finally 'Appreciations and Prophecies'.

B136   Sutherland, Millicent Duchess of *Six Weeks at the War*, London: The Times, 1914.

She left England on 8 August, intending to join the French Red Cross, but worked under the Belgian authorities instead. Set up at the Convent of Namur. On 23 August saw a sudden influx of wounded. Namur was invaded and set on fire, but the convent managed to avoid the blaze. The rest of the account describes her being forced by the Germans to leave Namur, and travelling around Belgium under German authority in an attempt to get either to France or to England. Managed the latter. A note informs her readership of her intention to return to France with a fully equipped motor ambulance.

B137   Swanwick, Helena M. *The War in its Effect upon Women: Women and War*, London: Union of Democratic Control, 1915. Reprinted New York: Garland, 1971.

Two essays, the first of which employs the interesting rhetorical strategy of beginning with the assertion that women and men alike feel the losses and impoverishments of war, but that women are less likely to experience exhilaration, because of their inevitable concern with the preservation of human life over the thrill of battle. She then works towards a more satirical style, condemning politicians and journalists for sentimentalising women and their role in war: 'The fiction of women's incapacity must have indeed bitten deep when it could be supposed that it required a "superwoman" to clip a ticket!' (5). Her main points are concerned with the future; with the need for men and women to co-operate in the development of a just social policy that rejects reactionary and repressive laws. The way towards this is to give women the vote. Finally discusses the work of the Women's Co-operative Guild, the WEA, the UDC, the WIL, all being concerned with enabling women's involvement in politics. She returns ultimately to the maternal argument.

The second piece argues that women suffer from war economically as well as personally, that their experience as mothers equips them with a value system that differs from men's in important details, that physical force, while its history implies the subjection of women and small nations, need not be abolished, but must come under the control of moral and intellectual forces. Women should have a part in this, and their education by suffragist and pacifist movements has begun to equip them appropriately. Again her strategy is to combine political and economic points with idealist hopes and emotive examples.

B138   Swanwick, Helena M. *Builders of Peace. Being Ten Years' History of the Union of Democratic Control*, London: The Swarthmore Press, 1924.

A descriptive and discursive account of the history of the UDC, discussing its ideals, cardinal points and most prominent members (E.D. Morel, Ramsay MacDonald, Norman Angell, Dr Marion Phillips, among others). Recounts the ways in which the aims of the movement were misunderstood, partly as a result of misleading government propaganda, analyses the organisation and methods of the Union; its co-operation with women's and workers' organisations, its being subject to DORA, to raids and spies. Swanwick and Vernon Lee were both early members of the organisation.

B139   Tayler, Henrietta *A Scottish Nurse at Work. Being a Record of What One Semi-Trained Nurse has been Privileged to See and Do During Four and a Half Years of War*, London: John Lane, The Bodley Head, 1920.

A Scottish woman with some talents (primarily linguistic), but no training, launches herself into the running of a Red Cross Hospital. Two years later she's off to Belgium, where she looks after refugee children (she speaks some Flemish), then to France, to work in a hospital for 'rapatriés'. From there she goes to Italy. First to Florence, where food is extremely scarce, and then to the Front (Montecchio Maggiore), where she looks after Austrian, Croatian, Polish and Roumanian prisoners – primarily medical cases. The account is mostly descriptive, but unusual for the amount of civilian and prisoner nursing, and in the time spent in Italy that she recounts. For the most part she feels privileged, and the patients grateful.

B140   Thurstan, Violetta 'A Woman's Adventures at the Front', *The Common Cause* 471, (9 October 1914).

Informs us that Thurstan was an organiser in the NUWSS before the war. She tells the story of passing through the German lines and finding herself in the middle of a skirmish between Belgians and Germans, and of entering a German camp. She managed this feat by pretending, first to be German, then Belgian. The object of the journey was to visit a nurse in her company.

See Field Hospital and Flying Column (C16) and her autobiography (C92).

84

B141   Usborne, H.M. *Women's Work in Wartime: A Handbook of Employments*, London: T. Werner Laurie Ltd, 1918.

The first half of the handbook lists possible fields of work for women (in agriculture, canteen work, teaching, as commercial travellers, doctors, policewomen, VADs, WAACs, etc) and gives contact addresses, details of training required, age range, qualifications needed, wages, hours and uniform. Also states whether that area of employment is newly open to women, developing, for the duration of the war only, etc. The second half provides accounts of various kinds of work, such as the civil service, the Red Cross, munitions work.

B142   Vaughan, G.E.M. *The Flight of Mariette, a Story of the Siege of Antwerp*, London: Chapman & Hall, 1916.

A refugee called Mariette has told the author the story of the siege of Antwerp, from the point of view of herself and her family, and the author has set it down. Mariette was engaged to a German officer before the war, which caused a rift with her foster brother: he joined up before it could be resolved. The threatened advance of the German army eventually materialises and Mariette, her grandparents, pregnant sister-in-law and small children (one of whom they lose), join the sad procession towards the Dutch border and eventually on to a boat bound for England. The book has a preface by John Galsworthy, who admires it for bringing to life the tragic experience of Belgian refugees.

B143   Walshe, Ellen 'With the "Well-Brought-Up" on the Land', *Blackwood's Magazine* 200, (October 1916): 403–12.

The experience of educated women, usually from towns, who take up land work during their holidays. It is not what they have been led to expect. They are asked to get up at 3.00 am, to work in the cold and the wet, to endure the jeering of the locals, who do not don the uniform of the Land Army. They are not appreciated. A different farm offers more pleasant conditions, but, come the hop picking season, they are not wanted: the 'London poor' are not to be done out of their working holiday.

B144   Walters, E.W. *Heroines of the World War*, London: Kelly, 1916.

Includes chapters on Emilienne Moreau (The Heroine of Loos), Sister Myra Ivanova, Mabel Dearmer, Sister Joan Martin-Nicholson, Phyllis Campbell, women soldiers, women doctors and war decorations.

B145   Ward, Helen *A Venture in Goodwill, Being the Story of the Women's International League 1915–1929*, London: Women's International League, 1929.

Begins with a vignette of Margaret Ashton, Catherine Marshall, Emily Leaf and Maude Royden, blocked at Tilbury Docks from attending the Hague Peace Conference, 1915. Then goes on to describe that conference, its resolutions, the subsequent delegations of women to neutral and belligerent countries. Notes that the British League was chaired by Helena Swanwick, with Irene Cooper Willis as honorary secretary and Maude Royden as vice chair. Describes the 'educational' nature of the work, the writing of pamphlets, speeches, the organisation of petitions and specific campaigns. Comments on their International Congress of 1919 in Zurich, which concluded that the Versailles Peace Treaty was sowing the seeds of further war.

B146   Ward, Mrs Humphry *England's Effort: Six Letters to an American Friend*, London: Smith, Elder & Co., 1916.

The Dedication (to Lord Kitchener) and the Preface by Lord Rosebery ensure that this is understood as a book intended to justify and celebrate England's war efforts. The letters make the point that England has been badly misunderstood and harshly judged in the USA, that real and imagined mistakes – drunkenness, strikes, losses in the Dardanelles, military incompetence – have been over-emphasised. Mrs Ward paints a counter-balancing picture of effort and activity. She has been permitted by the British government to visit the Fleet in the north, a munitions plant in the Midlands and the military zones of north-west France. She justifies England's lack of preparations on the grounds that war was neither desired nor expected, and describes 'a mighty movement afoot in the workshops of England' that will ultimately ensure victory. The visits were sanctioned by Gilbert Parker of Wellington House: this was part of the propaganda exercise to bring in the Americans on the side of the British.

B147   Ward, Mrs Humphry *Towards the Goal*, London: John Murray, 1917.

A sequel to *England's Effort*. A tour of the Western Front, written up in the form of letters to Theodore Roosevelt (who also provides an Introduction), with the explicit aim of describing to Americans the part played by England in the struggle. A narrative of progress, praising the ever-increasing strength and efficiency of the munitions industry, the army, the aviators and the women – British, French and American – who have played their part. Also includes statistics (supplied by the War Office), atrocity stories, letters from well-treated German POWs and from German women on the home front saying how poor conditions are there. Purpose: to encourage and then to applaud America's participation in the war. (America joined in at Easter 1917, approximately half-way through this narrative.)

B148   Webster, N.H. *Britain's Call to Arms: An Appeal to Our Women*, London: Hugh Rees, 1914.

Not seen.

B149   West, Rebecca *The Young Rebecca: Writings of Rebecca West 1911–1917*, selected and introduced by Jane Marcus New York: Viking Press (in association with Virago), 1982.

Sections V and VI contain articles and reviews published in the *Daily News* and *Daily Chronicle* during the war years, and which directly (and indirectly) relate to the war. West reviews, for example, May Sinclair's *Journal of Impressions in Belgium*, B.L. Hutchins' *Conflicting Ideals of Woman's Work*, *Their Lives* by Violet Hunt and *War, Peace and the Future* by Ellen Key, all in trenchant and witty terms, praising the gallantry and humility in May Sinclair's book, mocking the intellectually vacuous platitudes in Ellen Key's. There are also articles on women's war work and on socialism.

B150   Wharton, Edith *Fighting France: From Dunkerque to Belfort*, London: Macmillan, 1915.

A series of essays, written while carrying out charitable work, and published initially by Scribner's in New York. Begins with 'The Look of Paris', then moves on to ambulances and clearing hospitals 'In Argonne'. 'In Lorraine and the Vosges' describes having passed 'black holes that were homes' and 'chasms that were streets', but comments that the growth of flowers and vegetables seem to signify almost instant regeneration. Other essays are 'In the North', 'In Alsace' and 'The Tone of France'. Includes photographs that show the extent of some of the scenes of destruction. Predominantly descriptive rather than propagandist in tone.

B151   Willis, Irene Cooper *How We Went Into the War: A Study of Liberal Idealism*, Manchester and London: The National Labour Press Ltd, 1919.

The first of three consecutive studies of Liberal idealism as expressed in the speeches of leading politicians, and in the national press. Sets out to be, not an indictment of Liberalism, but an analysis of the self-deception practised by particular Liberals at the outbreak of war. Divided into sections as follows: (a) Pre-war Feeling, (b) The Leader Writers, (c) The Holy War, (d) The 'Reason' of it. Analyses the discourse, the well-known phrases ('Being in, we must win'; 'Every sword that is drawn against Germany is a sword drawn for peace', etc) and charts the shift in tone and argument from neutrality to the language of the 'Holy War'. Particularly interested in unpicking the relationship between Liberal unconscious self-deception, and 'reason'.

B152   Willis, Irene Cooper *How We Got On With the War*, Manchester and London: The National Labour Press, 1920.

The second in the series takes as its starting point the declaration from 'A.G.G.' (Gardiner, editor of the *Daily News*) in an open letter to the Northcliffe Press, that 'We Lost and You Won', meaning that the Liberal press had believed in and worked for peace, while the Northcliffe Press (*The Times* and *Mail*) had believed in and worked for war. Willis thinks that had the Liberals properly understood what they were saying, 'they would not have claimed so boldly throughout the war that their aims, not Lord Northcliffe's, prevailed'. Again, undertakes close readings of the *Daily News* (predominantly) relating to its coverage of the blockade, the mobilisation of neutrals, conscription, the Russian Revolution, and the coming of the end.

B153   Willis, Irene Cooper *How We Came Out of the War*, Bradford, London and Manchester: International Bookshops Ltd, 1921.

The final part of her study concentrates on the Armistice, the Peace Conference and the Treaty of Versailles. Her view is that 'their arrogant and irresponsible assumption that their aims were the prevailing ones, the utter absence of self-criticism, moral or spiritual modesty in their writings and speeches, made a terrible scene of intellectual disorder, a replica in the field of thought to the battlefield itself' (13).

B154   Willis, Irene Cooper *England's Holy War*, New York: Alfred A. Knopf, 1928.

The three volumes above were printed as a single volume in 1928. Her major point is that the Liberal papers (especially the *Daily News*) generated an idealism that was indispensable, not for mean-minded or hypocritical reasons, but because without it they themselves could not have borne the shock of war. 'There has been no more pitiable spectacle in the war than the spectacle of Liberals, at sea in reaction, clinging to the myth that their aims were supreme' (173).

B155   Wolsely, Viscountess *Women and the Land*, London: Chatto & Windus, 1916.

Concerned, not so much with immediate patriotic need, as with the long-term necessity of maintaining the health of the race. Foresees a future peasant class, working under the guidance of the socially-elevated woman, who will provide the appropriate materials and leadership.

B156   Women's Group Executive 'The War, Women and Unemployment', *Fabian Tract* 178, London: Fabian Society, March 1915. Reprinted in *Women's Fabian Tracts*, ed. Sally Alexander, London: Routledge, 1988.

Begins by commenting on the general lack of interest in women's unemployment on the part of government and institutions. Goes on to describe, favourably, the early work of the Central Committee on Women's Employment, and to outline why workrooms should not be in competition with commercially produced goods. Considers the relationships between women and business, concluding that British women have little power over the management of industrial practices, and makes comparisons with women in France. Concludes with the general point that until women in general take it upon themselves to study industry, and share in its administration, the economic position of women will not be on a sound basis.

B157   Woolf, Virginia *A Room of One's Own*, London: Hogarth, 1929. Reprinted London: Granada, 1977.

Woolf's famous disquisition on the relationships between women and fiction which, although not overtly about the war, mentions it as a turning point in the relations between women and men: 'When the guns fired in August 1914, did the faces of men and women show so plain in each other's eyes that romance was killed?'

B158   Woolf, Virginia *Three Guineas*, London: Hogarth, 1938. Reprinted Harmondsworth: Penguin, 1977.

The context within which this was written was the Spanish Civil War and the rise of fascism, rather than the First World War. It does, however, speak to a series of masculine dispositions, to power structures and to relationships to power, that are present in Woolf's writings, certainly from *Jacob's Room* onwards, and which continue to influence theoretical writings on women and war.

B159   Yates, L.K. *The Woman's Part: A Record of Munitions Work*, London: Hodder & Stoughton, 1918.

An account of women's entry into munitions work, their training, and the gradual improvement of facilities (canteens, rest rooms, even crèches). Comments on uniforms, the long hours, the dangers, the loss of former prejudices concerning gender and class. Describes the experience as a 'pilgrimage' providing the qualities needed by mothers of the rising generation.

B160   Yerta, Gabrielle and Marguerite *Six Women and the Invasion*, London: Macmillan, 1917.

The six women in question are the author, her mother-in-law, and her four sisters-in-law. They live mostly in Paris, but spend the summers in a village called Morny, in the neighbourhood of Laon, Île de France, and that is where their experience of invasion is centred. The men have gone off to fight, leaving the women to cope with the incursion of the enemy. They requisition food, land and ultimately, the house of the family in question. There are no 'atrocity' stories; the officers are mostly courteous, if intrusive. It is written in a spirited style, recounting the chattering of the sisters, their ruses to conceal their stores, and pursuing the enemy, with exclamation marks. A Preface by Mrs Humphry Ward conveys to her female compatriots the relative safety of their own position.

II   OFFICIAL PUBLICATIONS

This section provides references to reports of government committees and sub-committees on issues that concerned women and the First World War, and other relevant papers. The citation provides the full title and reference number, which were taken from the *General Index to Parliamentary Papers 1900–1949*. Sub-, and sub-sub-headings are also compatible with the General Index.

CIVIL SERVICE

B161   Report of the Sub-Committee appointed to consider the position after the war of women holding temporary appointments in Government Departments. 1919 Cmd. 199 xxix 153.

CLERKS AND OFFICES

B162   Report of the Committee appointed to consider the conditions of clerical and commercial employment with a view to advertising what steps should be taken, by the employment of women or otherwise, to replace men withdrawn for service in the military forces. 1914–16 Cd. 8110 xiii 1.

DOMESTIC EMPLOYMENT

B163   Report of the Women's Advisory Committee on the Domestic Service
Problem, together with Reports by Sub-Committees on training,
machinery of distribution, organisation and conditions. 1919 Cmd.
67 xxix 7.

MUNITIONS

B164   Interim Report on the Health of Munition Workers Committee on
Industrial Efficiency and Fatigue. 1917–18 Cd. 8511 xvi 1019.

WAR 1914–18

Diplomatic papers

B165   The Execution of Miss Cavell. Correspondence. 1914–16 Cd 8013
lxxiv 703.

B166   Deportation of Belgians. Correspondence with Belgian Minister. 1916
Cd. 8404 xxxiv 99.

Army and navy

B167   The Official Press Bureau. 1914–16 Cd. 7680 xxxix 535.

B168   Pennant, Miss V. Douglas. Correspondence. 1919 Cmd. 182; Cmd
254 xxxiii 813, 833.

Industrial, commercial and social

B169   Clerical and Commercial Employments (Employment of
Women).1914–16 Cd. 8110 xiii 1.

B170   Women's Employment During the War. 1914–16 Cd. 7848 xxxvii
669.

B171   Reconstruction (Women's Employment). Report. 1918 Cd. 9239 xiv
783.

B172   Women's Employment. Report of Board of Trade. 1918 Cd. 9164 xiv
767.

B173   Civil Service, Women in the. 1919 Cmd. 199 xxix 153.

B174   Women in Industry Report &c. from the War Cabinet Committee. 1919 Cmd 135 xxx 241.

Miscellaneous

B175   Sheehy Skeffington and Others, Treatment of. Report 1916. 1916 Cd 8376 xi 311.

B176   Imperial War Museum, Report 1918–19. 1919 Cmd 138 xxii 1187.

WOMEN

B177   Interim Report of the Central Committee on Women's Employment. 1914–16 Cd. 7848 xxxvii 669.

B178   Report of the Women's Employment Committee of the Ministry of Reconstruction. 1918 Cd 9239 xiv 783.

B179   Report of the Board of Trade on the Increased Employment of Women in the United Kingdom during the War, with statistics to April 1918. 1919 Cd. 9164 xiv 767.

B180   Report of the War Cabinet Committee on Women in Industry. 1919 Cmd 135 xxxi 241.

B181   Appendices, Summaries of Evidence &c. 1919 Cmd 167 xxxi 593.

C DIARIES, LETTERS AND AUTO- BIOGRAPHIES

I DIARIES

C1   Asquith, Lady Cynthia *Diaries 1915–18*, London: Hutchinson, 1968.

Cynthia Charteris, daughter of Lord and Lady Elcho, was born in 1887. She married Herbert Asquith, second son of Prime Minister H.H. Asquith, in 1910. Her diaries came to light after she died in 1960. They describe in considerable detail the texture of her life during the war years: her social circle, war news, literary and artist friends (among them D.H. Lawrence and John Singer Sargent), the political world, and the incursions of the war into the lives of her family: her younger brother was killed, her husband, serving in the RFA, was wounded.

C2   Bagnold, Enid *A Diary Without Dates*, London: Heinemann, 1918.

An impressionistic account of her experiences in the Royal Herbert Hospital, on publication of which she was dismissed. Comments on hospital discipline, and her ability to resist it; the sexless, lifeless nature of the trained Sisters; the 'ardent longing to be alike' of the VADs (34). Individualistic, anti-authoritarian, conscious of her class background and the independence this grants her.

C3   Brittain, Vera *Chronicle of Youth: Vera Brittain's War Diary 1913–1917*, ed. Alan Bishop with Terry Smart, London: Victor Gollancz, 1981.

Diary on which *Testament of Youth* was based. Covers prewar life and the first two years of war in detail, including her developing relationship with Roland, her arrival in Oxford, her decision to take up nursing, Roland's death, nursing in Malta. The year 1917 is represented only sketchily.

C4   Courtney, Kate (Lady Courtney of Penwith) *Extracts from a Diary During the War*, privately printed, 1927.

Balanced account of personal and political life. Kate Courtney was married to Leonard Courtney of Penwith, a member of the House of Lords. Among their social circle were Stephen Hobhouse, Norman Angell, Maude Royden, Arthur Ponsonby and Vernon Lee. She comments on the social and political aspects of the war, and includes some military reports. Gives an account of Women's International

League delegates to the Hague conference, UDC members, lords, generals, enlisted men, pacifists and WILPF meetings she has chaired.

C5   De La Grange, Baroness *Open House in Flanders 1914–18*, London: John Murray, 1929.

Translated from the unpublished French, by Melanie Lind, this provides an account of the various happenings, as a result of which the author earned the accolade 'Mother of the British Army'.

C6   De Lisle, Adele *Leaves From a VAD's Diary*, London: Elliot Stock, 1922.

Large format book, with illustrations. Divided into episodes, or 'characters' rather than dates, for example 'Mrs Figg', 'The Old Contemptibles', 'Jock' and 'Tubby'. The entries are mostly character sketches, or accounts of humorous incidents, particularly concerning the unpredictable, but amusing nature of working-class women. A good-humoured book by a narrator devoted to her patients and all who serve under her. She returns to New York at the end.

C7   *Diary of a Nursing Sister on the Western Front 1914–15*, Edinburgh and London: William Blackwood & Sons, 1915.

Published anonymously, although there is a suggestion that K.E. Luard might be the author. The Sister has had previous experience in South Africa. She has set off from Dublin, and is kept waiting in Le Havre, where she evokes an atmosphere of 'longing for work', while surrounded by rumours and returning sisters from occupied zones. She works first on ambulance trains, an experience characterised by not knowing what her orders are to be next, and punctuated by dead horses on the railway lines, by the ubiquitous lice, and by trying to get men on to the top bunks in the aftermath of the First Battle of Ypres. Later works with a field ambulance.

C8   Farmborough, Florence *Nurse at the Russian Front. A Diary 1914–18*, London: Constable, 1974.

This diary, in its original form, ran to about 400,000 words, which were later reduced by about one-half in order to be published. It is, nevertheless, an immensely detailed record of a nurse on the Russian Front, which conveys a love of the country and its people at the same time as it documents the desperate conditions that arise within a country at war.

C9   Houghton, Mary *In the Enemy's Country. Being the Diary of a Little Tour in Germany and Elsewhere During the Early Days of the War*, London: Chatto & Windus, 1915.

The author's Preface says that most of the war references in her diary have been omitted, leaving 'the ripples of the back-wash that dents and moulds the sand', and this is supported by Edward Garnett, whose Foreword comments on the way that the spirit of militarism is revealed in ordinary people. The diary begins in the summer of 1914, when the author and her husband are about to set off from Florence, in a newly-acquired car, for a motoring tour of Austria and Germany. The war news gradually filters through and their holiday mood is challenged by minor confrontations with officials, and odd scenes in wayside inns, until their car is seized and they are deported to neutral Switzerland.

C10   Kennard, Lady D. *A Roumanian Diary, 1915, 1916, 1917*, London: Heinemann, 1917.

Begins with a desire to travel to Roumania in order to find out about life there in the city and in the country. When war is declared (1916), the author joins a Red Cross hospital. There are accounts of the pace of life, the routines of the local people, air raids, of plans to leave as the likelihood of a German invasion increases – and of the final, and very hurried, evacuation. Finishes with a great sense of pride in the country – 'our little brother Roumania has grown into a man'.

C11   Macnaughtan, Sarah Broom *A Woman's Diary of the War*, London: Thomas Nelson & Sons, n.d. [1915].

An account that reveals the vanities and stupidities of women's war work as well as its value. She refers briefly to her experience with Mrs Stobart's operation in Antwerp, a hospital which had to be evacuated when the Germans invaded, and to her time with the Munro corps, which she joined before setting up her own soup kitchen, first at Furnes, then later at La Panne. Gives a good sense of the war fronts being on the move, before the trench lines were heavily established, and provides a variety of pictures of soldiers, of all nationalities, on the Poperinghe Road, of the pain of loss, of the strange freedoms that war provides. An interesting account, characterised by an irony that remains sympathetic.

C12   Mansfield, Katherine *The Journals of Katherine Mansfield*, ed. J. Middleton Murry, London: Constable & Co Ltd, 1954.

A compilation of journal entries, reading notes, unpublished drafts and unsent letters, edited by Mansfield's husband, John Middleton Murry. Much of this journal covers the war years. It reflects in detail on Mansfield's affair with Francis Carco, which took her into the army zones in France, 1915, comments frequently on the Lawrences, and describes the last visit of Leslie Heron Beauchamp, Mansfield's brother, before he died at the Front. His death affected Mansfield profoundly. She writes about him a great deal, remembers their shared past in New Zealand, and is driven to encapsulate in fiction 'the lovely time when we were both alive' (90). Murry notes that not one of Mansfield's friends who went to the war, returned from it.

C13   Miles, Haillie Eustace *Untold Tales of War-Time London: A Personal Diary*, London: Cecil Palmer, 1930.

Eustace Miles ran a well-known vegetarian restaurant in London. This account, by his wife, sets out to 'remind people of what a *wonderful* place London was in wartime' (Foreword). Comments on how much in demand she and Eustace were for advice and information about meatless food, and how she ran a choir, which gave concerts in hospitals (Endell Street among them) as well as at the restaurant. Lots of home front details and war news (Belgian refugees, lights dimmed in London, zeppelin raids), but rather sentimental in tone, as is betrayed by sub-headings such as 'The Heroic Aeroplane' and 'A Wonderful Visit to the Slums'.

C14   Millard, Shirley *I Saw Them Die: Diary and Recollections*, ed. Adele Comandini. London: George G. Harrap & Co. Ltd, 1936.

A retrospective account written by an American woman, in the form of original diary extracts and accompanying commentary. She joined the French as a nurse in Spring 1918, with no previous experience or training. Describes wounds and conditions in gory and sensationalist detail: 'As the last band comes off, a sickening mass spills out of the wide gash at the side of his skull. Brains!' (27). Also describes her romantic attachment to the glamorous French Dr Le Brun, an unwitting rival to 'dear old Ted', whom she really *does* love and ultimately marries. Is conscious of the bellicose context of 1936: 'To my son Coco, his friends and their mothers, I offer this simple record of the dark caravan that winds endlessly through the memory of my youth' (128).

C15   Sinclair, May *A Journal of Impressions in Belgium*, London: Hutchinson, 1915.

Accompanies the Munro ambulance corps (from which the Two Women of Pervyse originate) as a secretary and reporter. Part of her job is to write small articles for the daily papers. She is conscious of her own fear, her colleagues' lack of it. Reflects on her own changing attitude to authority, the boredom and inactivity of much of the experience, the (perverse?) motivations of Munro himself, the mounting 'ecstacy' of the war experience. Her stay with the corps was brief, but it finds articulation in many of her novels (most notably *The Romantic* but *see also Anne Severn and the Fieldings* A124, A125). It has been suggested that her age and disposition were unsuitable, and that Munro himself was responsible for truncating her trip. (*See* Mrs Belloc Lowndes *A Passing World* C78.)

C16   Thurstan, Violetta *Field Hospital and Flying Column: Being the Journal of an English Nursing Sister in Belgium and Russia*, London: Putnam's, 1915.

Thurstan was a trained nurse, who served first in Belgium and then joined a Russian Flying Column, going, at short notice, to wherever help was required, and working under the most inhospitable conditions. She went through some extraordinary and dangerous experiences, but records them in cosy language reminiscent of the nursery ('it was not a very pleasant walk, as bullets were flying freely and the mitrailleuse never stopped going pom-pom-pom' (59)). Thurstan was a NUWSS member. An account of her crossing the German lines appeared in *The Common Cause* (B140). She was awarded the Military Medal for bravery in evacuating the wounded after a British dressing station was shelled in Belgium, 1917. Accounts of her war experiences appear in Kent Carr *Women Who Dared* and McLaren *Women of the War* (B34, B95).

C17   Waddington, Madame Mary King *My War Diary in and Around Paris*, London: Murray, 1918.

Record of events concerning an American family in France covering the period 1 August 1914 to 28 February 1916: Mary Waddington was the wife of a diplomat in Paris, who set up workrooms for out-of-work women. Descriptions cover social, domestic and military events.

C18   Webb, Beatrice *Beatrice Webb's Diaries 1912–1924*, ed. Margaret Cole, London: Longman's, Green & Co., 1952.

Comments on the disturbing nature of war's 'coarse stimulus' to service for those who, ordinarily, are 'dully immune to any other motive but self-interest qualified by self-indulgence'. Has a vast store of knowledge and experience, and meets and comments on a number of people and situations, such as Bernard Shaw, the Fabian Society and Research Department, Haldane, Jane Addams, trades unionism, Lloyd George, DORA, the Military Service Act, the Roger Casement affair, Mary Macarthur, and so on. Remains intellectually detached; is reflective about the broader political situation and the place of Fabian principles – as well as the ability of the leading lights to articulate these and put them into action.

C19   Woolf, Virginia *The Diary of Virginia Woolf. Volume 1: 1915–1919*, ed. Anne Olivier Bell, London: Hogarth, 1977.

Frequent passing references to the war and its effect on her daily life. She came into contact with many who were active politicians in a way that she never claimed to be: Margaret Llewelyn Davies, Helena Swanwick, Sidney and Beatrice Webb and, of course, her husband Leonard. Many of her circle were pacifists; she hears the guns from where she lives in Sussex; meets German prisoners while out walking. These factors provide material for meditation, some of which finds its way into the diary; otherwise her novels bear witness to the fact that the war affected her profoundly.

II   LETTERS

C20   Aldrich, Mildred *A Hilltop on the Marne: Being Letters Written June 3 – September 8, 1914*, Boston and New York: Houghton Mifflin, 1915. London: Constable, 1915.

Covers the period from June 1914 to September 1914 and begins with the author explaining to her unnamed correspondent her desire to retreat, aged 60-ish, to somewhere quiet and peaceful, 'une paysage riante'. So she finds a house in Huiry, overlooking a splendid panorama and the Marne. The tranquillity is soon disturbed by evidence of the outbreak of war: the 'garde champêtre' who marches up the road, beating his drum and announcing general mobilisation. This is followed by the flight of local Germans, the closing of the shops. The surrounding area is evacuated, valuables are stored in hidden underground passages. She declines to leave and does what she can in the way of observing enemy movements, feeding and providing water for men, and housing officers.

C21   Aldrich, Mildred *On the Edge of the War Zone*, London: Constable, 1918.

Letters that cover the period from September 1914 to March 1917. Describes the intense winter cold, the booming of the guns in the distance, the gradual militarisation of the surrounding area. For some months, nothing happens, then large numbers of soldiers are billeted in the region.

C22   Aldrich, Mildred *The Peak of the Load*, London: Constable, 1919.

Begins April 1917, just after America has declared war. Continuing observations, troop movements, hears Big Bertha's assault on Paris, combination of war news and domestic details. Finishes, November 1918, with the sense of a new era on the horizon.

C23   Atkins, Thomasina *The Letters of Thomasina Atkins: Private (W.A.A.C.) – on Active Service*, London: Hodder & Stoughton, n.d. [1918].

Cheerful letters from 'Thomasina' to 'Peachie', recounting her experiences in England, and 'Somewhere in France'.

C24   Dearmer, Jessie Mabel *Letters from a Field Hospital*, with a memoir of the author by Stephen Gwynn, London: Macmillan, 1915.

The memoir by Stephen Gwynn is 73pp. long, and includes a transcript of Mrs Dearmer's own account of the events leading to her decision to join Mrs St. Clair Stobart's Serbian unit. Dearmer wrote and published novels, including children's books, and was involved in the theatre. She specialised in writing and producing 'morality plays'. Her husband, Percy Dearmer, was appointed Chaplain to the British Units in Serbia; her sons Christopher and the poet Geoffrey had already joined up when she too decided to go as a hospital orderly. She was a Christian, a friend of Maude Royden, and entirely innocent of bellicose spirit, as is suggested by the following: 'the hardest fight is to love the person you want to fight and to seek *his* good rather than yours. It sounds a platitude, but to-day it is Christ or Kitchener. What chance would Christ have to-day? Crucifixion would be a gentle death for such a dangerous lunatic' (159). Happy to be in charge of the linen tents in a mud patch of a 'hospital', she comments on social class, on preparations, precautions against fever and the beauty of the surrounding landscape. There are very few references to Stobart. She died of typhoid, July 1915, while in Serbia.

C25   Denholm, Decie (ed.) *Behind the Lines: One Woman's War 1914–18, the Letters of Caroline Ethel Cooper*, London: Jill Norman and Hobhouse, 1982.

Letters from a woman of English descent, born in Australia, who found herself in Leipzig at the outbreak of war, and did not leave. The weekly letters to her sister detail her day-to-day life in Germany, the increasingly difficult conditions and her friends. The question as to whether or not she was a spy remains unanswered.

C26   Lee, Vernon *Vernon Lee's Letters*, with a Preface by her Executor, privately printed, 1937.

The letters themselves do not cover the war period, but the biographical sketch, by Irene Cooper Willis, does. Useful, given the relative scarcity of biographical information about Vernon Lee.

C27   Luard, K.E. *Unknown Warriors: Extracts from the Letters of K.E. Luard, Nursing Sister in France 1914–1918*, London: Chatto & Windus, 1930.

A trained army nurse, in charge of a number of casualty clearing stations very close to the front line on the Western Front, October 1915 to Spring 1918. Differs from VAD experience in its proximity to the battle front (describes the effect of Arras, Passchendaele and the German advance in the Spring of 1918) and therefore the rapidity with which they receive the wounded – often only one hour after injury in the later stages of the war. Tone is concise, restrained, controlled. Comments on conditions: 'Water in some of the Wards is half-way up the legs of the beds' (201); particular cases: 'The boy who threw his brains on the floor died yesterday, and another is dying' (8); and the amount of work: 'The wards are like battlefields, with battered wrecks in every bed and on stretchers between the beds and down the middles' (158). Her camp is bombed and, during the German advance, evacuated. Interest lies in the fact that this is front line work performed by a woman: 'The older surgeons think it's dreadful having us there, but as the C.O. says, without us they couldn't carry on at all, so it's worth it' (324).

C28   Mansfield, Katherine *The Collected Letters of Katherine Mansfield, Vol. I 1903–1917*, eds Vincent O'Sullivan and Margaret Scott, Oxford: Clarendon Press, 1984.

Letters to friends and family in New Zealand describing London in wartime; letters to Francis Carco; a significant number of letters to Murry, some from Paris, where she was staying with Carco, having assured Murry that she was not interested in him. The Lawrences figure largely: they were close neighbours in Cornwall, 1916. Other letters to Koteliansky, Ottoline Morrell, Bertrand Russell, Dorothy Brett, Virginia Woolf.

C29   Mansfield, Katherine *The Collected Letters of Katherine Mansfield, Vol. II 1918–1919*, eds Vincent O'Sullivan and Margaret Scott, Oxford: Clarendon Press, 1987.

Numerous letters to Murry from Bandol (France) and Paris, where she was held up on her homeward journey by the German bombardment of the city in March to April 1918. Married Murry in May, 1918. Letters from Cornwall, and afterwards from their joint home in Hampstead. At the end of the war she thinks of her brother – and of Ottoline Morrell.

C30   Mansfield, Katherine *The Collected Letters of Katherine Mansfield, Vol. III 1919–1920*, eds Vincent O'Sullivan and Margaret Scott, Oxford: Clarendon Press, 1993.

Postwar reflections, many of them related to the novels Mansfield was reviewing, which Murry sent to her in the South of France, where she was trying to recover from her poor state of health. Detailed commentary on the discomfort that Woolf's *Night and Day* provoked in her: 'I feel in the *profoundest* sense that nothing can ever be the same that as artists we are traitors if we feel otherwise: we have to take it [the war] into account and find new expressions new moulds for our new thoughts and feelings' (10 November 1919).

C31   Stevenson, Betty *Betty Stevenson, YMCA. Sept 3, 1896 – May 30, 1918*, eds C.G.R.S. and A.G. Stevenson, London: Longmans Green & Co., 1920.

These are extracts from her letters and diaries, edited by her parents. Betty Stevenson looked after Belgian refugees in Harrogate, while taking driving lessons. Aged 19, she went out to join her aunt, who was managing a YMCA canteen in Paris – her mother joined her for a time. In April 1917, following a spell at home, she went back to France, alone, as a driver, mostly chauffeuring guests, lecturers, relatives, etc. She was killed one night in a raid, having stopped (with others) to take shelter. Her letters give the impression of her being cheerful, sunny, capable of working hard without making a fuss, and having a good relationship with her parents. She was posthumously awarded the Croix de Guerre avec Palme. She was 21 years old. (*See* Lois Vidal, *Magpie* C95; she knew Stevenson briefly.)

C32   Thompson, Tierl (ed.) *Dear Girl: The Diaries and Letters of Two Working Women 1897–1917*, London: The Women's Press, 1987.

The diaries of Ruth Slate and of Eva Slawson, and their letters to each other. They were both working women in London, who took part in some of the major suffrage rallies. The writings reveal their struggles with material circumstances, the search for self-confidence and their various ways of contributing to the major events of their time. The war occurs towards the end of the record, and reveals a growing commitment to pacifism.

C33   Woolf, Virginia *The Question of Things Happening. The Letters of Virginia Woolf, Vol. II: 1912–1922*, ed. Nigel Nicholson, London: Chatto & Windus, 1976.

Woolf was ill during the beginning of the war. She makes passing comments on it, on her dislike of patriotic sentiment, the senselessness of the militaristic mentality. The famous 'preposterous masculine fiction' comment occurs in a letter to Margaret Llewelyn Davies, 23 January 1916. Comments on air raids, the sounds of the guns heard from the Sussex Downs, Leonard's brothers, Lytton Strachey's tribunal, Leonard's exemption, Sassoon's poetry and protest, the Women's Co-operative Guilds, conscientious objectors, in the context of many rich letters to her sister, friends, and other family.

C34   Woolf, Virginia *A Change of Perspective. The Letters of Virginia Woolf, Vol. III: 1923–1928*, ed. Nigel Nicholson, London: Chatto & Windus, 1977.

Postwar reflections. Covers the period in which she was writing *Jacob's Room, Mrs Dalloway* and *To the Lighthouse*.

III AUTOBIOGRAPHIES

C35   Addams, Jane *The Second Twenty Years at Hull House*, New York: Macmillan, 1930.

Covers the years 1909 to 1929, and is predominantly concerned with social issues in an American context, but her account of the efforts for peace surrounding the Hague Peace Congress are important to an understanding of the phenomenon.

C36   Allen, Mary S. *Lady in Blue*, London: Stanley Paul, 1936.

Memoirs of one of the founders of the Women's Police Service. Describes her earlier suffragette experiences, being inspired by Annie Kenney, going to prison and embroidering 'Votes for Women' on the men's shirts they were required to stitch. When war broke out, she got in touch with Margaret Damer Dawson, and together they put forward a plan for a women's police service. They had a uniform, and were mostly involved in keeping 'shiftless girls' out of the grasp of military males, officiating at air raids and at munitions factories, where there were explosions. Recounts tales of indescribable disorder in the Strand following the Armistice, with drug dealers and white slave traffickers. They were asked to disband, and were sued when they refused. Covers a lot of postwar international work also.

C37   Ashwell, Lena *Myself a Player*, London: Michael Joseph, 1936.

Ashwell, the organiser of 'Concerts at the Front', was born into a seafaring family and was a student at the Royal Academy of Music. Before establishing the concerts she was briefly involved 'in that really wonderful and most comic organisation the Women's Emergency Corps'. The concerts were organised through the YMCA: Ashwell was to select the artists and meet the expenses. She speaks of pretty, well-dressed women, good music, gay and tender songs that would refresh the soldiers with the 'message that England cared for them'. Ivor Novello was one of the party in 1915 – he had just written 'Keep the Home Fires Burning'. Cicely Hamilton and Gertrude Jennings were also involved. Ashwell thought that the success of the concerts meant that the nation would understand the importance of the contribution of theatre to the human spirit: she hoped to transpose the experience, postwar, to the poorest people, but no funding was forthcoming, and the project foundered.

C38   Asquith, Margot *The Autobiography of Margot Asquith, Vol. II*, London: Thornton Butterworth, 1922.

Volume I (published 1920) covers her aristocratic upbringing in the Scottish lowlands, her family, friends, political connections, The Souls, her marriage to Asquith in May 1894, and finishes around 1906. This volume covers the crisis in the House of Lords, 1910, the war years, the coalition, the campaign of calumny conducted against the Asquith family in the newspapers, which led to Asquith's resignation. Refers also to the Landsowne Letter, of which she and her husband approved, despite its being rubbished elsewhere. It is based on letters and diary extracts and is thus immediate, and in places, quite moving, as in, for example, the account of Raymond Asquith's death. Many pen portraits of public figures (Kitchener stands out) and details of family life.

C39   Bagnold, Enid *Enid Bagnold's Autobiography*, London: Heinemann,1969.

Anecdotal, discursive autobiography that tells of her childhood, school (with Mrs

Huxley, sister of Mrs Humphry Ward), young ladyhood in London and at her parental home on Shooter's Hill, her experiences with Walter Sickert, her relationship with Antoine Bibesco, her war experience as a nurse at the Royal Herbert Hospital, from which she was sacked, and later her driving escapades in France. Minute detail on her war experience is lacking, but she presents an interesting picture of herself and her friends during the period, before moving on to her marriage and later success as the author of *National Velvet*, among other books and plays.

C40   Beauchamp, Pat *Fanny Went to War*, London: Routledge, 1940.

Covers much the same ground as *Fanny Goes to War* (B14), but there is more detail on her accident, which resulted in the amputation of one leg below the knee. Brings the history of the FANY up to date.

C41   Blücher, Evelyn Princess *An English Wife in Berlin: A Private Memoir of Events, Politics and Daily Life in Germany Throughout the War and the Social Revolution of 1918*, London: Constable, 1920.

A detailed and compassionate account by an Englishwoman, who married a German, Count Blücher, in 1907. They lived mostly in England until the outbreak of war, when the question of their nationality forced them to go (ultimately) to Berlin, where they were part of a colony of 'internationals' at the Esplanade Hotel. Describes the social environment, the difficulties of having relations on both fronts, her distress at local celebrations of German victories, her attempts to trace British friends and relatives who might have been captured and to send parcels to prisoners. Also describes an odd visit by Roger Casement, before he was charged with treason.

C42   Bocharskaya, S. and F. Pier *They Knew How To Die: A Narrative of the Personal Experiences of a Red Cross Sister on the Russian Front*, London: Peter Davies, 1931.

Not seen.

C43   Bondfield, Margaret *A Life's Work*, London: Hutchinson & Co. Ltd, 1948.

A rather stilted account of an extremely successful life. Before the war she was involved in union activity, and met Mary Macarthur in connection with the National Federation of Women Workers. She was involved in the Women's Co-operative Guilds, and was pacifist by inclination. During the war she turned her attention to problems regarding women's employment, worked with Mary Macarthur on the Queen's Work for Women Fund, and became assistant secretary of the NFWW. After the war she became the first woman cabinet minister in Ramsay MacDonald's government. The autobiography is presented more in the interests of providing information than narrative pleasure, but contains a great deal of detail.

C44   Botchkareva, Maria *Yaska: My Life as a Peasant, Exile and Soldier by M.B., Commander of the Russian Women's Battalion of Death*, as set down by Issac Don Levine, London: Constable & Co. Ltd, 1919.

This promises to be a 'true' version of the life of this semi-literate peasant, as told by herself, rather than related through the press. She is said to be innocent of politics and not, therefore, a counter-revolutionary: she wanted only to free Russia from the German yoke. She nevertheless presents a 'horrible picture of Bolshevism in action'. She tells the story of her peasant childhood and early adulthood; a hand-to-mouth existence, in which rape and abuse are all but commonplace. She enlisted as a soldier in the army by special permission of the Tsar, and when war broke out fought, and was decorated. She formed the Women's Battalion when discipline failed and the solders were refusing to fight. She was a strong believer in individual command. There were meetings with Lenin and Trotsky, street scenes, descriptions of Bolshevik atrocities. The tone leans towards sensationalism and melodrama.

C45   Bottome, Phyllis *The Challenge*, London: Faber & Faber, 1952.

Second volume of autobiography taking her to her marriage in 1917. She travelled a great deal, knew H.D., Ezra Pound and Richard Aldington. Good descriptions of London in Spring 1914 and of the impact of war. She worked at Hammersmith Hall, helping with Belgian refugees, and later with John Buchan at the Ministry of Information. Wrote her novels *Second Fiddle* and *A Servant of Reality* while there. Married in Paris, 1917 and had a comparatively lavish honeymoon in the south.

C46   Bottome, Phyllis *The Goal*, London: Faber & Faber, 1962.

Takes up the story in Paris following the honeymoon. Her husband, Ernan Forbes-Dennis, was seriously wounded, but cured by experimental drugs. She supported the Lansdowne letter – and went on to write an anti-war novel, *The Mortal Storm*, in 1937. She knew Gertrude Atherton, Alice Meynell, Ethel Mayne (writer and friend of Violet Hunt) and wrote a memorial pamphlet for Stella Benson, 1934.

C47   Britnieva, M. *One Woman's Story*, London: Arthur Barker, 1934.

An Anglo-Russian woman's account of her war experiences as a nurse with a mobile hospital unit on various fronts. No details of the revolution itself, but has more to say about her tribulations during the months following. Describes her escape to England and her return to Russia to search for her husband.

C48   Brittain, Vera *Testament of Youth*, London: Victor Gollancz 1933. Reprinted London: Virago, 1979.

Probably the best-known woman's story of the war. This autobiography tells of Vera Brittain's struggle to get into Oxford, her passionate, but youthful love for Roland Leighton, and the interruptions to her plans that war brings. She trained as a VAD nurse and served in England, Malta and France. One after the other, her lover, his two friends, and her cherished brother all died. She found consolation in work which, on the Western Front, was gruelling, occasionally humiliating, but never demanded of her the supreme sacrifice that the men of her generation were offering all around her. The war over, she returned to Oxford, having chosen to study history instead of English, haunted by the horrors of her own experience and a sense of being an unwanted piece of war wreckage in a world that wanted only to forget. It was here that she began her friendship with Winifred Holtby. The account ends with her marriage to George Caitlin.

C49   Brittain, Vera *Testament of Experience*, London: Victor Gollancz, 1959. Reprinted London: Virago, 1979.

An account of the years 1925 to 1950, in which Brittain gives a full account of her decision to write *Testament of Youth*, and the experience of re-reading diaries and letters that formed part of that process. Renders in detail the development of her feminism and pacifism in this period.

C50   Butler, E.M. *Paper Boats*, London: Collins, 1959.

E.M. Butler was educated in France and Germany before attending Cheltenham Ladies College and finally getting a place at Cambridge. During the early war years she was teaching at Newnham and, having spent some time fumbling with bandages, looking after Belgian refugees and being suspected of espionage (she spoke fluent German), finally she was asked to shepherd some Scottish Women's Hospital nurses across to Russia. Having rapidly acquired something of the 'intellectual beauty of the Russian language' (thanks to Jane Harrison) she set off, on Elsie Inglis's orders, to travel to, and to work in a hospital. She gives a moving account of working with Inglis, of Inglis's fierce devotion to her duties, and of the inspiration that engendered. She also speaks of her own love for Russia, its people and its language. A reflective, often witty account of one who never really 'saw herself' as an academic, but whose love of literary research earned her the Cambridge Chair in German.

C51   Butts, Mary *The Crystal Cabinet: My Childhood at Salterns*, London: Methuen & Co., 1937.

Describes her childhood in Dorset and her being sent away to school in St Andrews. Imbued mostly with a sense of the prewar world, which is one filled with myths and legends, presided over by a nurtured intelligence, and which 'the war deflected, made angry, anguished, reckless, as it did so many of us' (273). Interesting to read alongside her novel *Ashe of Rings* (A31).

C52   Cameron, Mary *Merrily I Go to Hell: Reminiscences of a Clergyman's Daughter*, London: George Allen & Unwin Ltd, 1932.

Characterises herself as having been born at midnight, as the new century came in, one of twelve children in a riotous family. She was expelled from school at the outbreak of war, and joined the St John's Ambulance Brigade. Went to France as a dishwasher and worked in various hospitals and ambulance convoys, often hobnobbing with doctors and royalty. Many schoolgirlish pranks. Back in England, got work as a welder in an aircraft factory, clerical work in the Air Ministry, and worked, postwar as an actress in South Africa, India, Hong Kong and finally America.

C53   Cannan, May Wedderburn *Grey Ghosts and Voices*, Kineton: Roundwood Press, 1976.

Self-consciously locates herself in the Victorian age and is quietly adamant about not moving with the times. This autobiography describes her happy childhood in Oxford (her father was Dean of Trinity College) with her sisters, one of whom is the novelist Joanna Cannan. She had (male) friends in the OTC or the regular army – one of whom was Bevil Quiller-Couch, son of Arthur, the Cambridge Professor of English – and was not going to lag behind in terms of preparation for an increasingly likely war. Hence her involvement in the Red Cross Voluntary Aid Detachment. When war was declared she worked briefly for Oxford University Press and took in Belgian refugees, then went to France to help run a canteen. She finally got a job in Intelligence in Paris and it was in Paris, after peace was declared, that she became engaged to Bevil Quiller-Couch, who died of pneumonia while still on active service in Germany only a month later. She is conservative, has no time for the likes of the Sitwells, had nothing to do with her conscientious objector cousin, Gilbert Cannan. She is better known for her poetry than her prose (some of her war poems have been reprinted in Catherine Reilly's *Scars Upon My Heart*, London: Virago, 1981, and in the *Oxford Book of Verse*); her style and her sense of belonging seem more suited to the Victorian age.

See Imperial War Museum archives (E22) and *The Lonely Generation* (A33).

C54   Cole, Margaret Isabel *Growing Up into Revolution*, London and New York: Longmans, Green & Co. 1949.

Autobiography of Margaret Postgate Cole, covering her childhood (Cambridge and Liverpool), education (the hated Roedean then Girton), her 'discovery' of socialism, war experience, marriage, General Strike, fascism, Spanish Civil War, Second World War. At the beginning of the war she taught at St Paul's Girls School London, but when, in 1916, her brother, Ray Postgate, was imprisoned as a conscientious objector, she 'walked into a new world of doubters and protesters' (59) and began working for the Fabian (later Labour) Research Department. It was here that she met her husband, G.D.H. Cole, and became involved in Guild Socialism. Among her acquaintances were, on the political side, Sidney and Beatrice Webb, George Lansbury, Rowland Kenney, Francis Meynell (son of Alice, and a conscientious objector), Ellen Wilkinson and Mary Macarthur; on the literary/artistic side Stella Bowen, Ezra Pound, Ford Madox Ford and Naomi Mitchison. A fascinating record of the debates surrounding socialism during and after the war. As well as for her political activity, Cole is noted for her poems (reprinted in *Scars upon my Heart*, 1981) and her detective novels, written with her husband.

C55   Daisy, Princess of Pless *By Herself*, London: John Murray, 1928.

A lengthy account (529pp.) of her life by an Englishwoman who married into German royalty, some years before the war. Covers twenty-five years of prewar experience: the ceremony, the servants, the life of a royal 'Beauty', who was one of the most notable fashionable ladies. When war came, she worked in a military hospital, but under suspicion: she was known as a foreigner. Towards the end of the war she watched her eldest son go out and fight against England.

C56   Dayus, Kathleen *Where There's Life*, London: Virago, 1985.

The second volume of her fascinating autobiography (*Her People*, 1982, was the first), covering the years 1914–45. She was still at school when war broke out, but describes the fact that suddenly every one had plenty of money, whether from factory work, or from taking in the washing of workers. Food was fairly scarce, so a considerable proportion was spent on alcohol. There were many scandals regarding Australian and Canadian troops, and local married women. Dayus looked for a factory job on leaving school, aged 14, in 1916, and (after being molested by a doctor from whom she had to obtain a medical certificate) found work pressing out trouser buttons for the army. She worked so productively that they reduced the piece rate, which caused her to leave. Following that she tried a variety of jobs, with varying success, and ended up in the enamelling trade. The postwar depression began immediately and continued to 1939.

C57   Dayus, Kathleen *All My Days*, London: Virago, 1988.

This volume covers most of the life of Kathleen Dayus, who was born in the back streets of Birmingham, 1903. The account begins with her youth, comments on the availability of work during the war, and on the sexual education with which the older women in the factories attempted, rather unkindly, to provide her. There were plenty of jobs in factories, making uniforms etc., that temporarily lifted living standards: 'Nothing but war, it seemed, could provide employment for starving people, and now the war was over, the people were starving again' (71). She married, had five children, was widowed and had to give up her children to a Dr Barnado's Home until she was sufficiently set up to get them back. Covers Second World War experience, and a later, happier marriage.

C58   Fawcett, Millicent Garrett *The Women's Victory and After: Personal Reminiscences 1911–1918*, London: Sidgwick & Jackson, 1920.

Her personal account of how the vote was won. It begins in 1911 and discusses suffragist strategies and tactics up to the war, pausing occasionally to dwell on particular figures. Mrs Harley, for example, is credited with being the originator of 'The Pilgrimage' campaign (1913); she went on to work for the SWH, and was killed in 1917 by a Bulgarian shell. Gives a general account of the war relief work undertaken, implying that there was little or no difference of opinion as to what the stance of the NUWSS should be when war broke out. Drs Flora Murray and Louisa Garret Anderson are singled out for praise, as is Elsie Inglis, and the SWH movement – the only voluntary organisation to run under the auspices of a suffrage society. In this account men of all kinds, from government officials to commercial magnates, and female anti-suffragists are converted to the belief that women should have the right to vote, by the wonderful example set by women's war work.

C59   Fawcett, Millicent Garrett *What I Remember*, London: T. Fisher & Unwin, 1924.

An account of a long life, dominated by Fawcett's commitment to the advancement of women. Millicent Garrett was born into a large family in 1847. Her father, a merchant trader, was sufficiently forward-looking to encourage her older sister, Elizabeth (later Anderson) in her desire to become medically qualified. One of

Elizabeth's friends was Emily Davies, who founded Girton College. The narrative covers Millicent's school years in Blackheath, her marriage in 1867 to Henry Fawcett, and their life in Cambridge and London, until Henry's death seventeen years later. Lots of detail regarding friends, family and political acquaintances – most of whom are concerned with the suffrage movement, which, of course, dominated her life. The war occurred relatively late in her life and it is covered in two chapters, which refer to women's war relief work and the winning of the vote.

C60   Forbes, Lady Angela *Memories and Base Details*, London: Hutchinson & Co., 1921.

An account of her life from her birth (1876) until immediately after the war. Comments (unfavourably) on Germany before the war, on the London bicycling craze (c. 1895), on the short-lived nature of many aristocratic marriages (her own ended in divorce). Her first novel, *The Broken Commandment*, was banned by libraries for immorality. Began first aid classes on the outbreak of war, as she was asked to go to Dr Haden Guest's hospital in Paris, where, initially, '[t]here were more nurses than patients' (169). Many comments on the role of aristocratic ladies in the war effort: 'Lady Colebrooke belonged to the strenuous contingent ... she was immensely proud of her overtime' (170). Set up a 'club' in Etaples, for the use of soldiers, independently of the YMCA. Same milieu as Monica Grenfell, Lady Hadfield, the Duchess of Rutland. General commentary on the progress of the war.

C61   Forbes, Lady Angela [Lady Angela St Clair Erskine] *Fore and Aft*, London: Jarrolds, 1932.

Mostly postwar experience, but includes a resumé of her previous life, of which she says 'The war brought out a capacity for organisation which I had not suspected ... I developed during my four years in France a positive liking for hard work.' She started a training centre for disabled soldiers when she returned from France, but the scheme did not last. Found herself belonging to 'no particular generation' after the war: she lived a different kind of life from her sisters, the Duchess of Sutherland and Lady Warwick, but is very knowledgeable about 'Society' and how it adapted to postwar conditions.

C62   Furse, Katharine *Hearts and Pomegranates. The Story of Forty-Five Years, 1875–1920*, London: Peter Davies, 1940.

Dame Katharine Furse GBE, RRC, was responsible for developing the VAD department at Devonshire House, and, later on, for founding the WRNS. Her autobiography tells of her childhood as the daughter of the writer, classical scholar and Magdalene fellow John Addington Symonds, much of which was spent travelling and visiting, amongst others, the Leslie Stephens. She married the painter Charles Furse (who died in 1904, after they had had two children), knew the Northcliffes, and was a friend of Rachel Crowdy. Tells the story of her part in the VAD, her early training, the short notice given to assemble a party of twenty nurses to go to Paris in October 1914, the nature of the service at the beginning – in particular her insistence on 'seriousness' and uniforms. She came up with a number of schemes for the training and recruitment of women, many of which were rejected. Resigned from the VAD and began work with the WRNS in 1917. Articulates the excitement of having a role in the war, the frustration of knowing that women's employment could be so much better organised, if the authorities were only willing.

C63   Gwynne-Vaughan, Dame Helen GBE, LLD, DSc, *Service with the Army*, Hutchinson & Co. Ltd, n.d. [1942]

An account of her experience with women's army organisations, which gives a brief history of women's involvement in previous wars, before focussing on the WAAC. Describes her introduction to the command structure of the WAAC: Mrs Chalmers Watson, the first Chief Controller, was the sister of Auckland Geddes, at that time Director of Recruiting. Gwynne-Vaughan (at that time Head of Botany at Birkbeck, and studying medical bacteriology) knew Louie Garrett Anderson, Mrs Watson's cousin, and was invited to take over operations in France. Includes lots of minute details on titles, badges, uniforms, status and pay; deals with the objection to the employment of women, the ambiguities of their status and duties in France; and comments on questions of discipline, the need for sensitivity and compassion, and the false charges of immorality to which her organisation was subject. Professional, rather than confessional, account.

C64   Hamilton, Cicely *Life Errant*, London: J.M. Dent, 1935.

Described by her biographer as 'one of the most uninformative autobiographies ever written' (H33: 4), this is, indeed, a very reticent account of one of this century's more accomplished women. Hamilton was an actress and a playwright; she wrote and spoke for the suffrage cause, co-founded the Women Writers' Suffrage League and composed the words for Ethel Smyth's 'March of the Women'. During the war she worked as an administrator for the SWH until 1917, when she joined Lena Ashwell's organisation, 'Concerts at the Front'. She spent some time as a member of the League of Nations Union, was involved in the International Women's Suffrage Alliance, and later wrote for *Time and Tide*, finally becoming one of its directors. The novel of hers which is most often characterised as a 'war novel', *William – An Englishman* (A50), she, in fact, describes as a 'suffrage' novel, conceived as a critical response to the enthusiastic, but ignorant insistence on belli-cose rhetoric on the part of suffrage and other campaigners. The autobiography was written in the 1930s, and in common with, for example, Virginia Woolf's *Three Guineas*, displays a distaste for mass organisation that might usefully be placed in the context of that political period. Hamilton characterises herself very firmly as an 'individual' and appears particularly to deplore the organisational principles of any movement of which she has been a member: 'the dangerous attraction of membership, comradeship, is that it gives free rein to passions and vices which, as individuals, we are bound to hold in check' (74). She thus distances herself from the major campaigns and organisations with which she has been involved and produces a book that refuses to celebrate some of her major achieve-ments.

C65   Hamilton, Mary Agnes *Remembering My Good Friends*, London: Jonathan Cape, 1944.

Account of her upbringing in Manchester (where Helena Swanwick was a friend), Aberdeen and Glasgow. Read Economics at Newnham, where her confidence and awareness of social inequalities and determination to fight them developed.

Describes the shattering effect of the outbreak of war, the instinctive (although faintly self-righteous) pacifism of herself and those of her circle, the reaction of the ILP, which she joined about a week before war was declared. She worked for the UDC, was a friend of Irene Cooper Willis and with her met Bertrand Russell, Arthur Ponsonby, E.D. Morel, Ramsay MacDonald, and other frequenters of Philip and Ottoline Morrell's establishment at 44 Bedford Square. Comments on the galvanising effect of the Russian Revolution, and on postwar politics. She became a Labour MP in 1929.

Provides a convincing portrait of the political naivety of those of her circle in the early war years (this, of course, from the perspective of 1944), and comments that the characters in *Dead Yesterday* (A51), although criticised for being incredible, were an accurate portrait of those with whom she associated: earnest, politically minded, but ignorant and unprepared.

C66   Hutton, Isabel Emslie *With a Woman's Unit in Serbia, Salonika and Sebastopol*, London: Williams & Norgate, 1928.

Long account (302pp.) of the five and a half years' of work of an Edinburgh doctor for the SWH. She sees the distinctiveness of this publication as lying in its account of the advance of the Serbians in 1918 and the defence of the Crimea in 1920. Describes first her work in France, 1915, as Assistant Medical Officer and Pathologist to a SWH unit in Troyes, and then her work in Serbia. Worked in Salonika, in Macedonia, commanded a hospital at Ostrovo and then one in Vranja, where conditions were (initially) dreadful. Mentions barely registering the Armistice. Much detail of Serbian customs and culture, and of nursing the wounded and typhus/malaria cases. Comments on the work of Mrs Florence Harley, Olive Kelso King, Flora Sandes, Evelina Haverfield, Elsie Inglis and the 'thousand-dollar-a-minute girl', Kathleen Burke. First person retrospective narrative with excerpts from diaries and letters. Includes photographs.

C67   Hutton, Lady Isabel *Memories of a Doctor in War and Peace*, London: Heinemann, 1960.

Provides a longer perspective on the material outlined in the publication above, including her prewar medical education in Edinburgh, and her postwar experience in the Crimea and Vienna, and, following her marriage which barred her from some jobs, in Armenia, India and Yugoslavia.

C68   Jacob, Naomi *Me – A Chronicle About Other People*, London: Hutchinson, 1933.

Irreverent, amusing account by one predisposed more to theatrical than to military conventions. She describes herself as a suffragist and a socialist, who had been manager and secretary to 'a bill topper' in the music halls. She knew Masterman and was aware (while they were both staying in Selsey) that he was being visited by Lloyd George. Her reaction was to get an alarm clock, place it in a biscuit tin, and put it under the bungalow where they were staying. She joined the Women's Emergency Corps while Viola Meynell was there as a temporary typist, and characterises its atmosphere thus: 'Elderly females from Cheshire would come with some recipe handed down by their great-grandmother for making excellent meat pies from cabbage stalks and old boots.' She subsequently became a supervisor at a munitions factory, the one (she claims) in which Rathbone's *We That Were Young* was set.

C69   Jacob, Naomi *Me Again*, London: Hutchinson & Co., 1937.

A further garrulous and quirky account of her life. Spends time on her childhood, and her brief experience as a teacher, before hitting the road as part of a music hall troupe. Passes over her earlier war experiences and concentrates on munitions work: excess profits, the (unfounded) rumours about inflated wages. She left the industry having contracted TB, and went to recovery near the Lakes in Italy, where she stayed, postwar, trying to write and find stage work. Discusses her attitudes towards Hitler and fascism: she is Jewish.

C70   Jameson, Storm *No Time Like the Present*, London: Cassell & Co., 1933.

An autobiographical memoir, covering her upbringing in Whitby, her time at Leeds and London Universities, and her impressions of the postwar age. She provides a good account of prewar London, where she was at university as a postgraduate, having taken a first in English from Leeds. Provides few details of her own war experience, but has a number of observations to make on the event and its effects. Her brother, having earned the medaille militaire, DCM and MC was shot down: 'In 1932, what lying, gaping mouth will say that it was worth while to kill my brother in his nineteenth year?' She is horrified by the Peace, and, like Vera Brittain and a number of others, has a strong sense of belonging specifically to a war gener-ation: war 'stripped my generation of its leaves and branches, leaving the bare maimed stem'; 'The gulf which divides the women of my generation and their men who fought in the war is impassable on any terms.' She can't see that women's involvement in politics thus far has changed anything; is fully convinced that the next war is on its way, that women should not kill other women, and that she would endeavour to keep her son out of another war. Discursive rather than docu-mentary.

C71   Jameson, Storm *Journey From the North*, Vol. I, London:
             Collins & Harvill Press, 1969. Reprinted London: Virago, 1984.

A great deal more detailed than her 1933 memoir, this lengthy autobiography renders her life during the war, which was spent mostly following her (first) husband around and living in barely-adequate lodgings, caring for her much-loved son, and desperately desiring something larger from life than a cramped, domestic existence. This volume follows her through her breakthrough into the literary world in the 1920s, and up to the second war. Volume II continues the story.

C72   Jermy, Louise *The Memories of a Working Woman*, Norwich:
             Goose & Son, 1934.

The life story of Louise Jermy, who was born in 1877. Her mother died when she was in her second year, and she got on badly with her stepmother. Her childhood is characterised by family arguments, poor health and hard work. She got TB of the hip, which disabled her, but did not prevent her from going into service. This enabled her to leave home. She married, eventually, and had two boys. Covers war years, but not in great detail. More useful as contextual evidence of life in service. Has a Foreword by R.H. Mottram, saying 'This Memoir is said to be the first auto-biography written by a Women's Institute member.'

C73 Kaye-Smith, Sheila *Three Ways Home*, London: Cassell and Co., 1937.

The 'three ways home' of the title are: love of her part of the country, love of writing, and Catholicism. Tells the story of her upbringing, her determination to write, her success with *Sussex Gorse*, her fifth novel, which she wrote on the advice of W.L. George. Was not absorbed by the war; disliked the 'patriotism', but felt uneasy with conscientious objectors. Did some war work – made bandages, sold tea, worked in a War Office department, but having no-one 'in' it, she was more preoccupied with her fiction. The sound of the guns over Sussex inspired *Little England*. Married a clergyman after the war, continued to write, had major success with *Joanna Godden*.

C74 Kenney, Annie *Memories of a Militant*, London: Edward Arnold & Co., 1924.

Born 1879, one of eleven children, into a happy, harmonious family in a Lancashire village, most of whose occupants were employed by a cotton factory. Kenney left school at 13 to work, and first saw Christabel Pankhurst at a suffrage meeting. The book is dominated by the suffragettes' major campaigns, with Kenney as their second-in-command. In August 1914 the Pankhursts, in typically autocratic style, decided on a pro-war policy – and this didn't please all. It was decided that Kenney should go to the USA so that at least one of them should be safe if Paris or London were invaded. She thus toured some of the US, speaking of suffrage issues. Came back and spoke on the Balkans, then responded to Lloyd George's suggestion that a women's procession should be organised. Left the move-ment after the 'Khaki election', in which Christabel stood.

C75 Lawrence, D. *Sapper Dorothy Lawrence, the Only English Woman Soldier, Late Royal Engineers 51st Division 17th Tunnelling Company*, London: Lane, 1919.

The story of a woman who failed to get a job as a war correspondent and who, instead, cycled around France until she managed to enlist the support of some 'chivalrous' soldiers who found her a uniform, a billet (a ruined cottage, only a cabbage patch away from enemy trenches), and permitted her to join them in laying mines. She was eventually betrayed, cross-examined and deported. Describes those who helped her as 'my little army' and can't emphasise enough that 'immorality' was out of the question.

C76 Lockwood, Mrs Josiah (Florence) *An Ordinary Life, 1861–1924*, London: Mrs Josiah Lockwood, 1932.

Covers her childhood in Plymouth, her time as an art student at the Slade in the late 1880s, following which she made something of a living by working to commis-sion and teaching. At the age of 40 she married Josiah Lockwood, a Yorkshire cloth manufacturer. By chance she heard Mrs and Adela Pankhurst speak on women's suffrage, and this sparked a keen interest. Her war years were spent in Yorkshire. She became involved with the UDC, carried out relief work and spoke at a Women's Peace Crusade meeting; her husband's mill made khaki. She tells of the Scarborough bombing and of raids in London. She maintained an eccentric, because often isolated, resistance to war.

C77   Londonderry, Marchioness of *Retrospect*, London: Frederick Muller Ltd, 1938.

Begins with an account of her childhood and upbringing in Stafford House and Clarence House, in an atmosphere of politics and established wealth. Her aunt was Millicent, Duchess of Sutherland. Gives a brief account of the successes of women's organisations during the war, and describes her own involvement, initially as 'Colonel-in-Chief' of the WVR, and later in the development of the Women's Legion, of which she was the first president. Comments generally on women's success, on the spirit of comradeship that their work inspired, and on events and personalities in the war.

C78   Lowndes, Mrs Belloc *A Passing World*, London: Macmillan & Co. Ltd, 1948.

A discursive and anecdotal account of her life, which centres on the years 1914–18, but through the lens of the intervening period, which includes the Second World War. Margot Asquith had been a family friend for some years, and through this close connection, Lowndes was very close to the centre of political power when war broke out. Describes the Asquiths, Haldane, Lloyd George, Grey; the views from Westminster Bridge when the first zeppelin attack produced fires in London, having narrowly missed Woolwich Arsenal; May Sinclair – suggests that she put up the funding for the Munro ambulance corps, and was ejected at Munro's request; lots of parties – political, country house, and otherwise; and, of course, her own novels.

C79   Mackworth, M.H. (Viscountess Rhondda) *This Was My World*, London: Macmillan and Co. Ltd, 1933.

Describes childhood, adolescence (boarding school), young ladyhood (Somerville), marriage, and her gradual liberation from the drawing room via, initially, militant suffrage activity (she was imprisoned at one stage) and, during the war, action as business manager to her father, who did work of national importance at the Ministry of Food. Provides a rare account of the sinking of the *Lusitania*: both she and her father were on board and survived. Worked for the Ministry of National Service in 1918 and later formed the Six Point Group and founded the feminist magazine *Time and Tide*.

C80   Mitchell, Hannah *The Hard Way Up. The Autobiography of Hannah Mitchell, Suffragette and Rebel*, ed. Geoffrey Mitchell, with Preface by Sheila Rowbotham, London: Virago, 1977.

Just one brief chapter on the war in a fascinating, working-class autobiography. Mitchell was born in 1871 in Derbyshire, joined the Pankhursts in 1905 and describes her experience of violence by young thugs and the absence of police protection at suffrage meetings. Supported the NCF and WIL during the war. Her son was a conscientious objector and was exempted from combatant service. She later became a city councillor and then a city magistrate in Manchester.

C81   Mitchison, Naomi *All Change Here*, London: Bodley Head, 1975.

A volume of memoirs describing her prewar and wartime young ladyhood. A member of the famous Haldane family (her uncle was Richard Haldane, Secretary of War for the Liberal government), she spent these years in Oxford, slightly overshadowed by her talented brother, and over-protected by her mother. She passed her nursing exams, however, and escaped to London for a while to do VAD work in St Thomas's hospital, until she caught scarlet fever and had to return home. She received a limited education in science as a 'home student' at Oxford University. She married, young, in 1916 and had her first baby the year after. She had yet to discover the socialism, feminism and the drive to write for which she is now so well known, and the memoirs are characterised by a lively tone, a desire to escape chaperonage (which she managed, through devious means), and a consciousness that she was very young.

C82   Montefiore, Dora B. *From a Victorian to a Modern*, London: E. Archer, 1927.

Socialist and suffragist, Dora B. Montefiore was widowed when her children were aged 5 and 2. She was born into a large, wealthy family in Surrey, was married out in Australia, where she first became involved in women's suffrage, then returned to England after the death of her husband. She worked first with the NUWSS, then changed her allegiance to the WSPU in order to pursue more militant tactics: she was one of the first to refuse to pay income tax. At the outbreak of war, she joined a Cantine Des Dames Anglaises, under the French Croix Rouge, where she organised a canteen, and contributed to the subsistence of a VAD who worked with her. Records mostly personnel difficulties – thieving chefs, ungracious officers – but is also conscious that French soldiers who mobilised early heard nothing from their families who had been forced to evacuate their homes. She left when her son came over to England from Australia. He died after the war, from the effects of gas poisoning, and she continued to work for the Labour movement until bronchial asthma finally slowed her down.

C83   Morell, Lady Ottoline *Ottoline at Garsington. Memoirs of Lady Ottoline Morrell 1915–1918*, ed. and introduced Robert Gawthorne-Hardy, London: Faber & Faber, 1974.

Opens with her arrival at Garsington, designing, painting and decorating the scene of so many meetings of artists, politicians and thinkers during the war years, which was home to a number of conscientious objectors. Has a lot to say about D.H. Lawrence and Frieda, Bertrand Russell, Aldous Huxley, Katherine Mansfield, Virginia Woolf, Lytton Strachey, Duncan Grant, Maynard Keynes, Mark Gertler, David Garnett, Dora Carrington and Gilbert Cannan. Mary Agnes Hamilton visited, as did Siegfried Sassoon (he came with Robert Graves, at the time of his protest), Clifford Allen, Asquith and an excessively polite and restrained T.S. Eliot. Provides lots of detail on Garsington life, and on society and aesthetics discussions that took place there.

C84   Pethick-Lawrence, Emmeline *My Part in a Changing World*, London: Victor Gollancz, 1938.

The story of her life from her birth (1867) until 1937. Most of the book is concerned with her part in the militant suffrage campaign. She was a member of the WSPU until 1912, when the Pankhursts decided on a policy of autocracy and the destruction of private property. Pethick-Lawrence continued, with her husband, to edit *Votes for Women*, which became the organ of the United Suffragists during the war. During the war she became a pacifist, visited America on the advice of Rosika Schwimmer, and became acquainted with Jane Addams and the Women's Peace Party. She joined Addams and American delegates to the Hague Peace Congress (April 1915) on the *Noordam*, the ship that brought them from the USA to the Hague and thereby permitted Pethick-Lawrence to be one of the few British delegates to the congress. There is an account of the congress, its resolutions and subsequent deputations to rulers of belligerent and neutral countries, accounts of her peace work, the progress of the new franchise bill, and of her defeat in the postwar 'Khaki' election.

C85   Ruck, Berta *A Story-Teller Tells the Truth*, London: Hutchinson & Co., 1935.

Describes her upbringing in India, Wales and Liverpool, her scholarship to the Slade, marriage to the writer Oliver Onions, and the early journalism which led to her career as a 'story-teller'. Was in London and Wales during the war; saw a zeppelin shot down by Captain Robinson; collected material for *The Land-Girl's Love Story* while in Wales – her own 'tiny bit of useful propaganda'. Describes this in some detail – in places repeating the language in which the novel is written. Other than this, there is little about the war. A very anecdotal autobiography, punctuated with cheerful vignettes. Makes no claims for herself as an artist or a thinker.

C86   Russell, Dora *The Tamarisk Tree: My Quest for Liberty and Love*, Elek Books, 1975. Reprinted London: Virago, 1977.

The volume covers Dora Russell's early life, from 1894 to 1935. This covers the war period, part of which was spent in Cambridge, where she became aware of the views of C.K. Ogden, and did some reviewing for *The Cambridge Magazine*; the later part was spent in London, where she lived and studied (having obtained her first from Cambridge). Bertrand Russell and H.G. Wells come into the story, which is set in the context of a radical, 'Bohemian' London existence. She later spent some time in Paris, and visited Russia, following the revolution.

C87   Sandes, Flora *The Autobiography of a Woman Soldier*, London: H.F. & G. Witherby, 1927.

This account of the eccentric experiences of an all-round outsider begins: 'When a very small child I used to pray every night that I might wake up in the morning and find myself a boy.' Her prayers are pretty nearly answered when, having joined the ambulance unit attached to the 2nd Infantry Regiment (Serbian Army), they reach the point beyond which no ambulance may travel, and she makes the transition from dresser to Private. She is treated 'as a kind of mascot', but nevertheless advances up the bare, stony hills, 'rests' for hours in funk holes, joins in the scraps (and gets wounded), and feasts on bread and onions with the others. She is also a successful fundraiser. She gets demobbed in 1922, having been promoted to Captain.

C88 Sharp, Evelyn *Unfinished Adventure: Selected Reminiscences from an Englishwoman's Life*, London: John Lane, The Bodley Head, 1933.

Describes her childhood in London, time spent travelling, her movement in literary circles when older, and her work for the *Manchester Guardian*, her suffragette activity (she was imprisoned) and her friendship with Elizabeth Robins. There is a chapter on the war years, which mentions that she did some work on the land, visited Garrett Anderson and Flora Murray's hospital in Wimereux, and continued to edit *Votes for Women*, while running a club for women and girls in London. Her attitude to the war was broadly pacifist. She, among others, was a tax resister, and spent some time accompanied in her flat by a surprisingly pleasant and sympathetic bailiff, until he had to do the right thing and remove her furniture.

C89 Squire, Rose E. *Thirty Years in the Public Service: An Industrial Retrospect*, London: Nisbet & Co Ltd, 1927.

The career of a factory inspector, who became Director of Women's Welfare. When war was declared, all investigations, prosecutions of employers and future plans were halted. Squire was diverted onto the Health of Munition Workers Committee in order to plan how to increase production while maintaining health and promoting moral and physical welfare. Consists mostly of personal comments on her own career moves, night visits, working with high explosives, but also on the difference of scale in welfare provision that the war brought with it.

C90 Swanwick, Helena M. *I Have Been Young*, London: Victor Gollancz, 1935.

Born in Bavaria, 1864, Swanwick had three brothers, one of whom was Walter Sickert. She obtained a scholarship to study economics at Girton. Around 1905, she joined the North of England Suffrage Society, where she worked with Margaret Ashton, Kathleen Courtney, Maude Royden, Elsie Inglis and Catherine Marshall, among others. Became editor of *The Common Cause* in 1909. The account contains a great deal of reflection on gender and war. Her own war experience, following the split in the NUWSS, was dominated by work for the UDC (where she worked with Mary Agnes Hamilton, Irene Cooper Willis and Vernon Lee) and the British section of the Women's International League, the executive of which included Catherine Marshall, Kathleen Courtney, Emmeline Pethick Lawrence, Isabella Ford, Margaret Ashton and Ethel Snowden. Her principles were firmly socialist, and concerned with educating women, rather than 'wip[ing] up the mess made by men' (316). This is a fascinating story of political life in suffragist, socialist, and internationalist pacifist circles. She knew not only those mentioned above, but also Vera Brittain, Winifred Holtby, Evelyn Sharp, Margaret Llewelyn Davies.

C91   Thomas, Helen *World Without End*, London: William Heinemann, 1931.

The story of Helen Thomas's relationship with the poet Edward Thomas, their life together, their children, the poetry that they shared. Culminates in an extraordinarily moving account of her husband's departure for the Front, following his signing up with the Artists' Rifles.

C92   Thurstan, Violetta *The Hounds of War Unleashed*, St. Ives, Cornwall: United Writers Publications, 1978.

Recollections of the events told in *Field Hospital and Flying Column* (C16). Covers the same material (nursing in Belgium, 1914, being deported to Denmark, taking the 'Lapland Express' to join a mobile unit in Russia), but in a more contemplative mood, and one that conveys her later understanding of her experiences, rather than the immediate effect of them. The section on her Russian experience gives an indication of her emotional engagement with the country – the deprivation of the people, the gathering unrest – which is brought to a rather tragic climax with the death of her friend Nicky, the loss of their equipment and the disbanding of the unit.

C93   T'Serclaes, Baroness de *Flanders and Other Fields*, London: Harrap & Co., 1964.

Her memoirs, covering a miserable childhood and failed early marriage in Singapore, from which she returned, with her son – and discovered the joys of motorcycling. When war broke out, she had been trained as a cook, a nurse and was an expert mechanic: perfect qualifications to join an ambulance corps. She joined Hector Munro's unit (along with Mairi Chisholm, Helen Gleason, Lady Dorothie Fielding and May Sinclair), and describes early weeks in Belgium, transporting the wounded. Her conviction that shock could worsen physical injuries led her (with Mairi Chisholm) to establish an advance dressing station, which became the famous Cellar House at Pervyse, only five yards from the trenches. She provides a detailed account of work there, conditions, funds needed, visitors (Marie Curie and Ramsay MacDonald, for example) – until they were eventually gassed out. Agreed to work for the WRAF, which she rejoined in the second war, having spent the intervening period earning a living for herself and her son. 'This life of mine has been a bungled affair', she says. 'Only in time of war have I found any real sense of purpose and happiness' (213).

C94   Tynan, Katharine *The Years of the Shadow*, London: Constable, 1919.

Begins before the war, but mostly accounts for her life during the war years, in Ireland. Recounts a number of conversations (one with Frank Sheehy Skeffington), comments on the success of her poem 'Flower of Youth', on the rebellion, daylight saving, and her two sons, who joined up.

C95   Vidal, Lois *Magpie*, London: Faber & Faber, 1934.

A curate's daughter, one of a large family, the remains of which were living at Boar's Hill, Oxford when war broke out. Restless, she took a job in a hospital kitchen in Southsea, and later found work in the War Office in London, where she lived with her mother and sister. Her brother was killed. She went over to Le Havre to work in Intelligence during the day, and at the YMCA canteen in the evenings, which provided some close encounters with barely reputable soldiers. At Etaples she was in charge of the relatives of the wounded, and met Betty Stevenson. Land work back at home took her into the postwar period, which was characterised by vagabonding, a variety of low-paid jobs and risky relationships, until she was finally persuaded to write it down. An unusual account – especially of postwar years.

D JOURNALS

This section provides a brief synopsis of some of the journals and magazines that provide reflections on the war. Descriptions are limited to the war years. David Doughan and Denise Sanchez's *Feminist Periodicals, 1855–1984* (I11) offers a more comprehensive guide to publications with some feminist content, but therefore excludes the more conservative penny weeklies, which were the source of numerous strategies for managing war's distresses. For information on holdings the reader is referred to the *British Union-Catalogue of Periodicals*, although the British Newspaper Library at Colindale can be considered a generally reliable location.

D1   *Britannia*

The organ of the Women's Social and Political Union, succeeding *The Suffragette*, which ceased publication in August 1914. Published weekly. The very name *Britannia*, 'For King. For Country. For Freedom', betrays a shift in direction on the part of the Pankhursts towards pro-government and deeply patriotic activities. Initially the war is greeted as 'God's vengeance upon the people who held women in subjection', but soon appeals are made to the patriotism of militant women, whose 'love of country is necessarily strong' (iv, 97, 16 April 1915: 3). The editors demand that man should 'prepare himself to redeem his word to women, and to make ready to do his best, to save the mothers, the wives and the daughters of Great Britain from outrage too horrible to mention' (iv, 98, 23 April 1915: 25). Most articles concern the war, patriotic meetings, the Pankhursts' speeches. The editors were Christabel and Emmeline Pankhurst, Flora Drummond and Annie Kenney. Ceased publication in 1918.

D2   *The Common Cause*

The organ of the NUWSS, proclaiming 'Women's Suffrage the Common Cause of Humanity'. The suspension of political activities is announced regularly and the journal includes accounts of the NUWSS's wartime activities: workrooms, maternity centres, etc. Produces serious articles, not just on the organisation of the relief of distress caused by the war, but on women's work in industry, women's changing social role as a result of the war (articles by, for example, Susan Lawrence, B.L. Hutchins), as well as reviews and correspondence. Regular contributors include Ray Strachey, Cicely Hamilton, Clementina Black, Eleanor Rathbone. There is an article by C.K. Ogden, 26 February 1915, based on *Militarism Versus Feminism*. Arguments for and against a pacifist attitude to war are well aired before the actual split in the NUWSS leadership in 1915. Published weekly; editors included Helena Swanwick, Clementina Black, A. Maude Royden.

D3   *The Egoist*

Formerly called *The New Freewoman, An Individualist Review*, this influential, avant garde, literary magazine, was edited by Dora Marsden, assisted by Richard Aldington. Harriet Shaw Weaver also edited and funded the enterprise. Includes work by, for example, H.D., William Carlos Williams, Amy Lowell, Charlotte Mew. An article in the 1 September edition, 1914, by Richard Aldington, predicts 'mental indolence' as a characteristic of war art and is weary at the thought of the large number of sentimental novels that are likely to pour out, all on the same subject and all lacking in artistry.

Dora Marsden is a regular contributor, as is Madame Ciolkowska, who writes a regular piece called 'Fighting Paris'. May Sinclair has a poem published in the special imagist issue, 1 May 1915: 'After the Retreat'. Storm Jameson also occasionally contributes.

D4   *The Englishwoman*

A serious journal, dedicated to issues concerning women's advancement, and seeking to emulate the weighty, intellectual magazines concerned with art, literature and culture. Followed the lead of the NUWSS which, in the early months of the war, decided to suspend political activities and concentrate on relief work. An editorial in the September 1914 issue (no. 69) puts it in the following terms: 'For the present THE ENGLISHWOMAN [....] will be used to fire publicity, so far as lies in its power, to various schemes and methods of relief work, and will endeavour to represent the opinion of the large number of women who feel to the full the horrors of war, who ardently desire peace, but yet who would not buy it at the price of honour.'

There are lengthy articles on relief work, home economy, the necessity for women to be trained in their various roles in the war. Early articles reflect on, for example, the neglect by the authorities of trained VADs, the experiences of women such as Elsie Inglis and Violetta Thurstan (both of whom are contributors) and general 'problems of the day'. Esther Roper contributes to the debate concerning the economic emancipation of women (no. 99, March 1917: 206–12). Other articles are concerned with travel, book reviews, the nature of literature during the war. Mrs Fawcett was a regular contributor and, in June 1915, contributed an article on the relationship of the NUWSS to the Hague Congress, questioning the latter on constitutional grounds and concerned that, although its resolutions might have been generally appealing, there was no practical indication of how they might be carried out. Publication was monthly, and the editorial committee consisted of Frances Balfour, Mary Lowndes, Edith Palliser and M.M. Strachey, with E.M. Goodman as Acting Editor.

D5   *Everywoman's Weekly*

A new penny weekly, launched in March 1915. Aimed to be 'a friend to every woman' (editorial, I, 1, 27 March 1915: 1) and set about this by providing lots of household hints, advice on shopping and childcare, recipes, knitting and sewing patterns, stories, etc. Has a greater emphasis than, for example, *Woman's Own* on new career openings: a regular feature is called 'The War and the Woman Worker' and details the experiences of lift attendants, engineers, gardeners, dispensers as well as the more conventional nurses. Maintains the line, though, that women should not be paid as much as men, because 'The majority of us are not competent' (iii, 54, 1 April 1916: 42). Another striking feature is the 'weekly war chat with the women of Britain' from Horatio Bottomley, editor of *John Bull*.

D6   *Jus Suffragii*

Monthly organ of the International Woman Suffrage Alliance. Mary Sheepshanks was the editor. The IWSA president was the American Carrie Chapman Catt; Millicent Garrett Fawcett was the vice president. Early articles are on women's involvement in the war, and on women's work for peace – contributors include Ogden and Florence, Margaret Sackville and Sheepshanks herself. Anti-war organisations, such as the UDC, are discussed and welcomed. Tends to concentrate, in 1917, on suffrage issues in the light of the suffrage reform proposals in England. Regular reports from Great Britain, Australia, France, Germany, New Zealand, Norway, The Netherlands, Russia, Switzerland, Sweden, United States. Maintained international communications under intensely difficult conditions.

D7   *Mother and Home*

A penny weekly which concentrates on women's maternal role, saying 'This is a "war work", a work for "king and country"' (ii, 47, 1 January 1916: 499), and suggesting that it has been 'more repressed than encouraged during the last thirty or forty years' (ii, 48, 8 January 1916: 526). Little directly about the war: tends to concentrate on quite detailed advice on childcare.

The Suffragette see Britannia.

D8   *Vogue*

First British imprint, May 1916. Priced at one shilling, it is considerably more expensive than the penny weeklies and maintains a glamour, irony and aloofness about the war. Regular features on Society, the fine arts, the stage, special features on clothes, country estates, etc., but fashion and the fashionable dominate: '*Vogue* is fashion's Taube; it keeps a watchful eye on the battlefield. Do the lines of fashion shift and change – *Vogue* knows. Do the couturiers launch a stirring advance – *Vogue* knows. *Vogue* is a courier, and comes from Paris to drop bombs of fashion on expectant readers. And *Vogue* is not censored. It does not come from "Somewhere in France"; it comes from Paris' (47, 10, 15 May 1916: 33).

Later issues have a little more related to aspects of war economy: how to grow attractive vegetables in the garden; how to use cheaper dress fabrics; how to attire your 'butleress' and 'footwoman' in the absence of their male equivalents.

D9   *The Vote*

Weekly organ of the Women's Freedom League, edited by Charlotte Despard. (The Women's Freedom League was a dissident group of the WSPU, formed in 1907.) A number of articles on women's pacifist instincts, some based on the same arguments used in *Militarism Versus Feminism*, some more broadly Christian. A substantial publication.

D10   *Votes for Women*

Organ of the United Suffragists. Edited by Emmeline Pethick Lawrence. The United Suffragists were another break-away group from the WSPU, and included the Pethick Lawrences, Henry Nevinson – chair of the National Council for Adult Suffrage – Evelyn Sharp and George Lansbury, who was a leading light in the syndicalist movement. Articles on Mrs Pethick Lawrence's visit to America (on return from which she attended the Hague Peace Congress), on feminist pacifism, on aspects of women's war work and on the treatment of soldiers' wives.

D11   *The Woman at Home*

Early issues comment on the paper shortage and on the reduced volume of advertising, 'owing to the sudden and complete collapse of various forms of trade'. Combines awareness of the work of figures such as Mary Macarthur and Lilian Barker with more conventional romances by, for example, Annie S. Swan and Berta Ruck. Includes accounts and photographs of women's war work – from the more glamorous society ladies to those who took part in Macarthur's scheme – hints on wartime nutrition, health and nursing. Also includes articles by May Sinclair and Rebecca West, and reprints Olive Schreiner's 'Woman and War'.

D12   *The Woman's Dreadnought*

Organ of the East London Federation of Suffragettes. Edited by Sylvia Pankhurst and produced weekly. Speaks to and for the women of the East End, demanding, for example, that all food should be controlled, that men and women should be found work and paid at trades union rates, that women should get equal pay, that the moratorium on debts should cover those under £5, that working women should be on committees concerned with food prices, employment, relief – and, of course that all women should get the vote. Advertises the cost-price restaurants and babies' milk centres, etc, founded by Sylvia Pankhurst. Articles by Sylvia Pankhurst or by working women. Became *The Workers Dreadnought*, 28 July 1917, its general principles now being socialism, internationalism, votes for all. Opposed to a negotiated 'capitalist' peace. The ELFS became the Workers Suffrage Federation in February 1916, and then the Workers Socialist Federation in June 1918. The journal reflects an increasing involvement with the development of revolutionary socialism.

D13   *Woman's Own*

Priced at one penny, this is a low-budget comforter and advice manual to women affected in whatever way by war circumstances. Initially it emphasises knitting and sewing patterns, encouraging women to help out the soldiers via the Red Cross. It is usually dominated by Jeannie Maitland's homely advice on all matters practical and emotional, from removing difficult stains to tracing a missing soldier. Articulates the ethic of the 'Angel in the House': 'The great responsibilities of creating that quiet, wholesome happiness lies on the wife and mother. She must be kind, tactful, wise, and self-sacrificing if she is going to satisfy the heart-hunger of the young for something outside themselves' (4, 116, 17 July 1915: 1). Many recipes advising on butter substitutes and ways of economising while maintaining nutritional value. Regular stories. Some refer to the war, for example 'The Traitress: A Stirring Love Story of the Great War', serialised from September 1914. Urges women and girls *not* to be seduced by the glamour of war either into inappropriate war work or, worse still, into inappropriate war weddings. Very much the converse of *Vogue*. Lower middle class, homely, conservative.

D14   Woman's World

A penny weekly, issued every Monday. Dominated by a Christian ethic of loyalty, courage and cheerfulness, led by those such as 'Colonel Nurse Rachel', who forms and leads the 'Regiment of Mothers', and the (male) 'Bachelor of Experience', who delivers straight-from-the-shoulder chats to 'Sweethearts, Wives and Mothers of the British Empire'. One issue includes a free French conversation lesson, to be sent to 'your soldier lad' in case he gets lost. Alongside the lists of verbs, this includes such phrases as 'You must lubricate the wheels' and 'This shop looks very neglected' (520, 4 September 1915: 394).

D15   The Woman Worker

Produced monthly, this was the official organ of the National Federation of Women Workers. Concerned mostly with the campaigns of the NFWW for better working conditions for women in the light of changes wrought by war. The editor was Mary Macarthur, and her views predominate.

D16   Women's Industrial News (1895–1919)

Organ of the Women's Industrial Council. Clementina Black, an active campaigner for women in industry, was president of the WIC, and occasionally edited the *Women's Industrial News*. Usually publishes one to two articles on women's work and a selection of reviews of pieces on politics and employment that have women's interests at the centre.

E ARCHIVE MATERIAL

As indicated in the Introduction, this section does not aim to provide exhaustive references to archive collections of women's writing. Instead, it provides detailed accounts of two major collections: the Imperial War Museum in London, and the Liddle Collection in Leeds. There are also brief references to other libraries which the researcher may find useful. For further First World War manuscript material the reader might consult Mayer and Koenig *The Two World Wars. A Guide to Manuscript Collections in the United Kingdom. The Libraries Directory* contains further information on a much larger scale (*see* I24 and I19, for full references).

I   IMPERIAL WAR MUSEUM

Address: Imperial War Museum
            Lambeth Road
            London SE1 6HZ

Tel: 0171 416 5000 (main switchboard)
            0171 416 5342/4 (Dept of Printed Books)
            0171 416 5291 (Dept of Documents)

The Imperial War Museum has an excellent collection of books, memoirs, letters, diaries and other relevant documents and artefacts relating to women's involvement in the First World War. The museum has seven departments, four of which are located in the Main Building: Art, Documents, Exhibits and Firearms, and Printed Books. The Film and Video Archive, the Photograph Archive and the Sound Archive are housed in the All Saints Annexe, five minutes' walk away. For the purposes of this bibliography, focussing as it does on women's written versions of the war, I shall concentrate on the Departments of Printed Books and of Documents.

The Museum's Reading Room is located in the dome at the top of the building. Should you wish to consult material, you should phone for an appointment at least one day in advance and, depending on the level of information you can give, and the access arrangements for the materials requested, a reading place will be reserved for you and materials will be ready for consultation. You are almost certain to be reminded at some point that the site of the Imperial War Museum was originally the site of Bethlem Hospital – otherwise known as Bedlam – and the process of being accompanied through corridors, in a slow, silent lift, and up narrow staircases to the imposing circular dome, will inevitably lead you to ponder about the proximity of war to madness, of madness to research and of research to incarceration. But by then there's no turning back ... at least, not without an escort.

To research women's writing of the First World War, you should make appointments separately with the two departments named above. (If your remit is broader, and you want to include women's more general experience, the Department of Sound Archives is highly recommended.) There is a collection called 'The Women's Work Collection', which holds material on women's contributions to the war, and this is held by the Department of Printed Books. This particular collection does not, however, include all personal memoirs, diaries, etc., most of which are held by the Department of Documents. I shall clarify the distinctions below.

DEPARTMENT OF PRINTED BOOKS

The Women's Work Collection

This is a collection of documents, pamphlets, press cuttings, official reports, government reports, records, memos, etc. regarding women's work – official, unofficial, paid, unpaid – in the war. The collection was initiated by the Women's War Work Sub-Committee of the Imperial War Museum, during and after 1919, of which Lady Norman was the Chairman, and Miss Agnes Conway was the secretary. The material is now on microfilm and the microfilms are arranged alpha-numerically in the card index room of the Reading Room.

There are at present two catalogues to the collection, one entitled the Women's Work Inventory, the other the Women's Work Collection: General Index. The former gives a comprehensive outline of the material held on the file. Entries are listed alphabetically (e.g. 'Army', 'Belgium', etc.) and give a numerical file reference and a description (e.g. 'Employment 45.18 Pamphlet: To Women War Workers, homely advice in regard to the maintenance of their health and comfort'). To list all the entries would be to reproduce the entire catalogue: some of the file names are as follows: Army, Belgium, British Red Cross Society, Employment, Food, France, Land, Local Records, Munitions, Prisoners, Serbia, Suffrage and Politics, Welfare, WRNS.

The files of the British Red Cross Society, for example, contain detailed information about VAD organisation, ideals, recruitment procedures, much of which was written by Katharine Furse and is worthy of detailed scrutiny. Other entries similarly open up areas of organisation, expectations of women, ways of managing change, that can shed a huge amount of light on the official procedures, conflicts and attempts to ease women's entry into the larger world over which the First World War officiated.

The **General Index** is less complete and less useful as a blow-by-blow account of the collection. It is, however, helpful if you want to look up a particular person, place or organisation. Again, the list is alphabetical (e.g. 'Agriculture, women in'; 'Accrington Observer and Times'; 'Ashwell, Lena, Concert Parties at the Front: Press cuttings') and each entry should contain a cross-reference to the microfilm file in which it can be found (e.g. 'Holmes, Miss Constance C. Lady Inspector, Army Pay Department FI Army 4. 1–2'). This Index does also contain references to some books which are not on film and which therefore are not cross-referenced. In this case you will need to consult the card catalogue and fill out an order form, and will probably have to wait for your books to be brought up.

Parts of the catalogue are automated; others are not, but I must add here that the librarians and archivists are very willing to help with any kind of question or enquiry.

The book collection is substantial. The card catalogue, located in the Index room, which you pass through in order to get into the Reading Room, is not fully automated and is divided into 'old' and 'new' authors. To order a particular book you have to go through the process described above. The waiting period is not usually very long.

DEPARTMENT OF DOCUMENTS

This department holds memoirs, diaries, letters and other miscellaneous documents (certificates, passes, some photographs, autograph books, etc.) deposited with the Imperial War Museum by individuals (as opposed to organisations). There is a card catalogue to the collection, and you should specify which section of it you would like to see. This will be brought to you or reserved for you if you specify in advance. The classification 'women' contains the cards which should cover most of the files by women contributors. You could cross-check and/or specify by asking for sections on, for example, medical, VADs, trade and industry, relief and welfare, civilian conditions, etc. The archivists are very happy to help and advise. Each card contains a brief – or sometimes quite detailed – description of the contents of the file. The waiting period is approximately 30 minutes once you have placed an order (by filling in a form); you are allowed four files at any one time and photo-copying will be done for you on request.

The following is an outline of the files held. The collection, of course, is a growing one, although it is the Second rather than the First World War that continues to receive larger amounts of material.

E1   Adair-Roberts, Miss W.

TS account of her holiday in Switzerland, covering details of her return journey on news of war. Papers relating to her service as a Captain in the Women's Legion (initially the WVR), including reports, correspondence, photos and press cuttings covering the work carried out by her company 1914–17. Winifred 'Winks' Adair-Roberts had been a member of the WSPU and played a part in smuggling food to Mrs Pankhurst when she was in hiding. She resigned from the Women's Legion in 1917 and turned down an invitation to join the WAAC, as she was 'nine-tenths a pacifist' by this stage. Papers include a monograph, entitled *Winifred Adair-Roberts* by her niece, Jane Lidderdale, privately printed, 1983.

E2   Adams, Mrs M.H., TS Memoirs, 1977.

Parents were supporters of women's suffrage, which took up much of their lives prewar, then Mrs Adams worked as a VAD for six months, on the land for a while and then became a driver for Vickers Arms Factory.

E3   Airey, Miss Edith, MS Memoir, n.d.

Interesting account of a woman brought up in a Sussex village, who took up land work on the local country estate in 1915. Describes the various kinds of work, the impact of the seasons, the mansion becoming a Red Cross hospital. Later took on munitions work.

E4   Bale, Mrs M. MS Memoir, 'Memories of the Women's Land Army 1916–1919', n.d.

When her husband was posted to Malta, she and her sister took up land work, and made a market garden.

E5   Barclay, Miss M., Report, 12pp.

Copy of an anonymous report on the Serbian retreat of October to December 1915, probably by one associated with the SWH. The account is extremely critical of the Serbian General Staff and government, and their incompetent handling of the retreat: 'The state of confusion here is beyond description.'

E6   Barnard, Miss W.M.

Thirty files of MS letters written to her by thirty-eight correspondents, March 1912 to June 1946, serving mostly on the Western Front, also in Egypt.

E7   Barnett, Miss C.U.

Thirty-five long and detailed MS letters written to her family in England while she was serving as a voluntary nurse with the Friends' (Emergency) War Victims Relief Committee in France, firstly at their convalescent home and later at the FWVRC maternity hospital. Worked here with Dr K.S. McPhail.

E8   Battrum, Mrs M. (née White).

Papers relating to Edith Cavell and to Mrs Battrum's experiences as a nurse in Belgium, including letters written by Edith Cavell, an account of Cavell's career and of the writer's own escape from Belgium in 1915.

E9   Bawtree, Miss V.

TS transcription of her diary (7pp.) 1916–19, containing observations on 'Daylight Saving' (about which most people are glad, she says, although her Aunt Millie is a little indignant), zeppelin raids, comments on conscientious objectors (she appreciates that they have consciences, but doubts their ability to reason sanely), on wartime restrictions (price rises, eating margarine instead of butter) and her thoughts on the progress of the war. Highly critical comments on the peace settlement.

E10   Bickmore, Miss.

MS essay (8pp. with TS transcript, 7pp.) written in January 1918 by a nurse about life on an ambulance train in France. References to conditions on board, the work of the nursing staff, the daily routine and the difficulties caused by the secrecy surrounding destinations and starting times.

E11   Bilbrough, Mrs E.M., MS Diary, 96pp., July 1915–November 1918.

Diary contains occasional entries recording incidents of the war and her own experiences as a civilian in Chislehurst, Kent. Her husband was a member of Lloyds: the diary thus permits an insight into the feelings of a wealthy woman concerning the government, air raids, food shortages, conscription, conscientious objectors. Illustrated with newspaper cuttings etc.

E12   Bingham, Mrs R. TS, Memoir, 354pp., 1930s. Microfilm copy.

Covers her experiences as the wife of a Regular Army Staff Officer, 1910–19, including return journey from Switzerland after outbreak of war; canteen work for YMCA in Dieppe; domestic life with children in France; life on the home front, with reference to food shortages and spy scares.

E13   Blackstock, Miss M.

Correspondence (85pp.) in English, French and German, dated June 1915 to March 1920, received by a nurse who served in Serbia (1915) and in various London hospitals (1916–17).

E14   Bowles, Miss A., MS Diary, 47pp., 1916–17.

Covers her service as a nurse on the Balkan front, October 1916 to May 1917, including voyage to Salonika on HMS *Britannic*. Appalling conditions in hospitals.

E15   Brettell, Lieutenant F.A.

Copies of letters (c. 320) between Brettell and Peggy, his future wife, who worked as a driver with the Women's Legion.

E16   Brown, Miss M.A., 3 MS Diaries, 104pp., 153pp., 228pp., May
               1915–January 1918.

These diaries, kept by a staff nurse in the QAIMNS (R), cover her voyage to Alexandria, her service in Egypt, her experiences nursing casualties from the Dardanelles, her service on other hospital ships in the Mediterranean and in India.

E17   Brunskill Reid, Mrs M.

Papers relating to the Women Signallers Territorial Corps, including correspondence regarding the school of women signallers, pamphlets, lists of members, etc.

E18   Burford-Hancock, Lady, MS Notebook, 41pp., 1917–18.

Contains accounts of her experiences on duty during enemy air raids at a Red Cross first aid post located in Earls Court tube station.

E19   Burleigh, Miss C., Memoir, 4pp., plus letters and photos.

Concerning her employment with her father's timber firm in the USA, 1914–16, and with the US Army in France.

E20   Calwell, Mrs G., 2 MS Letters.

Written by a passenger on the SS *Galician* during the voyage from South Africa to the UK.

E21   Campbell, Miss E., MS Diary, 37pp., 1915–19.

Covering her experiences as a nurse in the QAIMNS including a voyage from Australia to Alexandria, and service on hospital ships in the Mediterranean, plus work in Egypt and India.

E22   Cannan, May Wedderburn, TS Memoir, 'Recollections of a British Red Cross Voluntary Aid Detachment, No. 12, Oxford University, March 26th 1911–April 24th 1919', 1971.

Gives the history of VAD, No. 12, Oxford, of which her mother was the first Commandant. May Cannan joined it in 1911, having passed the necessary first aid examinations. Comments on the ridicule with which they were greeted, the inefficiency of the War Office when war was declared, and the good work that, ultimately, they were allowed to do, despite poor relations with some of the trained nurses.

E23   Castle, Mrs O., 'First World War Reminiscences of Mrs O. Castle', MS. 1978.

Munitions work for two years, then volunteered for the WAAC. Describes the flu epidemic of 1918, and an outbreak of diphtheria at the Bostall Heath WAAC camp.

E24   Cavell, Edith.

Important collection of diary entries regarding her work at a Brussels clinic helping wounded over the frontier to Holland.

E25   Clarke, Miss C.W., published account, 71pp., 1919.

Photocopy of privately published account of her service as a nurse's aide with the American Red Cross, in France.

E26   Clarke, Miss M., MS Diary, 265pp., May–July 1916.

Covers her service as a naval nursing sister in the Grand Fleet hospital ship *Plessey*.

E27   Courtney, Dame Kathleen, MS Letters, contemporary.

There are 114 letters to family and friends written during travels and periods of relief work in the Mediterranean, the Aegean, Corsica, Vienna, Czechoslovakia.

E28   Cowper, Mrs L.C. (née Neill).

Collection of memoirs, essays, poems and letters describing her service as a welfare worker at a French Red Cross canteen near Verdun, and then as a VAD driver with a Motor Ambulance Column, stationed at Étaples.

E29   Cozens-Walker, Miss M., Diary.

Diary covering her service as a VAD in Salonika. Account of the social life there.

E30   Creighton, Miss L., MS Diary, 183pp., 1916–17.

Well-written diary concerned with her work with the Serbian Relief Fund. Comments on conditions, strained relations with Red Cross reps in Serbia and contacts with members of the SWH.

E31   Crozier, Miss G.A.D., 3 MS Letters, July 1916–January 1919.

Written by a nursing sister to her former landlady in Pembroke. References to work and living conditions.

E32   Dalgleish, Miss P., TS Memoir, n.d.

Describes various experiences encountered while serving as a WAAC in Calais, including reaction to air raids, etc.

E33   Dalton, Charlotte (Mrs G. Mackay Brown) (c. 1975), 'The First World War Scrapbooks of Mrs G. Mackay Brown by Charlotte Louise Fitzgerald Dalton, RRC', TS.

Detailed account of service abroad by a former commandant of a VAD unit in Bedford. Describes discipline, the adventurous who, supplied with wire cutters. snipped their way out to meet young men in the forest, the detail of daily routine, pay, accommodation, etc.

E34   Dayrell-Browning, Mrs M., 3 MS Letters.

Letters to her mother describing her observation on the night of 2–3 September of the air raid by zeppelin LS1 and its destruction; her successful application to become a translator and her work writing subversive propaganda leaflets to be dropped over Hanover and Schleswig-Holstein.

E35   Denys-Burton, Miss M., TS Memoir, n.d.

Narrative, illustrated with contemporary photographs, covering the experiences of a baronet's daughter as a VAD at Woodcote Military Relief Hospital, Oxfordshire.

E36   Dodsworth, Miss C. and Miss E., Diary.

Describes VAD work in Rouen, in Brighton and en route for Egypt, when the ship on which they were travelling was torpedoed.

E37   Downer, Mrs E. Memoir.

Brief account, describing her enlistment in QMAAC, October 1917, and details of her service until June 1919 as a clerk at Boulogne Docks.

E38   Doughty-Wylie, Mrs L.O., 26 MS Diaries.

Series of diaries detailing service in France, as directrice of an Anglo-Ethiopian Red

Cross Hospital, as matron of a hospital on Lemnos and on Thasos, and of her work in graves registration in Turkey.

E39   Duke, Miss E.B., TS Diary.

Transcript of a diary with brief entries recording her experiences as assistant radiographer with an SWH Unit in Serbia.

E40   Dunbar, Miss D.M., TS Memoir, n.d.

Account of her service career in the WRAF, 1918–19 (and later in the WAAF/WRAF October 1939 to August 1954).

E41   Edis, Miss O., TS Account.

Photocopy of an account of a four-week tour undertaken by a lady photographer in March 1919 to provide a pictorial record for the archives of the Imperial War Museum of work being done by British women in France and Belgium.

E42   Essington-Nelson, Miss A.

Album containing accounts of her work with the Catholic Women's League tending Belgian refugees, later working as an assistant at Princess Louise's Convalescent Home for Nursing Sisters, at Hardelot.

E43   Farmborough, Miss Florence, MS Diaries, 109pp.

Cover her service as a nurse with the Flying Column of a Russian Army medical unit. Provided the source for her published reminiscences, *Nurse at the Russian Front* (C8).

E44   Farrier, Miss R., MS Letters; MS Memoir, 1982.

Eleven letters (plus one by her sister) to her father in the army describing school activities. Reminiscences of wartime childhood in London.

E45   Fawcett, Miss M.

Printed booklet (144pp.) including edited diaries and extracts of letters written by her August 1916 to July 1917, describing work as an orderly with a London unit of the SWH.

E46   Fernside, Mrs E., MS Letters.

Letters (129) written from her home in Fulham to her son serving with the Royal Artillery, providing details about civilian conditions, riots, violence, food shortages, allotment schemes, Christmas, war loans, etc.

E47   Ferrar, Miss D.

Collection of official papers relating to her enrolment and service in the WLA (Agricultural Section). Kent 1918–19.

E48   Field, Miss D., MS Diaries 1915–18; Letters; Misc. Items.

Collection of documents relating mainly to her service as a VAD nurse in France and Italy during the First World War (and as an ambulance driver in the Second World War).

E49   Foster, Miss M.G., MS Letters.

Collection of 17–18 letters regarding her service as a nurse in the Territorial Force Nursing Service in Salonika. Comments on conditions, climate, the monotony and insularity of nurses' lives.

E50   Freedman, Rosa, TS Memoir, 'Memories of a Land Girl in the First World War', 1978.

One of ten children, who left school aged 13 to go into domestic service, and found considerable liberation being part of a mobile gang of land girls. Work and locations were thus varied. Detailed descriptions of muck-carting, fruit picking, threshing, etc.

E51   Fyfe, Miss Georgie, MS Letters.

Eight letters written during her service in France and Belgium with Dr Munro's Red Cross Ambulance Corps, and later as a supervisor of the Belgian Relief Fund's work. Describes Munro as 'a great Idealist' and adds that her job is to see that his ideas are carried out practically. There is a reference to Miss Macnaughtan and a letter from Dorothie Fielding, but no comments on the other women. Fyfe was awarded the Croix de Guerre for devotion to duty in Flanders.

E52   Gamwell, Miss A.M.

Collection of papers regarding her service in the FANY as a sergeant in the Motor Ambulance Corps.

E53   Garland, Miss A.

Short narrative and 1916 diary descriptions of experiences as a VAD at a military hospital in Herne Bay, Kent, plus three voyages on the hospital ship *Britannic* (which was torpedoed and sunk).

E54   Gibson, Mrs M.A.C., MS Letter.

Photocopy of a letter from the Unit Administrator of a QMAAC camp, Abbeville. She was awarded the Military Medal for gallantry and devotion to duty during a raid on the camp in 1918.

E55   Gifford, Miss J.H., Memoirs, 1930s.

This bound volume of memoirs covers experiences in Belgium during the war.

E56   Gilmore, Miss M.I.

Papers relating to her service in the WAAC and QMAAC in Britain and France, 1917–19.

E57   Glenny, Miss A., 'Montenegrin Adventure', 115pp.

Account consisting of sixty letters written to her mother while serving as a VAD in Montenegro January to December 1915 and March to December 1920.

E58   Goodliff, Miss P.E., MS Letters.

This is a collection of sixty-two letters by a VAD, written to her family during her service as a secretary in the Department of Wounded and Missing Inquiries Overseas. Includes details of conditions, entertainment, descriptions of the ruins of Poperinghe, Ypres, Armentieres and Bailleul. Plus miscellaneous items.

E59   Greenwood, Miss W.

Photocopy of TS transcript of an account covering her service in QAIMNS at Dartford War Hospital, May to October 1916.

E60   Grey, Nurse Elsie P.

Extracts from a diary and letter written while serving as a nurse with the New Zealand Expeditionary Force in England and France, September 1916–September 1917.

E61   Griffith, Miss L.J.D., Memoir, c. 1919.

Bound illustrated memoir, covering her service as (amongst other things) Private Secretary to Dame Katharine Furse, Welfare Supervisor at the Ministry of Munitions, Member of the French War Emergency Fund, running a canteen. Plus collection of passes and other miscellaneous documents.

E62   Haigh, Miss I., MS Letters.

Letters (144) written to her parents, while serving as a VAD in Wales, Egypt, Palestine. Very detailed and informative about social life.

E63   Haire-Foster, Mrs R., TS Account, 3pp., n.d.

Interesting account of her service as commandant of a group of General Service VADs in Salonika 1918. (General Service VADs were usually working class.) Describes conflict with principal matron in Salonika and relations with military authorities.

E64   Harkness, Lady, TS Account, 12pp., n.d.

Account of her service as a QAIMNS Nursing Sister in England (1914–17), and then in Cairo and Jerusalem.

E65   Harling, Miss E., MS Notebooks.

Eight exercise books kept by her as a young girl in Wye, Kent, including copies of headlines and newspaper cuttings which amount to a regular account of the progress of the war and how it was portrayed to civilians. Brief comments concerning her employment in the RFC, 1918.

E66   Harrison, Miss H.A., TS Memoir, n.d.

Brief memoir of experiences in BRC VAD hospital No. 56, in Kent.

E67   Harrison, R.F., TS Account, 3pp., [1988].

Recollections of his boyhood in East London. His father was a serviceman; his mother was sent 4/6 a week by his father's former employers. His mother had another child in January 1915, which made their finances even tighter. At one point she did 'home work', stitching khaki material, but her machining skills were not good and she kept breaking the needles. Her son became an errand boy. Describes fetching the coal from a bay, 'manned' by women.

E68   Harrold, Mrs M., MS Memoir, n.d.

Describes zeppelin attacks, which made her nervous enough to apply to do land work, in the country. Works in Somerset and Kent, pulling flax, bandaging trees, threshing.

E69   Harry, Sybil, MS Letter.

Photocopy of letter written while working with French servicemen in a hospital in Samur.

E70   Hastings, Miss E., Diary.

Covers her service with the Territorial Nursing Service in Glasgow, her voyage to Salonika and service in hospital there. Details of social activities.

E71   Hay, Miss D., Letters, 1915.

Interesting collection of letters written to friends describing experiences with Dr Bennett's Red Cross Hospital Unit in Vrnjatchka Banja, Serbia, January to October, 1915.

E72   Haylock, Miss F.M.

Small collection regarding her being awarded the British Empire Medal for service with the GPO London Telephone Service during air raids, 1918.

E73   Henry, Dr L., TS Account, 41pp., n.d.

Interesting account of SWH unit at Royaumont, France, covering the development of the SWH from the Scottish Women's Suffrage Societies, the history of the Abbaye at Royaumont and work of the SWH there.

E74   Higgins, Miss D.E., MS Letters, February 1916–June 1917.

Letters (57) written to her parents in Lincolnshire, concerning her VAD service in Rouen as a radiographer and radiotherapist.

E75   Hill, Miss C.A.

Material relating to her work as a secretary with MI5.

E76   Hodges, Miss K., TS Memoir, 178pp., 1934.

Lively account of her opportunistic engagement as a driver with the SWH on the Roumanian Front, then as part of a Russian Unit on the Galician Front. Worked under Mrs Haverfield; Dr Inglis was in charge of the whole unit. Takes an exuberant pride in the power and energy of women like herself, and gives a striking account of the Serbian retreat. Notes attitudes towards the Russian Revolution. Returned to Britain in 1917 and became a YMCA driver, first in London, then in France. Very good account. Immensely detailed, good sense of narrative, large in scope, good humoured. Conveys a sense of being permanently on the move.

E77   Holland, Miss G., MS Journal, c. 300pp.

Covers experiences as an ambulance driver in Belgium. Was attached, briefly to Dr Munro's Ambulance Corps, and, in Serbia was with Mrs St Clair Stobart's Unit.

E78   Home Front Diary, MS, Anonymous, 1916.

Barely legible account of extremely repetitive days, involving getting up, having breakfast, seeing Fred off, going to work, doing the dusting, answering the phone, having lunch, doing Mr Campkins' accounts, doing letters, having tea, maybe going out in the evening, going to bed.

E79   Hutchinson, Beryl, TS Account, 34pp., n.d.

Service with FANY working as an ambulance driver on Calais Convoy, 1914–17, and at St Omer, 1917–19.

E80   Ingram, Miss M., TS letters, May–July 1915.

Photocopies of five letters covering her sea journey to Athens and on to Salonika. Worked as a dispenser in Serbia.

E81   Jeffery, Miss M.

Draft of the book *Auntie Mabel's War* (1980). Including documents relating to her service as a qualified nurse in France.

E82   Jones, Mrs G.A.

Semi-official diary kept as Deputy Controller WAAC, responsible for the Expeditionary Force Canteen in France, 1918–19.

E83   Kaye, Mrs G., Letter to her sister Eileen, Autograph Letter, Signed, 24 January 1940.

Munitions work at Vickers and Woolwich Royal Arsenal. Was a Principal Overlooker. Describes a zeppelin being brought down.

E84   Keen, Mrs D., MS Memoir, n.d.

Brief reminiscences of a Norfolk woman, written when she was approximately 84. Details of the RNAS camp at Swan's Lodge, Holt. Recalls the story of herself and a friend cycling down to the camp with a bottle of whisky for the men there, who were 'perfect gentlemen' and appreciated what the girls had done. Served subsequently as a pay clerk in the WRAF and as a police woman in London.

E85 Kenyon, Miss K.M.R., MS Diary, March 1917–August 1918.

Covers her service as a VAD at Camiers, describing duties, discomforts, outings, sadness at deaths. Transcript included.

E86 Kenyon, Miss W.L., TS (transcript) Diary.

Personal diary covering VAD service as head cook in Tonbridge, Bar-le-duc and Rivigny, and as a nurse at Catterick Camp Hospital and King Gerfe's Hospital. Includes description of destruction of a zeppelin over Rivigny.

E87 Kersley, Miss E.M.

Miscellaneous papers relating to her service as a VAD.

E88 Lea, Sister E.W.B., MS Letters, September 1915–July 1916.

Forty-seven letters to her family written during her service with QAIMNS (R), covering nursing Dardanelles victims.

E89 Leared, Mrs R.I.

Account of her WAAC service as an ambulance driver in France, 1914–17.

E90 Lecher, Miss L.M.

Miscellaneous documents regarding VAD service and work with the Women's Legion Motor Section.

E91 Line, Mrs D.B.G., TS Memoir.

Covers her work as a search clerk with MI5, 1915–17. She tried for Oxford, but her family suffered a financial loss and, by invitation, she was interviewed for MI5 instead. Her job was to sort information on spies and traitors and to supply links, as appropriate, to requests from sub-departments. Describes lively, happy working and living conditions, and took pleasure in having access to London's rooftops. She left in 1917, but not before introducing her friend, the poet Elinor Jenkins, to the job. Jenkins was published by Sidgwick and Jackson in 1915: she died in the postwar flu epidemic.

E92 Littlejohn, Miss D.H., Letters.

Five multi-page letters by a cook with SWH in France 1914–15. Contain detailed descriptions of her work and its problems.

E93 Lorimer, Miss E.C., Diary, 99pp.

Copy of a diary covering her voyage to Serbia, her work as a probationary VAD in Belgrade, evacuation and return to England.

E94   Ludlum, Miss M., MS Diary, 381pp., 1917–18.

Photocopy of a diary covering her experiences as an American Red Cross aide en route to, and working in France, 1917–18.

E95   McCann, Mrs Dorothy, TS Account: 'The First World War Memoirs of Mrs D. McCann, VAD', n.d.

Detailed account of work at No. 18 General Hospital, near Étaples. Describes excitement at the work, the charming, but strict Matron, working in the mess, strategies to avoid lice, the perils of sleeping in bell tents, the atmosphere of friendship and enjoyment of the work.

E96   McNeill, Dr M.L., Diaries and Letters, 1916–17.

Copies of five diaries and sixty-seven letters covering service with the SWH in Salonika, October 1916 to May 1919. Detailed descriptions of conditions.

E97   MacPhail, Dr K.S. Letters, 1916.

Interesting collection of letters covering service with the Serbian Relief Fund on the Marne, in Corsica and in the Haute Savoie, January to December, 1916. Strongly committed to the Serbian cause. Letters contain descriptions of work, Serbs' plight and criticisms of the SWH.

E98   Manning, R.B., MS Diary entitled 'Diary of Ruth M. Manning, VAD', 24 April 1917–3 September 1918.

Served at the 14th Stationary Hospital, Wimereux, joined Dame Maud McCarthy's staff in Abbeville, and finally went to Lady Gifford's Convalescent Home at Hardelot. Trained as an almoner after the war.

E99   Marie Georgine, Reverend Mother, TS (transcript) Letters, 1914–1918.

Long detailed letters by an English-born nun at a Belgian convent during the war. Covers billeting of Belgian soldiers, coping with refugees, the arrival of the German army and life under occupation.

E100   Marx, Miss C.M., MS Notebooks; Letters.

Three notebooks and two files of correspondence regarding her service a member of the Red Cross attached to the British Mission in France, 1918–19. Did work on repatriation of British prisoners of war and location and registration of war graves.

E101   Mascall, Mrs E.M., TS Memoir, 212pp., 1972.

Bound memoir, including illustrations, covering life on the home front (among other things).

E102   Mayne, Mrs C., MS Notebook, 51pp., 1935.

Account of her service as a qualified nurse with a British Hospital in Belgium,

1914–15. Refers to Dr Munro's Unit and to Mrs Knocker and Miss Chisholm at Pervyse.

E103   Mullineaux, Mrs A., TS Diary, c. 100pp., 1918–19.

Excellent diary covering service as American Red Cross nurse with the French 'Service de Santé', May 1918 to July 1919. Describes work with US soldiers and aviators, social life and refugee work.

E104   Neale, Miss R.A., TS Account.

Lively and amusing account of her experiences as a member of an all-girl concert troupe. The problems, the privations, the hostilities. …

E105   Neville, Miss Amy, MS Letters.

Seventy-six letters written to her family while serving as a VAD in France. Mostly expressing how happy she is with the work and conditions.

E106   Nicol, Dorothy, TS Memoir 'Memoirs of a VAD 1915–1917', 70pp., n.d.

Communicates a strong sense that her nursing work at Camiers made her feel the romance of war, despite its desperate sadness. Describes the (menial) work she was given by an unwelcoming Sister, but this is mitigated by a general sense of comradeship, reverence for the wounded men and a new self-confidence.

E107   Paterson, Sister J., MS Diaries.

Three pocket diaries kept during service as a nursing sister in QAIMNS (R) in France and the Mediterranean.

E108   Pease, M.S. Diaries and other Papers.

Five volumes of diaries kept by Pease during his internment in Ruhleben. Interesting for the correspondence between him, his parents and, particularly, Helen Bowen-Wedgwood, a pacifist involved with the Fabian Society, Women's Trades Unions and land work.

E109   Peile, Mrs L., MS Notebook, 234pp.

Contains almost daily diary of her life in Margate with her young daughter. Descriptions of raids, both by air and by destroyer, on the coast.

E110   Pemberton, Miss E.B., MS and TS Letters.

Photocopies of approximately 130 letters written to her parents, while serving as a VAD in France at rest stations, a small hospital, a convalescent home for nurses and as a quartermaster for a Red Cross Motor Ambulance Convoy. Also served with the Metropolitan Special Constabulary, London (1917), helping the public to shelter during air raids.

E111   Pearson, Mrs F., Memoir, 1p., 1988.

Very brief account of her service with Women's Forestry Section near Amersham, Bletchley and Yorkshire, 1917–18.

E112   Peck, Miss A., TS Memoir, 50pp.

Photocopy of memoir of service with an American Red Cross mobile canteen, September to December, 1918, in France.

E113   Peterkin, Miss M.B., Diary, 59pp., 1914–15.

Covers service as a Red Cross Sister at No. 9 General Hospital, France. Conditions plus harrowing descriptions of suffering of wounded. Rumours of German atrocities.

E114   Pickford, the Honourable Dorothy, MS Letters.

Forty-eight letters to her sister written while serving as Assistant Administrator with WAAC (and QMAAC) in France. Letters deal with administration, discipline, social activities.

E115   Pinninger, Miss A.J., TS Memoirs, 100pp., n.d.

Extracts from undated memoirs concerning her service and social life in France with French Red Cross, and in Serbia and Russia at a military hospital. Witnessed the Serbian retreat and heard Lenin speak at mass meetings.

E116   Plaistow, Mrs P.E.

Passport and brief account of experiences as a secretary at the Allied Mission in Paris.

E117   Pocock, G.M. and L.C., MS Diary; Memoir, 24pp.

Notebook with diary notes and reminiscences relating to her experiences as a governess in Russia, 1917–18, describing experiences culminating in her evacuation via Moscow to Japan, with Lady Muriel Paget's Red Cross Unit. Includes miscellaneous documents and husband's diary.

E118   Proctor, Miss E.H., MS Letters, 1917–19.

Thirty-five letters written by a VAD and nursing orderly during her service with a SWH unit.

E119   Prunell, C.M., MS Diary, 1917.

Diary of a land worker that opens with a section from *Piers Plowman*. Notes hearing the first cuckoo, the arrival of the swallows, etc. Includes sketches and photographs, and is heavily involved with documenting rural detail.

E120   Quinlan, Mrs E.E., MS Memoir, 3pp.

Memoir of service as a clerk with WAAC in France 1917–19. Includes miscellaneous items.

E121   Rathbone, Miss I.R., MS Diaries, 330pp., June–Oct 1918.

Three diaries covering her voluntary canteen work in the 3rd Army YMCA Rest Camp at St Valery-sur-Somme, 1918. Very detailed accounts of daily life and routine, social activities, attitudes towards women's war work. Articulates the feeling that the young, 'respectable' women ought to act as the moral protectors of the equally young soldiers. In a passage about 'ladies of easy virtue' she comments that their presence would be easier to bear if it were only the older military men who made use of their services; the fact that the younger boys did so too was deeply affecting. Articulates the consciousness that although they act as 'sisters' to these soldiers, in fact they hardly know them.

The diaries form the basis for parts of *We That Were Young* (A99), Rathbone's semi-autobiographical novel, first published in 1932; reprinted 1988. There are large, faint crosses on some pages, lines in red ink on others, and further indications such as 'much shorter', or 'see P's diary' elsewhere.

E122   Reading, Eva, Marchioness of, MS Letters.

Approximately 608 letters written to her husband, providing a detailed, daily record of her activities, thoughts and emotions during their separation.

E123   Reeves, Miss S., MS Diary, 75pp., February–April 1916.

Covers her service as a VAD attached to the 1st British Ambulance Unit for Italy.

E124   Rendell, Miss F.E., MS Letters (plus transcript); MS Diary, 1917, miscellanous documents.

Over eighty letters to her family, written while serving as a nurse with the SWH in Russia and the Balkans, 1916–19. Diary for part of 1917. Was a member of the suffrage movement, worked closely with Dr Elsie Inglis and Dr Chesney. Gives good insight into work of SWH in the face of administrative difficulties etc.

E125   Rice, C.J., Letters, 1915–17.

Four letters from Sister Rice QAIMNS, at Alexandria, 1915–17.

E126   Rochdale, Lady Beatrice, TS (transcript) of Diary, Journal and various letters, 1915.

Photocopies of material from 1915 covering her voyage to Egypt via Marseilles and life in Cairo, where her husband, who commanded the 6th Lancashire Fusiliers, was stationed.

E127   Rose, Dr Jean, MS Diary, 1917–18.

Vivid account of life with SWH unit at Ostrovo, Macedonia, October 1917 to May 1918. Anecdotes about camp life, observations of local customs and accounts of outings and entertainments.

E128   Ross, Miss J., TS (transcript) Diary, 69pp., 1916–17.

Well-written diary covering her experiences as a cook with the SWH, her journey to Salonika, meeting Flora Sandes, and journey home via Italy.

E129   Royds, Miss K.E., MS Letters, Diary extracts, 1915.

Over sixty-five letters and diary comments relating to her passage to Salonika via Malta and Athens, in October 1915, with a SWH unit. Experiences working with Serb refugees. Miscellaneous documents.

E130   Rubery, Miss E.T., MS Letters, 87pp.

Thirteen letters by a VAD regarding her journey via France and Italy to Egypt, her service in Egypt and also covering the disturbances in Upper Egypt, March 1919. Includes MS Diary and miscellaneous papers.

E131   St Clair Stobart, Mrs, MS Diary (plus bound TS transcript),
             October–December 1915.

Covers her experiences in command of a flying Anglo-Serbian field hospital during the Serbian retreat, 1915. Vivid account of the work and the conditions. Basis for her book *The Flaming Sword* (B134).

E132   Scott, Miss F., Letters and Memoir.

Fifteen letters plus an account entitled 'Experiences in Serbia' by a Red Cross nurse with Lady Paget's Relief Hospital in Skopje, Serbia, February to May, 1915.

E133   Seale, R.

Photocopies of *The Limit* (August and October, 1918), the works magazine of White and Poppe National Shell Filling Factory, No. 10, Coventry. Articles on social activities, girls' work and lives. Plus cartoons.

E134   Shave, Miss C.F.

Papers relating to her service with the Forage Guard.

E135   Sheppard, Miss E.E.

Documents relating to her service as a telegraphist in the WAAC (later the QMAAC) at Le Havre, June 1917 to September 1919.

E136   Smellie, Lieutenant-Colonel L.P.

Six MS letters and one fragment of an MS letter from Miss Flora Sandes, an Englishwoman who served as a sergeant in the Serbian Army.

E137   Sowerbutts, Miss E.F.M., TS Memoirs, 580pp.

Three volumes of memoirs covering the period from her childhood (b. 1896) until the 1950s. Includes an account of her work as a shorthand typist and her membership of the WVR, during the war.

E138   Starr, M., TS Diary, 96pp., 1915–16.

Bound diary, written in the form of letters home while serving as a Canadian VAD with a SWH unit at the Abbaye de Royaumont, September 1915 to January 1916.

E139   Stephens, Miss P.L., 'My War Service Diary During World War 1 1914–1918'.

Covers her work in munitions factories in Birmingham, Southampton and Lincoln and then as a motorcyclist for the RAF. Good photos.

E140   Stevenson, Miss D.I.K.

Miscellaneous papers concerning her service in France as a voluntary welfare worker, 1916–18.

E141   Storey, Miss G.

Correspondence referring to the fund she set up to provide soldiers at the Front with Bovril.

E142   Tait, Miss A.S.

Material relating to work with the Red Cross and St John's Ambulance Association in Bangalore.

E143   Tarring, Miss F.E., MS Journal, 360pp., 1914–19.

Covers the period September 1914 to December 1919, and is written in the form of instalments addressed to 'Hilde'. She was a tutor to the son of one of Hungary's oldest families. Comments on conditions on the Russian and Roumanian Fronts and in Hungary.

E144   Taylor, Miss Olive M., MS, 'Recollections of the Great War 1914–1918', n.d.

Vivid account of her work on the land, in munitions (poor conditions, spy scares, loss of sexual innocence, a fire and explosions) and for the WAAC. Lots of detail, and a strong sense of personality.

E145   Thomas, Mrs A.A., TS Memoir, 40pp., n.d.

Photocopy of her memoir of experiences as a VAD in military hospitals in India. Refers to QAIMNS colleagues, social activities and life under the British Raj, and to hospitals in Mesopotamia. Comments on her West Indian and West African patients.

E146   Thompson, Miss D.J., TS, 129pp.

Account recording her experiences as a secretary in the Wounded and Missing Enquiry Department of the Red Cross in Rouen and Étaples.

E147   Tisdall, Miss C.E., TS Reminiscences, 55pp.

Bound reminiscences of a VAD attached to a London District Ambulance Column.

E148   Tower, Miss W.L.B., MS Journal, 47pp., 1914–16.

Records an account of life in the Isle of Wight during the early stages of war (spy scares etc.) and then life in London.

E149   T'Serclaes, Baroness E. de, MS Diaries, 1914–15.

Three diaries covering the period from September 1914 to January 1915, during which time Elsie Knocker (as she then was) and Mairi Chisholm worked with Munro's Ambulance Corps and subsequently established their front line dressing station at Pervyse. Includes drafts for articles, photo albums, etc. See also *The Cellar House of Pervyse* (B105) and the Liddle Collection.

E150   Trembath, Miss M.G., Diary 1917–18.

Short diary plus papers relating to the voyage of a nurse to India and on to Mesopotamia, November 1917 to March 1918.

E151   Turnbull, Miss M.E., MS Letters, plus Diary.

Two letters plus a pocket diary of a VAD in France and Malta. Plus miscellaneous documents.

E152   van den Bergh, Miss A.J., TS Memoir, 21pp., 1990.

Describes German air attacks on Antwerp, and German occupation. She was the daughter of the Consul-General for the Netherlands in Belgium.

E153   Wagstaff, Miss C.H., MS Reminiscences, 8pp.

An account of life in the WAAC, 1918.

E154   Watkins, Miss Amy, MS Memoir, '1914–18 First World War', n.d.

Land work. Atmospheric description of 11 November 1918.

E155   Wedgwood, J.C. Baron of Barlaston.

Letters from his daughter, Helen Bowen Wedgwood, concerning her work with conscientious objectors, her service with the Land Army and standing for election. (*See also* M.S. Pease, E108.)

E156   West, Miss G., Diaries, 1914–17.

Cover her experiences as a VAD cook (1914–16), setting up a canteen at Farnborough, then joining the Women's Police, where she served as an officer in munitions factories. A very fluent account which includes a description of seeing a zeppelin being brought down in October 1916. Lively, animated descriptions of trying to find work in London (as a cook, a Lyons bread cart driver, a seater in a restaurant) before applying to be a woman police officer for the wage of £2 per week. Works in Chester and in Wales and gives detailed descriptions not only of her own work in the munitions factories, but of the 'girls" work and conditions, commenting on their liveliness, cheerfulness and on the many 'characters' among them.

File includes photos of Women's Police, of Red Cross workers and of Miss West's dog, Rip, who was allowed a pass into the works' canteen.

E157   Whiffen, Miss O., Notebooks.

Notebooks written while working as a physiotherapist. Contain experiences and poems of the soldiers.

E158   Whitaker, Ruth, TS Memoir: 'The First World War Memoirs of Miss R. Whitaker', c. 1970.

Clergyman's daughter, served as a VAD nurse in England, Malta and France. Conditions and areas of responsibility varied enormously. Claims to have nursed Ford Madox Hueffer while at Rouen. Lengthy, detailed account, reflecting on patriotism, unselfishness of the soldiers, unpredictability of VAD service. Supervised National Kitchens and Restaurants in south-west London.

E159   White, Miss A.W., MS Reminiscences, 7pp.; and MS Letters.

Photocopy of reminiscences of experiences as a personal secretary to the Deputy Director of Operations at the Admiralty, 1918–19. Letters written to her by friends.

E160   Wilby, Mrs E., TS Memoirs, 22pp., 1984.

Photocopy of memoirs describing her London childhood before the war and brief details of munitions work. She worked in a pub, where she was a little accident-prone, although well thought of, but left it for munitions work, to the distaste of her husband, who didn't like to see women in trousers. She didn't get on too well there, either: the toolsetter, apparently, had his favourites among whom she was not included.

E161   Williams, Miss Daisy, 'Adventures in Germany', 183pp., 1923.

Well-written account covering the period May to September 1914 in Germany, when the author was a 16-year-old schoolgirl living with her mother. Describes conditions, mood, 'spy mania'.

E162   Winterbottom, Miss A.D., Diaries, Letters, miscellaneous documents.

Seven diaries, correspondence, photos etc. relating to her service in Belgium as an ambulance driver, as a hospital administrator and as directrice of recreation tents. She met the Baroness T'Serclaes and Mairi Chisholm.

E163   Young, Miss G.E., MS Memoir, 12pp.

Covers experience as a waitress with the Women's Legion in England and Boulogne.

E164   Miscellaneous 60.

TS transcript of a letter by an unidentified American woman attached to the Red Cross, April 1918.

E165   Miscellaneous 947, MS Account, 5pp., n.d.

Brief account by Miss J Swann of experiences in WAAC.

E166   Miscellaneous 948, MS Account, 15pp., n.d.

Account of experiences as a worker in a munitions factory 1916–18, and in the WAAC, 1918–19.

E167   Miscellaneous.

Brief account by a Canadian VAD ambulance driver of one night's work at Étaples taking casualties from an ambulance train to a hospital.

E168   Miscellaneous [under 'civilian conditions'].

Anonymous diary (75pp. MS) kept by a London woman between July and September 1914. Describes home front life, with references to rumours, scares, price rises, hoarding, recruiting among the middle classes.

II THE LIDDLE COLLECTION

Address: The Liddle Collection
             Special Collections
             The Brotherton Library
             The University of Leeds
             Leeds LS2 9JT

Tel: 0113 233 5518 (Direct to Special Collections)

The Liddle Collection is presently located at the Brotherton Library, University of Leeds. It is an extensive collection of materials relating to personal experience of the First World War, and now extends to materials covering the Second World War also. The collection was built up by the former Keeper, Peter Liddle, over some years. It began as the project of an enthusiastic schoolteacher, moved with Peter Liddle when he took up a post at what is now Sunderland University, and has since been housed in the Edward Boyle and Brotherton Libraries at Leeds. Its character is built on the firm belief in the need to document the lives, experiences and responses of ordinary participants, which, in many cases, may contradict the mythicisation of the war as seen in postwar novels and films, in order that the true variety and complexity of responses to the war might be better understood. Peter Liddle has produced a number of books and contributed to some television productions based on the collection. He was the editor of *The Poppy and the Owl*, a journal which has now ceased publication, but which published material related to personal experience of the war, much of which derived from the archive itself.

Listed below are brief accounts of the holdings in the files relating to women's work, the domestic front, and the tape-recorded holdings. The catalogues contain cross-references as appropriate, and brief descriptions. The collection is continually expanding, so the material here, which is not exhaustive in any case, will almost certainly have been augmented by the time this volume is in print. Those wishing to visit the collection should contact Special Collections to request an appointment, giving professional status and reasons for wishing to visit – for example, research for personal or scholarly interest, publication, etc.

WOMEN'S CATALOGUE

E169   Ansell, Ada M.

TS and accompanying letter of July/September 1914. Diary covers experience in Belgium and France. Two Photographs of French troops and crowds at Gravelines, August 1914. Diary describes her arrest in Gravelines for spying, the crowds in the street, some silent, some crying, remembering 1870, as mobilisation begins.

E170   Beaumont, A.G.E.

St John nurse in Kitchener hospital, Brighton, and 17th General Hospital, Alexandria. Four autograph albums, photographs, one document and war medals.

E171   Black, Mrs M. (née Hale).

TS recollections of her mother as a QAIMNS nurse, of spies, army hospitals, and an air raid resulting in her mother's shell-shock. Includes photographs.

E172   Booth, Miss Mary.

Salvation Army with the BEF.

E173   Boyes, Miss Mary.

Women's Legion and FANY. Leaflets, photographs, booklets and further papers.

E174   Brown, Mrs Janet B.

Letters 1918–19, relating to her experience with Scottish Churches Huts.

E175   Brumwell, Mrs G.K.

TS article entitled 'The Masseuse', written 1918, commenting on the puzzled reactions of patients to these mysterious creatures, who aren't proper nurses. Plus addition made in 1971.

E176   Burgess, Nursing Sister.

Photocopy of a TS transcript of her diary, November to December 1917. Served in a hospital in Marseilles, and describes the trying attitude of the Captain during a voyage to Malta. The ship was torpedoed.

E177   Carlisle, Mrs Elsie M.

VAD nurse at No. 9 General Hospital, Rouen. Long 1916 letter about the work.

E178   Chisholm, Miss Mairi

TS recollections of one of the Women of Pervyse, who began as part of the ambulance corps of Hector Munro (whom she describes as 'a great feminist'). She describes setting up the cellar house, attending to cases of VD, which was routinely left unattended in its early stages, the confessions of soldiers, their courage and her own sense of being privileged to work in danger alongside them. (*See* index for cross-references.)

E179   Clarke, Miss M.

VAD nurse. Letters to her from soldiers; photographs.

E180   Cliffe, Mrs I.E.

Nurse, QAIMNS. Privately printed memoirs of her service in Egypt, India, Mesopotamia.

E181   Colston, Mrs E.F.

Photographs, FANY gazettes, papers and correspondence.

Tape recorded, PHL.

E182   Constable, Mrs E.

VAD. TS recollections expand on diary entries and discuss treatment of soldiers in ambulance room at munitions factory and in France. Describes a good working relationship with trained sisters. Diaries (two) describe day-to-day details, raids, care of soldiers etc. Letters, photograph album.

E183   Cook, Mrs Charlotte.

Nurse. Service with Friends Ambulance Unit, Dunkirk. TS recollections and photographs, Red Cross certificates.

E184   Courtauld, Dr E.

Served with the SWH in France, 1918–19. TS letters and photographs.

E185   Crowder, Mrs G.V.

Nurse, Red Cross VAD. Certificates and letters from her brother in the Canadian Army.

E186   Disney-Simons, Miss E.

Women's Legion. Documents, photos, shoulder flashes and badges.

E187   Dutton, Miss

Serbian Relief Unit. Letters, 1915, in Salonika and Serbia.

E188   Fair, Mrs E.B.E. (née Crouzet).

French civilian. TS memoir of her experiences.

E189   Faithful, Miss Edith.

Ambulance driver in Russia.

E190   Fidler, Miss Muriel.

Account (1915) of journey from Roumania to UK via Servia and Macedonia. Photo album.

E191   Fisher, Miss C.M.

TS, worked as a cook in Sofia.

E192   Folkard, Miss H.A.

VAD Nurse in No.36 General Hospital, Vertekop, Macedonia. Photos and commission of her later husband.

E193   Foss, Josephine.

TS recollections of teaching in China, 1914, and of a journey through Russia.

E194   Freshfield, Miss K.

Three volumes of diaries, plus TS recollections. VAD in France and Belgium. Describes her departure for France, with Mrs Furse, whose boy scout element she finds comical. Lots of details on patients, civilian and military, on relations between her and other nurses, recreation, illness, conditions, horrific injuries. Mentions Dr Inglis and Miss Crowdy. Diaries illustrated by line drawings.

E195   Furse, Dame Katharine GBE, RRC.

Photocopies of letters to Rachel Crowdy, her son, Paul, her sister, Madge, expressing how glad she is to have carried on with Red Cross work, despite the ridicule. Photocopies of correspondence between her and Sir Alfred Keogh, which is illuminating in terms of the establishment of the VAD, and their use abroad. There is also an article, 'Personalities and Powers', a statement explaining her resignation, and further papers relating to her time as director of the WRNS.

E196   Gibson, Mrs M.A.C.

Photocopied letters and related documents of a QMAAC nurse.

E197   Gladstanes, Miss Elsie.

WRNS. Photograph album, cap badge, pages from WRNS magazine.

E198   Goldthorp, Miss M.E.

QAIMNS Professional nurse at London Hospital. Three volumes of diaries, 1914–16. Sent 17 August 1914, with four others, to accompany the BEF. Describes conditions of departure, arrival in Rouen, posting to Versailles. Details of medical cases, rats and nightingales. Photographs. Good first volume; fewer entries in volumes two and three.

E199   Gould, Miss E.M.

Nurse with 1st British Field Hospital for Serbia, March to December 1915. Photos.

E200   Hardie, Mrs Mary.

Nurse at Middlesborough Infirmary and Langley Park Isolation Hospital. Christmas cards, postcards (humorous, patriotic), letters from ex-patients or their parents, photos, cuttings of sentimental, comic or patriotic verse and souvenir programme of Military Pageant at Ripon, April 1916.

E201   Henry, Dr L.M.

Doctor with SWH in France. Photo album, loose photos and further papers.

E202   Hogg, Mrs E.

VAD nurse. Diaries relating to experience in Hoddesdon and Thirlsone Castle Hospitals 1914–18. Missing 1915. Papers and correspondence.

E203   Hutchinson, Miss B.

FANY nurse. Scrapbook, recollections, autograph albums, papers, photos, cards, certificates.

Tape recorded, PHL.

E204   James, Miss M.M.

Sister in TFNS – BEF in France. Diary (1914) relating to experience in 14th General Hospital.

E205   Jameson, Miss R.C.

French Red Cross Nurse. MS and TS recollections. Postcards, photos and papers concerning nursing in France.

E206   Kenyon, Miss Winifred.

VAD nurse in Tonbridge and France. Photos and transcript of diary 1915–18.

E207   Lenanton, Lady (née Carola Oman).

VAD nurse, BRCS. Photos and papers. Tape recorded, PHL.

E208 Loveday, Miss Dorothy.

WAAC 1917–18. Letters to her former Headmistress, Miss Robertson.

E209 Lupton, Miss Elinor G.

VAD nurse, Ambulance de l'Ocean, La Parre, 1915. Letters. Sister of Elizabeth Lupton (*see* below).

E210 Lupton, Miss Elizabeth.

VAD nurse in No. 12 Field General Hospital, Rouen. Photocopied extracts from Diary January 1917 to January 1918. Describes arrival of Americans and resulting tensions, comments on discipline and on furtive meetings between sisters and officers. Describes the ongoing and severe tension between VADs and their superiors, particularly a Miss Stinson, a rigid observer of rules.

E211 Lynn, Mrs E.A.

St John's Ambulance Service in base hospitals in France and Italy. Recollections, photographs and papers.

E212 McCann, Mrs D. (née Brooks).

VAD nurse, 18th and 20th General Hospitals in France (Camiers), 1919–19.

E213 McLeod, Mrs E. M.

Nurse with 1st British Field Hospital in Serbia and later ASC ambulance driver. TS recollections, notes from 1915. *See also The Sphere*, 15 January 1916, *The Illustrated London News*, 7 August 1915, and *The Graphic*, 10 July 1915. Papers relating to nursing work in Serbia, and ambulance work.

E214 Mann, Miss K.

Matron on hospital ships evacuating wounded from the Dardanelles, and Serbians from Albania, crossing the Mediterranean and reaching Bombay. Photocopies of diaries, July 1915 to March 1917, plus photos and further papers.

E215 Marguerite, Sister.

Roman Catholic nun in occupied France, 1914–18. Illustrated memoirs. Nursed wounded, was held captive in Germany, returned to France, where she worked in a military hospital.

E216 Miall-Smith, Dr G.

Women's Imperial Service League Hospital at Tourlaville and Scottish Women's Hospital at Royaumont. Cuttings, photos and MS recollections.

E217 Milburn, Miss G.

VAD nurse. Worked in Hunstanton, Hull, Malton, Bethnal Green, Tottenham,

France and Germany. Letters, papers, albums, certificates, diaries, uniform badges etc.

Tape recorded, PHL.

E218   Miller, Miss.

Nurse, SWH. Photos, letters, poems and papers. SWH newsletters.

E219   Munday, Mrs F.

Employed in the Counter-espionage Office in Paris, and Naval Intelligence Department, Admiralty. Poem (verse rhyme) written while at work.

E220   Parker, Mrs M.

Driver, BRCS. MS recollections and photos.

E221   Potter, Miss A.

WAAC telegraphist. TS recollections, photos, cards, souvenirs.

E222   Pratt, Miss.

Nursing sister in India. Letters from soldiers she had nursed.

E223   Prentice, Mrs.

Driver, St John's Ambulance Brigade. MS recollections and photos.

E224   Puckle, Miss.

VAD Driver, and FANY service in Britain and France. Letters, photos, TS recollections, FANY gazettes.

Tape recorded, PHL.

E225   Robertson, Miss Winifred.

YMCA Hut, St Leonards School, Le Havre. Diaries, photos and papers, 1918–19.

E226   Selby, Miss E.M.

VAD nurse. Diary, papers, cuttings, 1918.

E227   Sidney, Dr Alex.

Driver, SWH. TS recollections and photo album.

E228   Simms, Miss F.B.

SWH nurse at Royaumont. Three 1918 letters.

E229   Slythe, Miss Alice.

TFNS nurse, Western Front. Eight diaries, from 1915, photos, concert programmes, etc.

E230   Smith, Mrs D.

Clerk, VAD General Service. Diary for service in Salonika.

Tape recorded, PHL.

E231   Smythe, Mrs Y.M.

VAD nurse in Britian and Rouen. Letters 1917–19 and photos. Letters from ex-patients, photos and scrap album.

Tape recorded, PHL.

E232   Stead, Mrs Madge (née Eaton).

VAD nurse in UK and No. 55 General Hospital, France. Diary 1918, 1919, photo album, TS memoirs.

E233   Thompson, Miss Muriel.

FANY Driver, St Omer Convoy. Describes driving in harsh conditions, during raids, often without lights. Socialising with officers. Backwash of the retreat; so many refugees.

E234   Thurstan, Miss Violet.

St John's Ambulance nurse in Belgium and Russia. Album of postcards sent home. Letters, photo album, documents relating to WRAF service, Jan 1919.

See index for cross-references.

E235   T'Serclaes, Baroness de.

Nurse with Munro Corps, and then independently, Belgium. Three slide boxes.

See index for cross-references; also Chisholm. Tape recorded, PHL.

E236   Towers, Miss.

Women's Legion. MS recollections, papers, photos.

E237   Vaughan-Phillips (née Dodsworth).

VAD. TS and MS recollections of the Misses Dodsworth, Western Front and Egypt. Photo album and re-written diary (original lost).

E238   Verney, Dr Ruth (née Conway).

SWH. Letters from Macedonian/Serbian Front, 1918–19.

E239   Ward, Mrs N. (née McClean).

WAAC. MS recollections of office duties at Army Post Office, Wimereaux. Describes disturbances following the shooting of an Australian soldier. Documents and letters relating to call-up, clothing, discharge certificate and further papers.

E240   Washington, Mrs Pat Beauchamp.

FANY Driver. TS recollections giving family background, sexual innocence while on active service, air raids. Photos, cuttings, concert programmes, etc.

See index, under Beauchamp. Tape recorded, PHL.

E241   Wherry, Mrs Albina.

Honorary secretary of Cambridge branch of VAD. TS recollections concerning army horses, voluntary workers (who turned up variously in resplendent jewellery or unmistakably in the garb of a 'Woman of the Town'), hospital work in Belgium (friction between the trained and the socially superior VADs), convoys, zeppelins. Varied experience. Was over service age when war began.

E242   Wilsdon, Mrs S.T. (née Apperley).

Nurse, Aldershot and Kantara, Egypt. TS recollections describing life as a nurse, and meeting and marrying her husband. Good diary, interspersed with letters and photos. Descriptive style; less on nursing detail than on way of life, journey to Egypt, social engagements, grief at brother's death, joy at falling in love.

DOMESTIC CATALOGUE

E243   Abson, Jessie.

Recollections, MS, 4pp. A child during the war (b. 1912). Recollections of family life in North London.

E244   Alexander, Miss K.

A child's scrapbook diary, written from her home in Broadway. Comments on refugees seen at Paddington station, agricultural work, some of the major events in the war. Tremendously detailed, including newspaper cuttings, photos, details of national as well as personal events. Use of language interesting. Collection also contains diaries by her brothers.

E245   Allen, Enid.

Recollections. Book-length TS, plus illustrations, entitled 'Her Boots Got her the Job'. Land work – WNLSC. Fictionalised.

E246   Armstrong, Miss O.

Diary kept by a lecturer in History and Economics, Trinity College, Dublin, 1915–18. Covers war news, Easter Rising and subsequent fighting; includes cuttings – a large number from the Roll of Honour.

E247   Barkworth, Miss E.M.

Schoolgirl. Diaries, 1913–19.

E248   Bernard, Mirs Mary Ellen (née Doidge).

Three diaries for 1917–18. Day-to-day activities: shopping in London, cello lessons; other musical events. Little detail, few subjective ruminations.

E249   Birnstingl, Ursula.

Friend of Peggy Hamilton. One drawing and extracts from MS private autobiography. Did some land work (dressed by her mother as a Millet peasant girl), drove an ambulance, went for an (amusingly recounted) interview with an amateur women's army corps. Worked, 1916–17, with Peggy at Weston Park, near Southampton Water, a munitions factory. Worked in Birmingham for a while – describes poverty and living by her wits in the tool room. Married her beloved Oliver, an RFC pilot, killed just before the Armistice. A well-narrated account.

See Peggy Hamilton *Three Years or the Duration* (B73).

E250   Booth, Florence E. (née Knight).

TS recollections, 3pp., of work in munitions in Kent and office work in Cricklewood.

E251   Bowes, Mrs D.

West Yorks girlhood recollections, 1914–18. Documents concerning her father's YMCA work.

E252   Bowman, Mrs Agnes (née Smithson).

MS recollections, 4pp. At the Quaker Boarding School, York, 1913–17.

E253   Box, Kathleen N. (née Charman).

TS recollections, 15pp. Girlhood in the country. Was 14 when war broke out. Her parents were tradespeople in the village.

E254   Brand, Mrs E. S. (Margaret Mann).

TS recollections, 8pp. Childhood in Ramsgate and London.

E255   Bristow, Mrs N.

MS recollections, photos, certificate. Initially did clerical work in the War Office, London. Decided in 1918 to change to outdoor work. Describes training to drive tractors, initial suspicion of farmers, Armistice. Regrets the lack of recognition accorded to land workers.

E256   Brookes, Dorothy.

TS recollections, 8pp. Childhood in the Cotswolds.

E257   Buck, Mrs Barbara.

TS of interview, 3pp. Was married to Evelyn Waugh's brother, Alec, who was also a well-known novelist. Had an influence on Evelyn while he was still at school. Her mother was a suffragette and a pacifist. She describes herself as a Communist. Her father was the writer W.W. Jacobs.

E258   Campbell, Dr Margaret W.H.

TS recollections, 17pp. A talk delivered to the Scottish Society of the History of Medicine, 1977. Graduated 1918, and became a house surgeon.

E259   Carlin, Miss E.E.

MS recollections 3pp. Sunderland area: school and billeting in a private house.

E260   Chambers, Miss K.

MS recollections, 3pp. Woman solicitor in London.

E261   Cockayne, Dame Elizabeth.

Recollections and documents relating to nursing.

E262   Colgrain, Madge, Lady.

MS recollections, 9pp. Travels between Egypt and England. Hospital support work.

E263   Collins, Mrs T.

TS recollections, 4pp. Girlhood in Devon, including comments on her patriotism and regard for Baden Powell's Scouting for Boys. Describes parents' attitudes to land girls. Self-mocking tone.

E264   Corbett Ashby, Dame Margaret.

TS recollections entitled 'War 1914–18' and 'A Lucky Accident, First World War'. Letters to her husband, to her mother, from her parents. MS recollections of prisoners in Isle of Man internment camp. MS recollections entitled 'Women's Work during First World War'.

E265   Courtney, Lady Kate.

Copy of her 'Extracts from a Diary During the War', printed for private circulation, December 1927.

See C4.

E266   Craven, Mrs Hilda (née Duckworth).

VAD at Crescent Hospital, Croydon, 1918–19. Diary 1914–22. Photos and further papers.

E267   Davison, Miss H.W.

TS recollections, ration books, recipes, cards, anti-German poem.

E268   De Valois, Dame Ninette.

Recollections. Transcript of tape recording. Commencing dancing career in Brighton and London. Worked in the kitchen in a hospital near Hyde Park when not on stage.

E269   Dillon, Miss N.G.

TS recollections, 7pp. Experience in north-east and as VAD in France.

E270   Duguid, Mrs B.

TS autobiographical account of her schooldays on Toedean and Crofton Grange throughout the war.

E271   Dunlop, Mrs May (née Justice).

VAD at Waverley Hospital, Farnham, Surrey. Diaries 1817–18, certificates, autograph albums, photo albums.

E272   Dyer, Miss Winifred.

Recollections. Interview. TS, 14pp. Worked in France as part of a Quaker unit, treating civilians.

E273   Farmer, Mrs M.A.

TS recollections, 14pp. Childhood in Jarrow; zeppelin raid.

E274   Featherley, Janet.

MS recollections, 8pp. Schoolgirl at Ursuline Convent in Forest Gate. Aged 11 when war broke out.

E275   Gilbraith, Dr G.R.

TS recollections, 3pp. Female student in Oxford – describes the negative attitude to her and her colleagues.

E276   Gordon, Mrs H.F.

TS recollections, 5pp. Brother interned in Germany.

E277   Green, Ada.

Papers and photographs referring to her munitions work and WAAC service, 1919–20. Scrapbook of newspaper cuttings with articles and photographs of women working at Woolwich Arsenal and the Women's Land Army.

E278   Hamilton, Lady Peggy (née Wills).

Munitions work. File contains good drawings, some by Ursula Birnstingl, some by Peggy, some taken from the *Illustrated London Times*.

See Birnstingl (E249 above) and Hamilton *Three Years or the Duration* (B73).

E279   Haworth, Lady.

TS recollections, 2pp. Childhood memories of zeppelins, food shortages, Canadian soldiers. Father was a silk merchant.

E280   Heenan, Mrs L.S.

Diaries of an Army Officer's wife, 1914–15. Voyage from India. War work and social life in England.

E281   Hill, Enid.

MS recollections, 14pp. A supporter of women's suffrage. Describes wartime zeppelin raids over Clapham Common, while still at school.

E282   Hutchinson, Gladys.

Diary written from the Manor House, Catterick, 1908–19. (Original plus TS copy.)

E283   Iliff, Phyllis Constance.

Journal (1918–22) of her poems of love and grief at the death of her sweetheart in July 1918. Moving expression of loss. Copies of poems by, for example, Swinburne, Shelley, plus Rose Macaulay's 'Many Sisters to Many Brothers'. Her own poems are not accomplished, but expressive. Plus photos, a locket/keepsake.

E284   Jones, Mrs E.J.

TS recollections, 3pp. Vivid memories of girlhood on East Yorkshire coast.

E285   Kennedy, Miss Cynthia.

Nurse, Norfolk war hospital; RFC driver. Papers, and letters from male friends.

E286   Lawrence, Mrs E.

TS recollections, 4pp. In Romsey and later as a nurse at Great Ormond Street Children's Hospital. Describes poor conditions, poor children and their parents.

E287   Liddle, Miss W.

MS recollections, 3pp. Describes looting of Germans' shops in Sunderland; bombardment of Hartlepool.

E288   Lunn, Dr Phyllis.

Schoolgirl and student during the war. Account of Scarborough raid. Christmas cards and papers, including her father's passport, allowing him to visit a hotel in Switzerland that would take released British wounded and sick POWs.

E289   Lynwood, Mrs.

TS recollections, 129pp. Hampshire war bride and RAF wife.

E290 McCann, Mrs Beatrice.

TS recollections, 2pp. Had a German pacifist staying at their house at the time war was declared. Worked as a secretary at a Red Cross Hospital near Tunbridge Wells.

E291 Macleod, C.E. Lilias.

MS recollections, 7pp. Clerk at the Admiralty. Gives details of pay, expenses, economies necessary while living on such a small budget.

E292 Macleod, Miss M.L.

File contains accounts of Molly and her twin sister Betty, who helped to run a canteen at an army camp in Cambridgeshire. There is a précis of contents of letters and diaries. Covers brothers' experience in the forces, the sisters' VAD work (story about Rose Macaulay endeavouring to keep her apron dry while cleaning the floor), stories of silly women visitors to soldiers, their father's anti-pacifist work. Their aunt works in munitions in Holburn. There is a long (largely unsympathetic) description of a meeting addressed by Sylvia Pankhurst. Molly does some agricultural work, and gives impressions of Gypsy Hill Training College.

E293 McPherson, Isobel.

MS recollections, 11pp. Thinks of the war as providing considerable opportunities for women.

E294 Mann, J. de L.

TS recollections, 4pp. Oxford graduate, did Admiralty work in London and Paris.

E295 Manning, Miss Ruth Beatrice.

TS recollections, 2pp. VAD in Cambridge and France. Trained as hospital almoner later.

E296 Marshall, Mrs V.

MS recollections, 2pp. Girlhood in Woolwich. Describes munitions workers.

E297 Mitchell, Mrs Clair.

TS recollections. Munitions worker in Manchester. Describes earning 8 shillings per week for making shells, then later £12 for driving an electric crane. Good detail.

E298 Morgan, Lady Marjorie.

TS recollections, 6pp. Father a Lieutenant Colonel, engaging in voyages to Lahore and Gibralter; fiancé/husband at war. Life in Dublin and with in-laws in Kent.

E299 Nash, Alice Henrietta.

MS recollections that fill an exercise book. Munitions work in Sunderland. Vivid description of an accident and of asking for a raise. Joined the WAAC; worked for the RFC in Kent. Lively, spirited account.

E300   Neagle, Dame Anna.

MS recollections, 1p. Father in Navy; raids in Forest Gate.

E301   Newton, Dr Olive Margaret Celia.

MS recollections, 2pp. From a Quaker family. Medical student and then casualty house surgeon in Birmingham, dealing largely with munitions casualties. Older brother a conscientious objector, younger brother member of Friends' Ambulance Unit.

E302   Payned, Mrs Doris.

TS recollections, 30pp. Chapter 3 refers to the war. Girlhood in Northampton; billeting soldiers; observes land girls; comments on better wages and conditions for working-class women.

E303   Pearson, Mrs G.M.

TS recollections, 7pp. Life in Yorkshire, Edinburgh and later in London as a secretary at the Ministry of Munitions, and a higher-paying private firm.

E304   Potter, Mrs O.

MS Recollections, 2pp. York, in an army environment. Future husband at Scarborough. London MI5 work.

E305   Reece, Mrs Ada.

Diaries 1900–63, plus additional papers. War material describes the atmosphere in London, panic buying, the concerns of her daughter's French companion, of her husband Dick and of her son Harold, who is at Cambridge. Comments on war news, on women's proper role, on German behaviour, war babies, munitions, women's work, etc. Interesting on the role of the wife and mother. Contains lots of detailed commentary on the activities of the family members.

E306   Robb, Mrs.

Notebook diary (1911–18) of a girl working in a photographic shop, in Kirkwall, Orkney, which is near Scapa Flow, the base for the British Dreadnought Battleship Fleet. Mentions security, contraband, Jutland, the drowning of Lord Kitchener, threats of a German naval raid, the Armistice. Combination of domestic and war commentary. Interesting perspective.

E307   Robson, Gladys.

Recollections, MS 7pp., 4pp.; TS 1p. Life in a working-class area, Newcastle. Became a delegate for the NUWW while working in a Newcastle factory. Describes a strike (illegal, of course, in wartime), and meeting Susan Lawrence at the station to negotiate an agreement.

E308 Rutter, Christine Sophie.

MS recollections, 18pp. Schoolgirl in City of London.

E309 Schuster, Miss Florence.

Letters to her father, Professor A. Schuster from Manchester University, concerning a memorial service. Photocopies of three diaries. Travelled in Europe (July 1914); worked at an Army Remount Centre and then as a postal van driver.

E310 Sebastian, Mrs H. (née Gosling).

TS recollections, 16pp., plus 7pp. insertions and corrections. Experience at school and waiting to go to Cambridge to study science.

E311 Swann, Miss F.M.

Recollections, 50pp. Volume privately printed. Student at Oxford.

E312 Sykes, Dr Eleanor.

MS recollections, 11pp. Girlhood in Manchester; sister a VAD. Detailed social commentary.

E313 Trefusis, Mrs B.M.

Diary and photographs, 1914–16.

E314 Tully, Mrs Stephanie.

TS recollections, 11 pp. (interview). Childhood on a farm, Boreham Wood, where German POWs worked.

E315 Turner, Dr Dorothy M.

MS recollections, 7pp. Childhood in Hull. Describes excitement at outbreak of war.

E316 White, Mrs Blanco.

Papers relating to work in the Ministries of Munitions and Labour.

See index for cross-references.

E317 White, Mrs V.M.

MS recollections, 9pp. Took up canteen work; became a VAD in a hospital in Sandgate.

E318 Williams, Dr Frances A.

MS recollections, 3pp. Girlhood in Sunderland, helped out at Quaker-run canteen before entering Manchester University medical school, 1917.

E319   Williamson, Miss Margery.

MS recollections, 1p., closely written over two sides. Childhood in Lancashire village. Describes unneighbourly treatment of a Quaker couple; the husband, a conscientious objector, was sent to jail. Sees the war period as providing women with an escape from domestic slavery.

E320   Woods, Miss T.C.

TS recollections, 3pp. Schoolgirl in Tonbridge. Developed friendship with the German POWs accommodated in the adjoining house.

E321   Wright, Dr Helena.

MS recollections, 4pp. Had a Polish father. She and her sister were medical students, and fell victim to 'spy-fever' on several occasions. Finally, having attained the position of House Surgeon, the author was dismissed because of rumours that she was German and accompanying doubts about her loyalty.

E322   Wynne-Eaton, Mrs Frances.

MS recollections, 7pp. Joined the Women's Hospital Corps along with Drs Flora Murray and Garrett Anderson. From 1916 led the life of an RFC wife – one of constant movement. Her husband was a major.

TAPE RECORDINGS

E323   Ainsley, Mrs.

Munitions work.

E324   Ashby, Dame Margery Corbett.

Raid on Lowestoft; suffrage, political and social work.

E325   Bagnold, Enid.

Auxiliary nursing. Became Lady Jones. Father a Colonel in the Royal Engineers. Drove for the FANYs in France. Insists that all her experience is in her two books, *Diary Without Dates* and *The Happy Foreigner*.

E326   Beauchamp, Pat.

FANY driver. See her account in *Fanny Goes to War* and *Fanny Went to War*.

See index under Beauchamp for cross-references.

E327   Birnstingl, Ursula.

Munitions work in the Midlands and Southampton; war widowhood.

See index for cross-references.

E328   Burnett, Mrs.

Munitions work at Gretna, 1916–17.

E329   Burton, Mrs.

Munitions at Morecambe and Gretna. Account of an explosion.

E330   Burton, P.

Munitions work.

E331   Chisholm, Miss Mairi.

Describes being more interested in mechanics than clothes. Met Elsie Knocker at a motorcycle rally, and rode off to join her in the Women's Emergency Corps without waiting for parental permission. Hector Munro apparently saw her riding through London, and traced her. Describes, vividly, the wounded men, and seeing pilots jumping from planes, in flames, over the battlefields.

See index for cross-references.

E332   Cole, Dame Margaret.

Labour Party research worker during the war. Born in Cambridge, went to school at Roedean and from there to Girton. Her brother was a conscientious objector; her father was patriotic: both she and her brother were disinherited.

See her autobiography *Growing Up into Revolution* (C54).

E333   Cummings, Miss M.M.

Munitions work. Zeppelin raid on Hartlepool. Father a shipyard riveter.

E334   Davis, Mrs E.

Munitions, Gretna.

E335   Farmborough, Miss Florence.

Was named after Florence Nightingale. Lived in Austria then Kiev as a governess/companion. Went to Moscow in 1910. Nursed in Russia during the war. Describes experiences in heightened tones; comments on social conditions in upper-class society in Russia.

See index for cross-references.

E336   Forster, M.

Munitions.

E337   Habble, Mrs E.

Munitions at Gretna.

E338   Hamilton, Lady Peggy.

Munitions at Woolwich, Birmingham, Southampton.

See index for cross-references.

E339   Lenanton, Lady (Carola Oman).

VAD in France.

See E207, above.

E340   Limerick, Dowager Countess of.

Nursing in home counties as a VAD.

E341   Mitchison, Dame Naomi.

Nursing, social life, married life.

See index for cross-references.

E342   Neagle, Dame Anna.

Aspects of life on the domestic front.

E343   Reeves, Mrs Mary.

Munitions at Gretna.

E344   Robson, Mrs J.

Munitions.

E345   Smith, Mrs E.M.

Munitions.

E346   T'Serclaes, Baroness de.

Nursing at the Front, 1914–18.

See index for cross-references.

E347   Whitaker, Miss Ruth.

VAD work in Devon, Exeter, Rouen and Malta.

III   BIRMINGHAM CENTRAL LIBRARY

Address: Central Library
            Chamberlain Square
            Birmingham B3 3HQ

Tel: 0121 235 4511

The Literature department of Birmingham Central Library has a special collection of war poetry. The card catalogue covers this material and also a reasonable collection of books and plays by women of the period. The History and Local Studies department holds a number of publications and documents relating to Birmingham in the First World War. There are scrapbooks, collections of photographs and locally published books telling of the war experience of particular companies or industries, which include sections on, or references to, the role of women in wartime. Birmingham was a significant producer of munitions and prominent in the motor trade – also important for war production. There is also material on trades for women and girls in the area, published reports of the local Mothers' Union and bound volumes of *Women Workers*, the quarterly magazine of the Birmingham branch of the National Union of Women Workers.

IV   TRADES UNION CONGRESS LIBRARY

Address: Trades Union Congress Library Collections
c/o University of North London Learning Centre
236–250 Holloway Road
London N7 6PP

Tel: 0171 753 3184

A collection of Labour and union material running from the late nineteenth century to the present day. The material is mostly in the form of pamphlets, documents, reports, etc. A catalogue directs the researcher to material filed in boxes, much of which is available on the shelves. There is a good collection of material relating to women's work during the First World War, particularly industrial work: a useful complement to the material on middle-class women held at the Imperial War Museum. Reports include: 'Draft Interim Report of the Conference to Investigate into Outlets for Labour after the War'; 'The position of Women After the War', compiled by the Standing Joint Committee of Industrial Women's Organisations; 'The Output of Women Workers in Relation to Hours of Work in Shell-making', Reports of the Industrial Fatigue Research Board; 'Women in Industry After the War' by B.L. Hutchins; the War Office publication *Women's War Work* (HMSO, 1916). There are also materials on the Women's Trade Union League, the Women's Co-operative Guild, the National Federation of Women Workers, and the library holds copies of all major journals published in connection with unions or labour organisations.

The *Gertrude Tuckwell Papers* is a collection of newspaper clippings and other reports collected by Gertrude Tuckwell and covering the first twenty years of the twentieth century. The material concerns women and their employment, mostly in industry, and is available on microfilm. There is a typewritten guide to the files, which are arranged under headings such as 'Unemployment in cotton factories through the European war', 'Women in Industry 1913–20', 'Married Women's Labour', and so on. The papers include material on Mary Macarthur, Margaret Bondfield, the National Union of Women Workers, unemployed women, women in new trades, in agriculture, on tramways and railways, as civil servants, telephonists, in munitions, and the cost of living, conscription, postwar unemployment, and so on.

Access by appointment only.

V   THE FAWCETT LIBRARY

Address: The Fawcett Library
             Old Castle Street
             London E1 7NT

Tel: 0171 247 5826

Probably the most useful general library for those researching into women's history and related subjects. The library holds a good stock of books, journals, theses, newspaper clippings and special collections relating to women's history. The atmosphere is friendly and welcoming, the staff invariably happy to share their extensive knowledge and to give appropriate advice.

VI   THE BRITISH RED CROSS MUSEUM

Address: The British Red Cross Museum
             Barnett Hill
             Wonersh
             Guildford
             Surrey GU5 0RF

Tel: 01483 898595

Holds materials on first aid and nursing, as well as biographies and personal memoirs and archives of county branches. Access by appointment only.

Part II

SECONDARY SOURCES

F

LITERARY CRITICISM

F1 Bazin, Nancy Topping and Jane Hamovit Lauter 'Virginia Woolf's Keen Sensitivity to War' in *Virginia Woolf and War*, ed. Mark Hussey, Syracuse, NY: Syracuse University Press, 1991.

Demonstrates the link between public and private acts of violence, between personal grief and political life, with reference to Woolf's major works, arguing that consciousness of war permeates her major writings.

F2 Beauman, Nicola *A Very Great Profession. The Woman's Novel 1914–39*, London: Virago, 1983.

A ground-breaking study which explores the lives of middle-class women as rendered through their fiction of the 1920s and 1930s. The first chapter, on war, discusses Vera Brittain, E.M. Delafield, Enid Bagnold, May Sinclair, Cynthia Asquith and Cicely Hamilton, among others, drawing attention to the fact that women were not asked to give up their lives, but displayed strength and compassion through other forms of endurance and self-sacrifice. Other chapters touch on the war (the book is organised thematically) and on writers, such as Woolf, Mansfield, Macaulay, West, who wrote about war.

F3 Beer, Gillian 'The Dissidence of Vernon Lee: *Satan the Waster* and the Will to Believe' in *Women's Fiction and the Great War*, eds Suzanne Raitt and Trudi Tate, Oxford: Clarendon Press, 1997.

A detailed study of the context and content – both ideological and structural – of Vernon Lee's War Trilogy, *Satan the Waster*.

F4 Bennett, Yvonne A. 'Vera Brittain: Feminism, Pacifism and Problems of Class 1900–1953', *Atlantis* 12, 2, (1987): 18–23.

Argues that Brittain's feminism was geared towards lifting restrictions on women of her own class and that her pacifism was based on a reordering of human and economic relationships that was to be achieved through education, and thus bore little relation to the lives of most ordinary people. The liberalism and optimism of these aims, then, reflecting as they did a sharply middle-class orientation, may have (unintentionally) retarded the growth of the feminist and pacifist movements in the UK.

F5   Benstock, Shari *Women of the Left Bank: Paris 1900–1940*, Austin: University of Texas Press, 1986.

Primarily about expatriate writers, publishers, booksellers, salonières, but the war remains an important context throughout. Makes some specific comments on women, modernism and the war with reference to Wharton and Stein.

F6   Bishop, Alan ' "With Suffering and Through Time": Olive Schreiner, Vera Brittain and the Great War' in *Olive Schreiner and After. Essays on Southern African Literature in Honour of Guy Butler*, eds Malvern van Wyk Smith and Don Maclennan, Cape Town: David Philip, 1983.

Analyses the influence of Olive Schreiner's *Woman and Labour* and *The Story of an African Farm* on Brittain's *War Diary* and *Testament of Youth*. Notes similarities in writing styles between the *Diary* and *Story of an African Farm*, and comments on the differences between Brittain's earlier writing and her retrospective account, *Honourable Estate*.

F7   Bishop, Edward *A Virginia Woolf Chronology*, Basingstoke and London: Macmillan Press, 1989.

The title is self-explanatory. A useful research tool.

F8   Blondell, Nathalie ' " It goes on happening": Frances Bellerby and the Great War', in *Women's Fiction and the Great War*, eds Suzanne Raitt and Trudi Tate, Oxford: Clarendon Press, 1997.

An essay that effectively introduces this neglected writer, and discusses the ways in which war is evoked and invoked in her writing, with particular emphasis on the ways in which English life veils, but cannot protect, those deeply affected by memories of war.

F9   Boxwell, D.A. 'The (M)other Battle of World War One: The Maternal Politics of Pacifism in Rose Macaulay's *Non-Combatants and Others*', *Tulsa Studies in Women's Literature* 12, 1, (Spring 1993): 85–101.

This essay sets Rose Macaulay's novel *Non-Combatants and Others* in opposition to the discourse of the 'militarised mother' that was characteristic of much pro-war propaganda. Daphne Sandomir is seen as representative of maternal pacifism, and the author argues that Macaulay conceives of pacifism as the alternative 'battle' of the First World War, which has the effect of questioning the assumption that pacifism is intrinsically governed by feminine ideology.

F10   Bracco, Rosa Maria *Merchants of Hope: British Middlebrow Writers and the First World War, 1919–1939*, Providence RI and Oxford: Berg, 1993.

A book that sets out to present an account of English memory of the war in fiction that lacked the quality to endure. She is providing an alternative to Fussell's view of war writing as 'ironic' and arguing instead, that the 'middle-brow' writers were concerned with an Englishness that had more to do with tradition and reconstruction than with modernism and rebellion. Provides large-scale and well-documented coverage of bestsellers, looking at the book trade, the publishing context, journalism and reviews, and referring to such authors as Phyllis Bottome, A.S.M. Hutchinson, Cicely Hamilton, Gilbert Frankau and Irene Rathbone (among many others).

F11   Breen, Jennifer 'Representations of the Feminine in First World War Poetry', *Critical Survey* 2, 2, (1990): 169–75.

Looks at David Jones, Isaac Rosenberg and Edward Thomas, examining 'the feminine' in their work, to see if they subvert accepted mythologies concerning women. Ultimately comments on the varieties of the feminine that they reproduce.

F12   Brown, Constance A. *The Literary Aftermath: English Literary Response to the First World War*, PhD thesis, Columbia University, 1978.

Examines the writings of Rebecca West, Rose Macaulay, Katherine Mansfield, Vera Brittain, Winifred Holtby and Robert Graves in terms of their relative detachment or involvement with the war.

F13   Brown, Constance, A. 'Dissection and Nostalgia: Katherine Mansfield's Response to World War 1', *The Centennial Review* 23, (1979): 329–45.

Argues that Mansfield's response to the war informs the two parallel paths that characterise her writing after 1915 when her brother was killed by a grenade. Only five of her seventy-three completed stories directly refer to the war, and only one of these, 'An Indiscreet Journey', is based on her own personal experience. The others either contribute to a picture of Europe as brittle, hard, perverse and brutal in being capable of producing the war, or depict New Zealand as an idyll, uncontaminated by the mechanistic horrors of warfare, as a tribute to her dead brother and to the lives they shared in their native country as children. Concludes that, in her own way, Mansfield was very much a war writer.

F14   Buck, Claire ' "Still some obstinate emotion remains": Radclyffe Hall and the Meanings of Service', in *Women's Fiction and the Great War*, eds Suzanne Raitt and Trudi Tate, Oxford: Clarendon Press, 1997.

An essay on inversion, patriotism and the war, with particular reference to 'Miss Ogilvy Finds Herself' and *The Well of Loneliness*.

F15   Buitenhuis, Peter *The Great War of Words: Literature as Propaganda 1914–18 and After*, London: B.T. Batsford Ltd, 1989.

A detailed examination of literary propaganda during the war, built around C.F.G. Masterman's secret meeting of literary figures in Wellington House, September 1914. There is little overtly about women's contributions, although Mrs Humphry Ward, Edith Wharton, Gertrude Atherton and Phyllis Campbell are mentioned.

F16   Burnett, Gary 'H.D.'s Responses to the First World War', *Agenda* 25, 3–4, (Autumn–Winter 1987–88): 54–63.

An essay that outlines H.D.'s early response to the war, arguing against the common assumption that she was so traumatised as to be unable to articulate a response until the second war. Draws on her work as editor of *The Egoist*, particularly her critique of the Futurist/Vorticist leaning towards the planes and sharp angles that for her signify mechanism and the terror of war. Develops the relation between poetics and politics in a war-defined world.

F17   Byles, Joan Montgomery 'Women's Experience of World War One: Suffragists, Pacifists and Poets', *Women's Studies International Forum* 8, 5 (1985): 473–87.

A reading of some of the poems in Reilly's anthology, *Scars Upon My Heart* (Virago, 1980), in the context of women's experience of and political reactions to the war.

F18   Byles, Joan Montgomery *War, Women and Poetry 1914–1945: British and German Writers and Activists*, London: Associated University Presses, 1995.

Chapter 1 synthesises the best-known scholarship on British women's reaction to war, with emphasis on the Pankhursts, the Hague Conference (1915) and the awarding of the vote. The second chapter focuses on the poems in *Scars Upon My Heart*, comparing particular images with those used by the soldier poets. The third chapter provides an account of interwar women's activity in Britain, and parallels the German situation, before moving on, in the last two chapters, to the Second World War.

F19   Cadogan, Mary and Patricia Craig *Women and Children First: The Fiction of Two World Wars*, London: Victor Gollancz, 1978.

Lively, incisive account of the representation of women and children in war fiction, keen to expose humbug and deplore cliché, but to praise wit and sensitivity. First World War writers included are Berta Ruck, Evadne Price, Enid Bagnold, Rebecca West, Winifrid Holtby, Vera Brittain, Brenda Girvin, Bessie Marchant, among others.

F20   Carr, Glynis 'Waging Peace: Virginia Woolf's *Three Guineas' Proteus: A Journal of Ideas* 3, 2 (1986): 13–21.

Argues that *Three Guineas* poses the essential questions for feminist theorists of war and non-violence. Written in the context of the need for women to oppose war and the forms of violence and oppression that encourage it.

F21   Cecil, Hugh *The Flower of Battle: British Fiction Writers of the First World War*, London: Secker & Warburg, 1995.

A study of the lives and writings of some less well-known First World War writers. The subjects are mostly male (e.g. Richard Aldington, Wilfrid Ewart, Gilbert Frankau), but there is a chapter on the Irish writer, Pamela Hinkson, who wrote some novels under the pseudonym 'Peter Deane'.

F22   Chapman, Wayne K. and Janet M. Manson 'Carte and Tierce.
Leonard, Virginia Woolf, and War for Peace', in *Virginia Woolf and
War*, ed. Mark Hussey, Syracuse, NY: Syracuse University Press,
1991.

Argues against the common assumption that Leonard and Virginia Woolf inhabited
'separate spheres' with neither infringing on the territory of the other, stating that
they collaborated on an article that was to articulate Leonard's stance on the war
and on the (nascent) League of Nations.

F23   Clarke, Ann Jennifer 'Know This is Your War: British Women Writers
and the Two World Wars', PhD thesis, *DAI* 50, 8 (February 1990):
2494A.

Uses an interdisciplinary approach to challenge the tradition that war stories
belong only to men. Examines the work of Rebecca West, Edith Sitwell and Vera
Brittain in order to elucidate their strategies for understanding war and their relationship to war.

F24   Condé, Mary 'Payments and Face Values: Edith Wharton's *A Son at
the Front*', in *Women's Fiction and the Great War*, eds Suzanne Raitt
and Trudi Tate, Oxford: Clarendon Press, 1997.

A detailed reading of Wharton's war novel, *A Son at the Front*.

F25   Cooper, Helen M., Adrienne Auslander Munich and Susan Merrill
Squier (eds) *Arms and the Woman: War, Gender and Literary
Representation*, Chapel Hill and London, University of North Carolina
Press, 1989.

A collection of essays on war writing, covering conflicts from the Trojan war to
those in the Middle East. The general aims are to examine the relationship between
war and gender as figured in literature, and to consider the complexities of women's
roles in conventional war texts. Four essays cover the First World War: James
Longenbach's 'The Women and Men of 1914', is concerned with the 'suffrage
battle', the 'modernist battle' and the 'Great War'; Jane Marcus's 'Corpus/Corps/
Corpse: Writing the Body in/at War' provides a general section on women's war
writing, followed by detailed discussion of Evadne Price's *Not So Quiet*; there is an
essay on May Sinclair's *The Tree of Heaven* by Laura Stempel Mumford; and one
on Willa Cather's *One of Ours* by Sharon O'Brien.

F26   Coroneos, Con 'Flies and Violets in Katherine Mansfield' in *Women's
Fiction and the Great War*, eds Suzanne Raitt and Trudi Tate, Oxford:
Clarendon Press, 1997.

Offers contextual readings of Mansfield's stories 'An Indiscreet Journey' and 'The Fly'.

F27   Cramer, Patricia ' "Loving in the War Years". The War of Images in
The Years' in *Virginia Woolf and War*, ed. Mark Hussey, Syracuse,
NY: Syracuse University Press, 1991.

Analyses the way in which sub-plots which have matriarchal or mythical content are interwoven with realist narrative in *The Years* in order to exemplify the political consequences of (patriarchal) domestic rituals, and to strengthen the female outsiders' resistance to male violence.

F28   Darrohn, Christine M. 'After the Abyss: Class, Gender, and the Great War in British Fiction of the 1920s', PhD thesis, Rutgers University, New Brunswick, 1996, *DAI 57*, 11 (May 1997): 4749A.

An analysis of class and gender in the context of the social disruptions that the war put in place. Looks at Mansfield, Woolf and Lawrence, taking as a 'touchstone' the image of the upper-class woman contemplating the death of the working-class man.

F29   Dickinson, J.E. 'Women Novelists and War: A Study of the Responses of Seven Women Novelists 1914–40', M.Litt. dissertation, University of Edinburgh, 1980.

Looks at Mrs Humphry Ward, Edith Wharton, Rose Macaulay, Storm Jameson, Vera Brittain, Winifred Holtby and Virginia Woolf in the light of their reactions to the war and their attitudes towards writing. Useful for biographical information and contexts.

F30   Farquharson, Janice Marie 'The Literary Experience of the Great War with Special Reference to the Western Front and the Home Front', PhD thesis, University of South Africa, 1987, *DAI 50*, 7 (January 1990): 2061A.

Uses a contextual approach with the aim of shedding light on social attitudes during the war, with a particular focus on the gulf between combatants and civilians. Refers to writers, poets, artists, critics and illustrators.

F31   Field, Frank *British and French Writers of the First World War: Comparative Studies in Cultural History*, Cambridge: Cambridge University Press, 1991.

Concerned to bridge the gap between literary scholars and historians and to articulate some similarities and differences between English and French experience of the war. Looks at male writers – Jean Jaures, Charles Peguy, Ernest Psichari, Brooke, Wells, Shaw, Romain Rolland, Lawrence, Rosenberg, Owen.

F32   Fussell, Paul *The Great War and Modern Memory*, New York and London: Oxford University Press, 1975.

One of the best known and most influential studies of First World War writing, this book sets out to explore the ways in which the war has been mythologised: the literary themes, conventions and resources that fuelled an understanding and the dominant memory of trench experience. Women's contributions are relatively few, but those books written by women since Fussell's (notably Tylee *The Great War and Women's Consciousness*) frequently refer back to it.

F33   Gardiner, Juliet (ed.) *The New Woman*, London: Collins & Brown, 1993.

Includes one chapter on 'Women's War'; extracts from poems, novels and non-fictional pieces by, for example, Vera Brittain, E.M. Delafield and Mrs Humphry Ward. Lacks bibliography and full publication details of extracts cited.

F34   Gilbert, Sandra and Susan Gubar *No Man's Land: The Place of the Woman Writer in the Twentieth Century*, vols I and II, New Haven CT and London: Yale University Press, 1988 and 1989.

Sandra M. Gilbert's essay 'Soldier's Heart: Literary Men, Literary Women, and the Great War', an abbreviated version of the chapter of the same name in vol. II, was first published in *Signs* 8 (Spring 1983): 422–50. The argument is that men were immobilised and emasculated by the war, while women were correspondingly liberated and joyful, having overturned 'the rule of patrilineal succession'. Land girls beam healthily, nurses acquire a new and secret glamour, the war was 'a festival of female sexual liberation'. The authors compile a great deal of (published) evidence to make their case. They have, however, been criticised for presenting a limited view of women's war writing.

F35   Gregory, Elizabeth 'Gertrude Stein and War' in *Women's Fiction and the Great War*, eds Suzanne Raitt and Trudi Tate, Oxford: Clarendon Press, 1997.

An account of Stein's experience of the war and of the more 'accessible' style in which she wrote about it, placing the military and the domestic on the same level. Comments that war had its pleasures for Stein.

F36   Hamer, Mary 'Mary Butts, Mothers and War' in *Women's Fiction and the Great War*, eds Suzanne Raitt and Trudi Tate, Oxford: Clarendon Press, 1997.

On Mary Butts's troubled relationship with her mother, her unusual writing style, and the effect of the war on her life and writing.

F37   Handley, William R. 'War and the Politics of Narration in *Jacob's Room*' in *Virginia Woolf and War*, ed. Mark Hussey, Syracuse, NY: Syracuse University Press, 1991.

Refers to Georg Lukács and Mikhail Bakhtin in order to explore relationships between genre, power and ideology in *Jacob's Room*. Argues that Woolf and Bakhtin provide formal mechanisms for a profoundly social and liberating art.

F38   Hanley, Lynne *Writing War: Fiction, Gender and Memory*, Amherst: University of Massachusetts Press, 1991.

A book about the power fiction has to shape and create memory, and one that sees First World War writing, and influential studies of it (notably Paul Fussell's *The Great War and Modern Memory*) as generating a particular understanding and definition of war writing. This is a book of critical essays, interspersed with fictional writings that aim to 'demilitarise our memories of war'. The essays kick off with a detailed critique of Fussell's book and refer elsewhere to Virginia Woolf, Doris Lessing and Joan Didion, among others, who have written about wars during this century from a variety of perspectives which don't necessarily privilege combat experience. The writer, in common with Woolf and others, sees bellicosity, hierarchy and aggression as dominant features of liberal higher education in the USA.

F39   Hargreaves, Tracey 'The Grotesque and the Great War in *To the Lighthouse*' in *Women's Fiction and the Great War*, eds Suzanne Raitt and Trudi Tate, Oxford: Clarendon Press, 1997.

Focuses on the understanding of Woolf's relationship to war, as revealed by a reading of the holograph version of 'Time Passes'.

F40   Haule, James M. '*To the Lighthouse* and the Great War. The Evidence of Virginia Woolf's Revisions of "Time Passes"' in *Virginia Woolf and War*, ed. Mark Hussey, Syracuse, NY: Syracuse University Press, 1991.

The author has discovered the typescripts of a version of 'Time Passes' that was submitted to a Parisian periodical. A reading of that version and the holograph reveals that significant revisions were made before final publication. These revisions include the drastic reduction of direct references to war, the elimination of associations between war and male brutality, and alterations to the 'character' of Mrs McNab.

F41   Henke, Suzette A. 'Virginia Woolf's Septimus Smith: An Analysis of "Paraphrenia" and the Schizophrenic Use of Language', *Literature and Psychology* 31, 4 (1981): 13–23.

An analysis of Septimus Smith's 'paraphrenia' (i.e. megalomania and withdrawal of interest from the external world) in the light of Freudian analysis of warfare, homosexuality and the effects of condensation and displacement in Septimus's use of language.

F42   Higonnet, Margaret 'Women in the Forbidden Zone: War, Women and Death' in *Death and Representation*, eds Sarah Webster Goodwin and Elisabeth Bronfen, Baltimore, MD: Johns Hopkins University Press, 1993.

Questions the orthodoxy that only men can write about war, as only they can experience or 'see' it. Analyses the gendering of war discourse. Refers to the black US writer Alice Dunbar Nelson, to Amy Lowell, Edna St Vincent Millay, Katherine Anne Porter, Willa Cather, Edith Wharton and Mary Borden.

F43   Hrisey, Dimitris Zegger *May Sinclair*, Boston: Twayne Publishers, 1976.

Critical study, evaluating Sinclair's merits as a novelist, and placing her in the context of the literary and intellectual movements of her time. A chapter on the 'war interval' deals with the *Journal of Impressions*, *Tasker Jevons* (examining the extent to which the hero was based on Arnold Bennett) and *The Tree of Heaven*.

F44   Hussey, Mark (ed. and introduction) *Virginia Woolf and War. Fiction, Reality, Myth*, Syracuse, NY: Syracuse University Press, 1991.

Collection of essays, mostly by American contributors, intended to refute the position that Woolf was apolitical and entirely uninfluenced by war. The First and Second World Wars, and the Spanish Civil War are covered in the light of Woolf's literary output – fiction (long and short) and non-fiction. A number of critical perspectives are represented – biographical, literary theoretical, phenomenological, manuscript study – some dealing with her best-known novels, others taking a more general perspective or looking at the collaboration between Virginia and Leonard Woolf. Contributors include Mark Hussey, Nancy Topping Bazin and Jane Hamovit Lauter, Karen L. Levenback, Wayne K. Chapman and Janet M. Manson, Roger Poole, Helen Wussow, William R. Handley, Josephine O'Brien Schaefer, Masami Usui, James M. Haule, Judith Lee, Patricia Cramer, Patricia Laurence. Published as part of the series 'Syracuse Studies on Peace and Conflict Resolution'.

F45   Huston, Nancy 'Tales of War and Tears of Women', *Women's Studies International Forum* 5, 3–4 (1982): 271–82.

An article that explores the connections between war and war narrative, concentrating on the (peripheral) roles played by women in these narratives and, in particular, on women's weeping as a source of both arousal and anxiety for the men who make war. Does not refer specifically to First World War literature, but to the *Iliad*, to an ancient Chinese fable and to the discourse of the Second World War.

F46   Hynes, Samuel *A War Imagined: The First World War and English Culture*, London: The Bodley Head, 1990.

A book that explores the 'Myth of the War': the imagined version of the First World War that evolved over the years following the Armistice, and that found articulation in novels, paintings, films and other cultural forms. Employs a very broad frame of cultural reference, and refers to a large number of women writers.

F47   Joannou, Maroula *'Ladies, Please Don't Smash These Windows': Women's Writing, Feminist Consciousness and Social Change 1918–38*, Providence and Oxford: Berg, 1995.

Feminist readings of interwar texts, from the perspective of the 1990s. Includes a detailed reading of Vera Brittain's *Testament of Youth*, arguing against reading it as a feminist text; material on Leonora Eyles and socialist feminism; on spinsterhood; on Woolf's *Orlando* and Hall's *Well of Loneliness*; on Rosamund Lehmann and Elizabeth Bowen; and on anti-fascist writing by Woolf and Burdekin. Most obviously concerned with the 1920s and 1930s, but the war, and attitudes to war in general, are present.

F48   Kelly, Katherine E. 'The Actresses' Franchise League Prepares for War: Feminist Theatre in Camouflage', *Theatre Survey: The Journal of the American Society for Theatre Research* 35, 1 (May 1994): 121–37.

The argument of this is that the League's activities during the war have been either simplified or overlooked. Documents the history of the Woman's Theatre, an organisation run by women stage managers and business managers, which evolved into the Women's Theatre Camps Entertainments. The aim was to create a women's theatrical agency, to provide a high standard of entertainment within the variety format, and to offer free concerts at hospitals and clubs. As a result, though, the suffragist allegiance of the organisation was subsumed under the war effort.

F49 Khan, Nosheen *Women's Poetry of the First World War*, Brighton: Harvester, 1988.

A critical study based on large-scale retrieval of women's First World War poetry. Thematically organised in order to explore the rich variety of women's responses to the war.

F50 Klein, Holger (ed.) *The First World War in Fiction*, London: Macmillan, 1976.

A comparative approach, analysing works by male writers from Britain, France, Germany, the USA, Italy and Austria-Hungary. Addresses the questions of truthfulness (as opposed to verisimilitude), of representativeness and of literary articulation of political attitudes. Essays on, for example, Mottram, Aldington, Barbusse, Remarque, Marinetti.

F51 Layton, Lynne 'Vera Brittain's Testament(s)' in *Behind the Lines*, eds Higonnet *et al.*, New Haven: Yale University Press, 1987.

Argues that Brittain's personalisation of the war involved a shift from male to female identification. Before the war her intimates were men (Roland, her brother); afterwards they were women – predominantly Winifred Holtby. This signals a shift in her 'feminism' from a self-concerned to a more broadly empathetic position.

F52 Lawrence, Karen 'Gender and Narrative Voice in *Jacob's Room* and *Portrait of the Artist as a Young Man*' in *James Joyce: The Centennial Symposium*, eds Morris Beja, Phillip Herring, Maurice Harmon, David Norris, Urbana and Chicago: University of Illinois Press, 1986.

Of interest in that it compares the protagonists' and the writers' relation to tradition, and analyses the nature of the relationship between protagonist and narrator in either case, concluding that the narrator of *Portrait* exercises power and privilege while Woolf's narrative strategies call into question 'the concepts of the male ego, patriarchal succession and narrative power'.

F53 Lee, Judith ' "This Hideous Shaping and Moulding". War and *The Waves*' in *Virginia Woolf and War*, ed. Mark Hussey, Syracuse, NY: Syracuse University Press, 1991.

Uses the argument advanced by Elaine Scarry, that all aesthetic activity has an ethical content because it originates in bodily, sentient experience, in order to interpret the relationships between war (destruction) and 'making' (creative imagination) in *The Waves*.

F54   Levenback, Karen L. 'A Chasm in a Smooth Road: A Study of the Effect of the Great War on Virginia Woolf', PhD Thesis, University of Maryland, 1981.

An examination of Woolf's writing in terms of its contribution to the written experience of the war on the home front. Argues that Woolf 'understood the war as destroying not only the values of the past, but the hope for the future' which was supported by those values.

F55   Levenback, Karen L. 'Virginia Woolf's "War in the Village" and "The War from the Street". An Illusion of Immunity' in *Virginia Woolf and War*, ed. Mark Hussey, Syracuse, NY: Syracuse University Press, 1991.

Examines Woolf's wartime reviews for the *Times Literary Supplement* and argues that Woolf came to realise that there was no protection in civilian life from the effects of war.

F56   Light, Alison *Forever England: Femininity and Conservatism Between the Wars*, London: Routledge, 1991.

As the title indicates, this focuses on between-the-wars writing, but the First World War inevitably plays a part in the imaginative landscapes of the writers concerned. There are chapters on Ivy Compton-Burnett, Agatha Christie, Jan Struther and Daphne du Maurier.

F57   Lyon, Janet 'Militant Discourse, Strange Bedfellows: Suffragettes and Vorticists before the War', *Differences: A Journal of Feminist Cultural Studies* 4, 3 (Summer 1992): 100–32.

Analyses the semiotic links between militant suffragettes and avant-garde artists, despite the overt distaste for the feminine on the part of the Vorticists. Points out the violence and bellicosity in both sets of rhetoric. Discourse anticipates the war-like images and strategies that were to become dominant with the First World War.

F58   Mackay, Jane and Pat Thane 'The Englishwoman' in *Englishness: Politics and Culture 1880–1920*, eds Robert Colls and Philip Dodd, Beckenham: Croom Helm, 1986.

A study of girls' and women's magazines, looking at the initial confusion in terms of appropriate role models on entering war, then exploring the fantasy role models, ideas of Empire, of honour and of womanliness.

F59   Marcus, Jane ' "No More Horses": Virginia Woolf on Art and Propaganda' in *Critical Essays on Virginia Woolf*, ed Morris Beja, Boston: G.K. Hall, 1985.

A defence of Woolf against Bell's accusation that 'She belonged, inescapably, to the Victorian world of Empire, Class and Privilege. Her gift was for the pursuit of shadows' (II, 186). Summons Woolf's experience at Morley, her leadership of Women's Co-operative Guild meetings, etc. and argues that, while Woolf criticises the union of art and propaganda as sterile, she nevertheless divides herself into artist and pamphleteer. Not directly relevant to the war, but relevant to Woolf's aesthetic practices.

F60   Marcus, Jane 'The Asylums of Antaeus. Women, War and Madness: Is There a Feminist Fetishism?' in *The Difference Within: Feminism and Critical Theory*, eds Elizabeth Meese and Alice Parker, Amsterdam and Philadelphia: J. Benjamins, 1989.

An analysis of women's self-representation in suffragette iconology, and the restitution of feminine stereotypes in the imagery of war propaganda. Takes on a detailed critique of Gilbert and Gubar.

F61   Mellown, Muriel 'Reflections on Feminism and Pacifism in the Novels of Vera Brittain', *Tulsa Studies in Women's Literature* 2, 2 (1983): 214–28.

A broadly descriptive account of Brittain's novels: *The Dark Tide* (1923), *Not Without Honour* (1924), *Account Rendered* (1945) and *Born 1925* (1948). Set in the context of Brittain's moral convictions, particularly her feminism and growing commitment to pacifism.

F62   Mellown, Muriel 'One Woman's Way to Peace: the Development of Vera Brittain's Pacifism', *Frontiers* 8, 2 (1985): 1–6.

A brief, explanatory, almost celebratory piece, drawing attention to Brittain's gradual fusion of feminism and pacifism, and different but related aspects of the same struggle against tyranny and oppression. Charts her disillusion with the League of Nations and the Labour Party, and her movement towards Christianity, symbolised by her support for Dick Sheppard's Peace Pledge Union.

F63   Meyers, Judith Marie '"Comrade-Twin": Brothers and Doubles in the World War I Prose of May Sinclair, Katherine Anne Porter, Rebecca West and Virginia Woolf', PhD Thesis, University of Washington, 1985.

Looks at the ways in which fictional and autobiographical 'heroines' apprehend combatant experience imaginatively, through brother and double relationships, in order to gain a sense of selfhood, of courage, and of the part they are to play in their social world. Takes each author in turn and offers detailed readings of her texts, taking into account feminist content and context in the light of the above.

F64   Miller, Marlowe Allyson 'Family, War and Writing: H.D., Virginia Woolf, and Marguerite Duras', PhD thesis, University of California, *DAI* 52, 8, (February 1992).

Uses a French feminist approach to analyse these three writers in the light of their negotiations with language, patriarchy and war.

F65   Millett, Fred B. 'Feminine Fiction' *The Cornhill Magazine* clv, 926, (February 1937): 225–35.

An interesting overview of women writers from the postwar period. Interesting for its contemporary judgements ('most of the novelists, at least of a secondary order, have been women' (225); '[h]er feminism, unhysterical as it is' (227)) and for the range of novelists that it covers (e.g. May Sinclair, Rose Macaulay, Sheila Kaye-Smith, E.M. Delafield, Clemence Dane, Dorothy Richardson, Dorothy Whipple, Virginia Woolf).

F66   Montefiore, Jan *Men and Women Writers of the 1930s. The Dangerous Flood of History,* London: Routledge, 1996.

Primarily concerned to review the role of memory in the construction of the 1930s period, and to restructure the male-dominated view of that period by inserting women, and broader social contexts into the picture. The First World War is mentioned in so far as it seems to delimit the landscape of 1930s writers and stands as a symbol of futility. It appears in autobiographies (notably Vera Brittain's and Storm Jameson's) and its language echoes through some of the poetry of the period.

F67   Moreland, Deborah Anne 'The Suffragettes, the Great War, and Representation in H.D.'s *Asphodel'*, *Sagetrieb: A Journal Devoted to Poets in the Imagist/Objectivist Tradition* 14, 1–2, (1995): 243–60.

Analyses the representations of the character Hermione in relation to images of womanhood in suffragette and First World War poster art. Provides a similar analysis of the nurses in the novel, and develops an argument which explores the alignment of pregnancy with battle.

F68   Neuman, Shirley '*Heart of Darkness,* Virginia Woolf and the Spectre of Domination' in *Virginia Woolf: New Critical Essays,* eds Patricia Clements and Isobel Grundy, London: Vision and Totowa NJ: Barnes and Noble, 1983.

Considers the war, in *Mrs Dalloway*, as a generalisation for the particularity of specific 'tyrants' and as a means of extending Marlowe's remarks to their 'furthest historical and cultural reaches'. Argues that what Maisie Johnson sees in Septimus as 'horror' is insanity born out of the experience of war, and that war is an extension of the 'idea' that Marlowe thinks 'redeems' the 'conquest of the earth'.

F69   Newton, Esther 'The Mythic Mannish Lesbian: Radclyffe Hall and the New Woman', *Signs* 9, 4 (1984): 557–75.

Puts 'mannish lesbianism', as exemplified most famously by Stephen Gordon, in the context of contemporary sexology, feminist rebellion against the constraints on women and the gendering of sexual desire.

F70   Orel, Harold *Popular Fiction in England 1914–1918,* Hemel Hempstead: Harvester Wheatsheaf, 1982.

A study of the novel as a popular genre during the war years, taking the line that 'novels were not the place to learn that the old order was passing forever' (3–4). Interesting contextual material on publishing, reviewing, literary journals, etc. Concerned mostly with male writers, but Mary Webb (whose novels do not overtly deal with the war) gets a chapter to herself.

F71   Otte, George 'Mrs Humphry Ward, the Great War, and the Historical Loom', *Clio: A Journal of Literature, History and the Philosophy of History* 19, 3, (1990): 271–84.

Readings of Ward as a conservative writer who, in propaganda and war novels alike, retains her class prejudices and resists imagining a world in which the role of women has radically changed. Concludes that Ward communicates a desperate faith in the resumption of the sort of history she can understand.

F72   Ouditt, Sharon *Fighting Forces, Writing Women. Identity and Ideology in the First World War*, London: Routledge, 1994.

This study examines a range of women's writings concerning the war, from institutional handbooks to the novels of Virginia Woolf. It explores the various ways, from the conservative to the radical, in which feminine identity is negotiated in order to enable or obstruct social change. The chapters deal respectively with the VADs, land and munitions workers, women in the domestic sphere, pacifists and Virginia Woolf, drawing on published and unpublished materials, memoirs, political writings, women's magazines and novels.

F73   Ouditt, Sharon 'Tommy's Sisters: The Representation of Working Women's Experience' in *Facing Armageddon. The First World War Experienced*, eds Hugh Cecil and Peter H. Liddle, London: Leo Cooper, Pen & Sword Books, 1996.

An exploration of the rhetorical strategies used to represent working-class women's experience in war writing, considering the rather derogatory images presented in some written propaganda in comparison with the narratives of progress that underpin some working-class autobiographies.

F74   Pickering, Jean 'On the Battlefield: Vera Brittain's *Testament of Youth*', *Women's Studies: an Interdisciplinary Journal* 13, 1–2, (1986): 75–85.

A reading of *Testament of Youth* as a resolution of private and public lives, of past and present. Brief comparisons made with other war memoirs by Blunden, Sassoon and Graves.

F75   Poole, Roger ' "We All Put Up with You Virginia". Irreceivable Wisdom About War', in *Virginia Woolf and War*, ed. Mark Hussey, Syracuse, NY: Syracuse University Press, 1991.

Relates Heideggerian phenomenological categories to the 'Time Passes' section of *To the Lighthouse* specifically, and more generally to Woolf's other novels, in order to explore her modernist vision, in the light of her understanding of the effects of war.

F76   Potter, Jane ' " A great purifier": The Great War in Women's Romances and Memoirs', in *Women's Fiction and the Great War*, eds Suzanne Raitt and Trudi Tate, Oxford: Clarendon Press, 1997.

An essay on the transformative power of war, as evidenced in the two popular writers: Berta Ruck and Ruby M. Ayres, and two memoirists: Kate Finzi and Olive Dent.

F77   Price, Alan *The End of the Age of Innocence. Edith Wharton and the First World War*, London: Robert Hale Ltd, 1996.

Using a biographical approach, this study provides an historical context for Wharton's humanitarian and literary achievements during the war. Follows her charitable work, her attempts to reduce suffering from TB, her 'propaganda' writing. There is a separate chapter on the use of war in her fiction. Comments in general on her social and aesthetic response to war.

F78   Raitt, Suzanne ' "Contagious ecstacy": May Sinclair's War Journals' in *Women's Fiction and the Great War*, eds Suzanne Raitt and Trudi Tate, Oxford: Clarendon Press, 1997.

A thoroughly researched study of pride, ecstasy, shame and humiliation, principally as a result of Sinclair's experience with the Munro Ambulance Corps.

F79   Raitt, Suzanne and Trudi Tate (eds) *Women's Fiction and the Great War*, Oxford: Clarendon Press, 1997.

A lively and varied collection of essays on women's fiction of the war period. The introduction makes it clear that the editors are interested in the differences among women and in the problems of considering 'woman' as a category. The volume includes re-readings of well-known modernists (Woolf, Stein, Mansfield, Wharton, H.D.), it introduces Mary Butts and Frances Bellerby, and looks again at writers such as Mrs Humphry Ward, Ruby M. Ayres, Berta Ruck and Vernon Lee, who were influential at the time. The essays are: Helen Small, 'Mrs Humphry Ward and the First Casualty of War'; Mary Condé, 'Payments and Face Values: Edith Wharton's *A Son at the Front*'; Suzanne Raitt, ' "Contagious ecstacy": May Sinclair's War Journals'; Jane Potter, ' " A great purifier": The Great War in Women's Romances and Memoirs'; Gillian Beer, 'The Dissidence of Vernon Lee: *Satan the Waster* and the Will to Believe'; Tracey Hargreaves, 'The Grotesque and the Great War in *To the Lighthouse*'; Nathalie Blondell, ' " It goes on happening": Frances Bellerby and the Great War'; Claire Buck, ' "Still some obstinate emotion remains": Radclyffe Hall and the Meanings of Service'; Con Coroneos 'Flies and Violets in Katherine Mansfield'; Mary Hamer, 'Mary Butts, Mothers and War'; Trudi Tate, 'HD's War Neurotics'; Elizabeth Gregory, 'Gertrude Stein and War'.

F80   Rose, Jaqueline 'Why War?' in *Why War? Psychoanalysis, Politics and the Return to Melanie Klein*, Oxford: Blackwell, 1993.

An exploration of the relationships between psychoanalysis, war and knowledge, taking in Freud, Clausewitz and Virginia Woolf (among others). It was originally delivered as a lecture on 19 January 1991, two days after the outbreak of the Gulf War.

F81   Schaefer, Josephine O'Brien 'The Great War and "This Late Age of
World's Experience" in Cather and Woolf' in *Virginia Woolf and War*
ed. Mark Hussey, Syracuse, NY: Syracuse University Press, 1991.

Comparison between *Jacob's Room* and *One of Ours* in which the former is seen
to depict the senseless waste of war, and the latter to give voice to the meaning and
purpose brought by war. Concepts of nationhood, social class and education are
brought in to elucidate the argument.

F82   Small, Helen 'Mrs Humphry Ward and the First Casualty of War' in
Women's Fiction and the Great War, eds Suzanne Raitt and Trudi
Tate, Oxford: Clarendon Press, 1997.

An essay on the relatively neglected propagandist and fiction writer, exploring
morality and censorship in her successful and influential propaganda books, and in
her slightly less well-received war novels.

F83   Smulders, Sharon 'Feminism, Pacifism and the Ethics of War: The
Politics and Poetics of Alice Meynell's War Verse', *English Literature in
Transition (1880–1920)* 36, 2, (1993): 159–77.

Discusses Meynell's poetic treatment of complex issues, such as parenthood, motherhood and pacifism, commenting that although she retained her feminism, her
pacifism waned during the war. Comments on Meynell's poem on the death of
Edith Cavell, on her interest in women's unvoiced experiences, in the context of her
conservative disposition, despite some radical opinions.

F84   Stark, Susanne ' "Exits" from Victorianism', dissertation, University of
Leicester, 1990.

A study of May Sinclair, which, while it pays attention to most of her output,
emphasises particularly her novel *The Tree of Heaven*.

F85   Tate, Trudi (ed. and introduction) *Women, Men and the Great War*,
Manchester, Manchester University Press, 1995.

This is an anthology of short stories concerning the war, by male and female
writers. Tate provides an introduction and biographical information on those
selected. The stories by women writers are: Sylvia Townsend Warner, 'A Love
Match'; Mary Butts, 'Speed the Plough'; Winifred Holtby, 'So Handy for the Fun
Fair'; Katherine Mansfield, 'The Fly'; Gertrude Stein, 'Tourty or Tourtebarre';
H.D., 'Ear-Ring'; Radclyffe Hall, 'Miss Ogilvy Finds Herself'; Gwendolyn Bennett,
'Wedding Day'; Woolf, 'The Mark on the Wall'; Wharton, 'The Refugees'; May
Sinclair, 'Red Tape'; Kay Boyle, 'Count Lothar's Heart'. Male contributors include
Faulkner, Aldington, Mulk Raj Anand, Hemingway, Lawrence, Wyndham Lewis,
Conrad, J.M. Barrie, Sapper, Arthur Machen, Kipling, Ford, Maugham. Useful
collection of material that is often hard to find.

F86   Tate, Trudi 'Gender and Trauma: HD and the First World War' in
            Image and Power: Women in Fiction in the Twentieth Century, London
            and New York: Longman, 1996.

Concerned with the civilian experience of war neurosis, linking H.D.'s miscarriage
in 1915, which she attributed to the news of the sinking of the *Lusitania*, to the
articulation of the gendered experience of war in a short story, 'Kora and Ka', and
in H.D.'s novel, *Bid Me to Live*.

F87   Tate, Trudi 'HD's War Neurotics' in *Women's Fiction and the Great
            War*, eds Suzanne Raitt and Trudi Tate, Oxford: Clarendon Press,
            1997.

A version of the essay cited above.

F88   Tate, Trudi *Modernism, History and the First World War*, Manchester:
            Manchester University Press, 1998.

Addresses the relationship between modernism and war writing, arguing that the
distinction between the two, when read alongside each other, begins to blur.
Analyses a range of texts: modernist fiction, war writing by combatants and non-
combatants, newspapers, political writing, medical and psychoanalytical writing.
In terms of women writers, pays particular attention to H.D. and Virginia Woolf.

F89   Thacker, Andrew 'Dora Marsden and *The Egoist*: 'Our War is With
            Words', *English Literature in Transition (1880–1920)* 36, 2, (1993):
            179–96.

Concerned primarily with the transition from *Freewoman* to *Egoist*, and Dora
Marsden's involvement in it. Comments on the part played by Pound in the transition and on the influence of T.E. Hulme and Bergson, which helped Marsden
develop her dislike of linguistic abstraction. Also concerned with the relationships
between feminism and modernism: Marsden rejected the term woman, saying 'Is
there such a thing as woman sensed from the inside?'

F90   Thomas, Sue 'Virginia Woolf's Septimus Smith and Contemporary
            Perceptions of Shell Shock', *English Language Notes* 25, 2, (1987):
            49–57.

An account of the Report of the War Office Committee of Enquiry into 'Shell-
shock' in relation to the experience and treatment of Septimus Warren Smith.

F91   Tylee, Claire M. ' "Maleness Run Riot" – The Great War and Women's
            Resistance to Militarism', *Women's Studies International Forum* 2, 3,
            (1998): 199–210.

Provides a detailed and convincing critique of Sandra Gilbert's argument as articulated in 'Soldier's Heart'.

F92 Tylee, Claire M. *The Great War and Women's Consciousness: Images of Militarism and Womanhood 1914–64*, Basingstoke and London: Macmillan, 1990.

Impressively wide-ranging and informative study of women's writings of the war, concerned with rectifying the androcentric bias in the study of war writing and, particularly, with examining women's myths of war experience. Covers a large number of writers, diarists, memoirists.

F93 Tylee, Claire M. ' "Munitions of the Mind": Travel Writing, Imperial Discourse and Great War Propaganda by Mrs Humphry Ward', *English Literature in Transition (1880–1920)* 39, 2, (1996): 171–92.

Focuses on *England's Effort*, pointing out that women were involved in the production of pro-war propaganda, and arguing that Mrs Ward's writing, like so much war propaganda, is fuelled by imperialist discourse.

F94 Usui, Masami 'The Female Victims of the War in *Mrs Dalloway*' in *Virginia Woolf and War*, ed. Mark Hussey, Syracuse, NY: Syracuse University Press, 1991.

A gendered reading of *Mrs Dalloway* which takes in London topography as well as providing historically contextualised readings of the main female characters in the novel, particularly Rezia Warren Smith and Doris Kilman.

F95 Woollacott, Angela 'Sisters and Brothers in Arms: Family, Class, and Gendering in World War I Britain' in *Gendering War Talk*, eds Miriam Cooke and Angela Woollacott, Princeton NJ: Princeton University Press, 1993.

An essay which examines brother-sister relationships in First World War narratives, comparing middle-class to working-class renditions of the relationship between young women and their combatant brothers. Notes that middle-class daughters relied on their brothers as mediators of the public world and were emotionally as well as financially dependent on them. Working-class women, on the other hand, often gained financial autonomy owing to the expansion in women's industrial employment, and seemed, in any case, less sentimentally attached to their siblings. The comment is made, however, that this impression may be emphasised by the fact that the writing of middle-class women was often self-reflective, whereas the accounts by working-class women were often made at the behest of another person and are concerned more with material than affective detail. Her argument is that the more involved – psychologically, financially and practically – with her brother, the more likely a woman was to construct herself as a passive observer of the war, and that this should be recognised as an interpretative strategy.

F96 Wussow, Helen 'War and Conflict in *The Voyage Out*' in *Virginia Woolf and War*, ed. Mark Hussey, Syracuse, NY: Syracuse University Press, 1991.

Argues that the paradigms of public and private conflict, of war and aggression within a patriarchal context, are played out in Woolf's prewar novel.

F97 Wussow, Helen 'The Nightmare of History: The Great War and the Work of Virginia Woolf and D.H. Lawrence', DPhil thesis, University of Oxford, *DAI* 53, 5, (November 1992).

Explores the significance of war and conflict in the writings of Woolf and Lawrence, tending towards an understanding of the part played by violence in the modern world.

F98 Zwerdling, Alex *Virginia Woolf and the Real World*, Berkeley: University of California Press, 1986.

A study that explores Woolf's social vision: her sense of the complex ways in which history, institutions, politics and society affect the interior and exterior worlds of her characters. Significant reference is made to the First World War, particularly in discussion of *Jacob's Room*, *Mrs Dalloway* and *To the Lighthouse*, but also in discussion of her non-fictional work and in her essays, diaries and letters. Provides very useful elucidation of references to social and historical events. Has a detailed index.

G

SOCIAL AND CULTURAL HISTORY

G1   Alberti, Johanna *Beyond Suffrage: Feminists in War and Peace, 1914–28*, London: Macmillan, 1989.

Uses a biographical approach to outline the lives and interests of fourteen women, all known to each other, who all had an interest in the suffrage and related issues. Chapter three focuses specifically on the war. The women are: Margery Corbett Ashby, Kathleen Courtney, Eva Hubback, Catherine Marshall, Emmeline Pethick Lawrence, Eleanor Rathbone, Lady Rhondda, Elizabeth Robins, Maude Royden, Evelyn Sharp, Mary Sheepshanks, Mary Stocks, Ray Strachey, Helena Swanwick.

G2   Armstrong, Alan *Farmworkers: A Social and Economic History 1770–1980*, London: B.T. Batsford, 1988.

Brief section on war context, commenting on prewar effect of laissez-faire policy on food production, and the loss of many labourers to the army; government intervention following the Lloyd George coalition; and the links between the War Agricultural Committees and the Whitehall planners. Comments on employment of women on the land, suggesting that there were more 'village women', whether full or part time, than land army women working as agricultural labourers. Useful general context, but little on the specific experience of women.

G3   Beddoe, Deirdre *Back to Home and Duty: Women Between the Wars 1918–39*, London: Pandora, 1989.

As the title suggests, a study of the interwar period. It characterises the period following the war as one in which women had made considerable gains, which were followed up by increasing pressures to return to traditional roles. A cultural and historical study, drawing on a wide range of primary sources.

G4   Bidwell, Shelford *The Women's Royal Army Corps*, London: Leo Cooper, 1977.

A history of the corps from its beginning in 1917, to the time of publication. Contains a lot of useful information, but lacks a full bibliography.

G5   Boston, Sarah *Women Workers and the Trade Unions*, London: Lawrence & Wishart, 1980; new edn, 1987.

A history of women and trades unions, covering the period 1874 to 1986. Chapter 4,

'Don't Blackleg Your Man in Flanders', deals with the war period, and outlines confrontations and negotiations between women and unions, unions and employers, Mary Macarthur and Sylvia Pankhurst, etc. Also details the activities of the NFWW, and follows the debates concerned with equal pay, maternity benefit, and DORA.

G6   Braybon, Gail *Women Workers in the First World War: The British Experience*, London: Croom Helm, 1981.

An account of the public debates surrounding working-class women's employment during the war, from a broadly socialist feminist perspective. The sources comprise government reports, union and trade journals, feminist journals, contemporary newspapers and contemporary books on the subject. Aims to demonstrate the consistency of male attitudes towards women's work, even under such exceptional circumstances, and the effect of this on work practices during and after the war. Covers women's entry into war work, the reorganisation of industrial practices, the question of pay, the attitudes of the unions, debates concerning welfare provision, the public image of women workers, issues of social class. The context is the relationship between capital and labour at a time when a legacy of government non-interference in workplace organisation collides with a new authoritarian machinery for running the war. Extremely useful and readable account.

G7   Braybon, Gail 'Women and the War' in *The First World War in British History*, eds Stephen Constantine, Maurice W. Kirby, Mary B. Rose, London: Edward Arnold, 1995.

A general essay, which sets out the broad lines of the debate between historians of women's involvement in the war. Braybon examines the effect of war on women's employment, and how women 'felt' about the war, concluding that improvements were only temporary, and commenting that responses are varied, and often depend on the nature of the source.

G8   Braybon, Gail and Penny Summerfield *Out of the Cage: Women's Experiences in Two World Wars*, London: Pandora, 1987.

The introduction outlines the authors' interest in letting women's voices speak for themselves, and draws broad comparisons between the two wars. The first half relates to the First World War. Outlines the basic shifts in employment patterns in 1914, covers issues relating to class, health, domestic life and demobilisation. Uses a large number of memoirs, autobiographies, published and unpublished first-hand accounts.

G9   Brittain, Vera *Lady into Woman. A History of Women from Victoria to Elizabeth II*, London: Andrew Dakers Ltd, 1953.

Begins with the Victorian inheritance of the woman of 1901, and works through the vote, politics, education, equal rights and pay, money, morals, marriage, war, peace, and writers, towards what she calls the human revolution. Comments on the success of women in work during the First World War, but in the context of the postwar attitude that removed the freedoms and elided the achievements. Doors were opened even wider in the second war, but Brittain retains the idea that women's natural impulse is to create and to save.

G10   Burnett, John (ed. and introduction) *Useful Toil: Autobiographies of Working People from the 1820s to the 1920s*, 1974. Reprinted London: Routledge, 1994.

Extracts from working-class autobiographies, most of which were previously unpublished. Several cover women's war work, and provide a rare articulation of working women's experience.

G11   Bussey, Gertrude and Margaret Timms *Pioneers for Peace: Women's International League for Peace and Freedom 1915–1965. A Record of Fifty Years' Work*, London: Allen & Unwin, 1965.

Accounts for the origins of the Hague Congress in 1915, names the major participants (e.g. Jane Addams, Aletta Jacobs, Rosika Schwimmer, Emmeline Pethick-Lawrence), describes the resolutions and the effects of the envoys sent out to governments, in the hope of gaining support for mediation. The USA's declaration of war in April 1917 ended hopes for a neutral conference of mediation. Describes the second congress, May 1919, at which the name was amended to Women's International League for Peace and Freedom.

G12   Byles, Joan Montgomery 'Women's Experience of World War One: Suffragists, Pacifists and Poets', *Women's Studies International Forum* 8, 5, (1985): 473–87.

A paper that outlines the difference of view between the various suffragist factions (the Pankhursts, Mrs Fawcett, the pacifists) and goes on to examine some of the poems in Reilly's anthology *Scars Upon My Heart* (Virago, 1981) by way of examining the experience of change wrought by the suffrage movement and the war.

G13   Carmichael, Jane *First World War Photographers*, London: Routledge, 1989.

A study of First World War photography, examining the roles of officials and amateurs and examining the control and dissemination of information on the various battle fronts and on the home front. Includes over one hundred reproductions from the archives at the Imperial War Museum.

G14   Ceadel, Martin *Pacifism in Britain 1914–1945: Defining a Faith*, Oxford: Clarendon Press, 1980.

Makes the distinction between 'pacifist' and 'pacificist'. A good account of the main antiwar movements – the No Conscription Fellowship, the Fellowship of Reconciliation, etc., and of their moral/political orientations. Useful context for women peace workers, as some were associated with groups other than the Women's International League, which the author believes, rather dismissively, to have been 'doctrinally too confused ever to become important' (61).

G15   Collett, Christine *For Labour and For Women. The Women's Labour League 1906–1918*, Manchester: Manchester University Press, 1989.

Has one chapter on the war, during which the Women's Labour League declined. Includes accounts of the work of Marion Phillips and Katharine Bruce Glasier.

G16   Condell, Diana and Jean Liddiard *Working for Victory? Images of Women in the First World War 1914–1918*, London: RKP, 1987.

An excellent collection of photographs, exhibiting women's roles during the war. With accompanying explanatory captions and introductions to each section.

G17   Cooke, Miriam and Angela Woollacott (eds) *Gendering War Talk*, Princeton NJ: Princeton University Press, 1993.

A collection of cross-cultural and multidisciplinary essays concerned with gender, discourse and war. Concentrates on twentieth century wars from the First World War to the Gulf War. Essays on the First World War by Angela Woollacott and Margaret R. Higonnet.

G18   Costin, Lela B. 'Feminism, Pacifism, Internationalism and the 1915 International Congress of Women', *Women's Studies International Forum 5*, 3–4, (1982): 301–15.

Outline of the collective action taken by women, across international boundaries, in time of war, to establish peace.

G19   Crofton, Eileen *The Women of Royaumont. A Scottish Women's Hospital on the Western Front*, East Linton: Tuckwell Press, 1997.

A history of an SWH unit, housed in the beautiful, but impractical thirteenth-century Abbey of Royaumont. The building was successfully converted into a modern hospital, where it functioned efficiently from January 1915 to March 1919, thanks to a well-qualified, flexible and dedicated staff, which included the writer and dramatist Cicely Hamilton among its number (she worked there as an administrator). The story is told to a large extent through the voices of the main protagonists, thus producing a variety of perspectives on the successes, failures, problems and solutions found by the unit. There is also a substantial biographical section.

G20   Culleton, Claire A. 'Gender-charged Munitions: the Language of World War 1 Munitions Reports', *Women's Studies International Forum* 11, 2 (1988): 109–116.

Analyses the representational strategies of written propaganda tracts, postcards, cartoons concerned with women and munitions work, arguing that women's work was persistently associated with maternal work or sexual instinct.

G21   Dakers, Caroline *The Countryside at War*, London: Constable, 1987.

A study which draws on a wide range of previously unpublished papers and family archives in order to depict the way the occupants of and traditions in the English countryside responded to the war. Includes chapters on agriculture; life and death in the manor houses, vicarages, schoolrooms and farms; and the countryside at peace.

G22   Darracott, Joseph *The First World War in Posters*, New York: Dover Publications, 1974.

Posters taken from the Imperial War Museum, representing artists of various nationalities. A brief introduction notes the various styles of poster art, the fact that posters were often part of a broader national campaign, sources of imagery, typography. Not a gender-based study, but useful as a general source book.

G23   Davin, Anna 'Imperialism and Motherhood', *History Workshop 5*, Spring, (1978): 9–65.

An exploration of the context of the new maternal role in the early twentieth century. Considers the drive to reduce the infant mortality rate, the need to improve the health and physique of soldiers, education for motherhood, women in the workplace, factors of class and poverty, all in the broader context of questions of Empire, of eugenics and of economics, given the challenges to Britain's international pre-eminence. Fascinating in itself, and useful as context for the roles and representations of mothers in First World War discourse.

G24   Elshtain, Jean Bethke *Women and War*, Brighton: Harvester, 1987.

A work of political philosophy that explores diverse discourses and the political claims and social identities that they sustain. The aim is to analyse the traditional Just Warrior/Beautiful Soul formulation that separates masculine from feminine, and forms the basis of narratives of conflict. The existence of female belligerence and male compassion clearly undermines the above dichotomy and initiates the analysis of ambivalences and complexities that are the subject-matter of the study. Resources include political works, first-person war narratives, poetry, novels, anthropology, myth. The study moves towards a reconceptualising of citizenship, informed by feminist thought.

G25   Enloe, Cynthia *Does Khaki Become You?*, London: Pluto Press, 1983.

A study of the relationship between women and military structures in Britain, the USA, Vietnam and the Falklands, from the Civil War to the Falklands War. Considers women as nurses, prostitutes, social workers, wives and mothers, examining the ways in which military structures depend on women at the same time as they marginalise them. Includes commentary on the First World War, but is concerned with gender and militarisation generally.

G26   Evans, Richard J. *Comrades and Sisters: Feminism, Socialism and Pacifism in Europe 1870–1945*, Brighton: Wheatsheaf Books, 1987.

European in outlook, and largely based on research into German feminist, socialist and pacifist movements. Chapter 5, centring on the Hague Peace Congress, provides an interesting perspective on internationalist pacifism.

G27   Garner, Les *Stepping Stones to Women's Liberty: Feminist Ideas in the Women's Suffrage Movement 1900–1918*, London: Heinemann Educational Books, 1984.

Primarily concerned to ask how the major suffrage organisations identified the oppression of women, and what solutions they proposed. In the context of war, comments on the split in the NUWSS, the antiwar attitude of the Women's Freedom League, the chauvinism of the WSPU, and the increasingly socialist-pacifist leanings of Sylvia Pankhurst's ELFS. Good as an introductory guide to where the priorities of the major suffrage groups lay.

G28   Gold, Marian *Wartime is Your Time: Women's Lives in World War I*, Edgeware, Middlesex: Hytheway Ltd, 1996.

An examination of women's lives during the war, with reference to women's magazines. The author provides a detailed account of women's magazines and analyses in them the contradictions and silences that were a part of managing the immense upheaval in manners, morals and social life.

G29   Gould, Jenny 'Women's Military Services in First World War Britain' in *Behind the Lines: Gender and the Two World Wars*, eds Margaret Randolph Higonnet, Jane Jenson, Sonya Michel, and Margaret Collins Weitz, New Haven: Yale University Press, 1987.

Brief account of the difficult relationship between women and the military in the war, from the (independently organised) First Aid Nursing Yeomanry (1907) to the Women's Army Auxiliary Corps of the British Army (1917). Comments on the reluctance of the mainstream to accept women in military positions, on the disagreements between women as to the direction any women's organisations should take, and the broader context of the crisis in combatant manpower.

G30   Harries, Meiron and Susie *The War Artists: British Official Art of the Twentieth Century*, London: Joseph, in association with the Imperial War Museum and the Tate Gallery, 1983.

Sets out to explain who commissioned the art, from which painters, where they went and under what conditions. Inevitably the study focusses on male artists (Muirhead Bone, Lavery, Nevinson, etc.), but there is a section that covers the visual documentation of women's activities and that mentions the artists Victoria Monkhouse, Nellie Isaac, Ursula Wood and Lucy Kemp-Welch.

G31   Haste, Cate *Keep the Home Fires Burning: Propaganda in the First World War*, London: Allen Lane, 1977.

A study of propaganda aimed at the home front. Discusses the means used to recruit troops, the active involvement of women's organisations in pro-war activity, atrocity stories, spy stories, propaganda for peace and the peace itself.

G32   Higonnet, Margaret and Patrice Higonnet, 'The Double Helix' in *Behind the Lines*, eds Margaret Randolph Higonnet, Jane Jenson, Sonya Michel, and Margaret Collins Weitz, New Haven: Yale University Press, 1987.

An essay arguing that gender functions as a parameter of political thought, as seen by the function of gender in wartime propaganda alongside defensive statist measures. This, when compared with the actual experiences of many women, shows how a disparity between those experiences and the prevailing ideology is revealed but not acted upon in war situations.

G33   Higonnet, Margaret Randolph, Jane Jenson, Sonya Michel, and
Margaret Collins Weitz, eds *Behind the Lines: Gender and the Two
World Wars*, New Haven: Yale University Press, 1987.

The introduction to this suggests that total war has acted as a clarifying moment,
revealing systems of gender in flux, and thus highlighting their workings. It looks
at the opposition of masculinity to femininity as a way of guaranteeing social
stability, but notes that there were extraordinary destabilising moments. These
were kept in check by the widespread notion that changes were for the duration
only and that ultimately women's claims were to be secondary to those of the
returning soldiers. The essays include: Joan W. Scott, 'Rewriting History';
Margaret R. Higonnet and Patrice Higonnet, 'The Double Helix'; Elaine Showalter,
'Rivers and Sassoon'; Lynne Layton, 'Vera Brittain's Testaments'; Jenny Gould,
'Women's Military Services in First World War Britain'; Steven C. Hause, 'More
Minerva than Mars: The French Women's Rights Campaign and the First World
War'; Karin Hausen, 'The German Nation's Obligations to the Heroes' Widows of
World War 1'; Sandra Gilbert, 'Soldier's Heart: Literary Men, Literary Women and
the Great War'. There are further essays on Anne Frank and on American and
European women in the Second World War.

G34   Holt, Toni and Valmai *Till the Boys Come Home: The Picture Postcards
of the First World War*, London: Macdonald and Jane's Publishers,
1977.

Over 700 reproductions, all annotated. An introduction gives a brief history of
postcard art. There are eight sections, one of which is on women at war, but many
of the others, of course, reflect gendered attitudes.

G35   Holton, Sandra Stanley *Feminism and Democracy: Women's Suffrage
and Reform Politics in Britain 1900–1918*, Cambridge: Cambridge
University Press, 1986.

An account of the activities of the democratic suffragists (i.e. not the WSPU),
including the war period. Notes relationships with the Labour movement, the
composition and orientation of the WILPF (of which Helena Swanwick was the
chair) and documents in detail the informal meeting preceding the Speaker's
Conference that recommended full adult suffrage for men and a measure of
women's suffrage. Extremely useful book, drawing significantly on the Catherine
Marshall papers as a window onto suffrage and labour politics of the time.

G36   Horn, Pamela *Rural Life in the First World War*, Dublin:
Gill & Macmillan, 1984.

Study of the reorganisation of the countryside, giving an overview of the prewar
situation, wartime agricultural policy, and reaction of farmers and land-owners to
the changes. Specific chapters on women and girls on the land; soldiers on the land;
and the employment of prisoners of war and enemy aliens.

G37   Kamester, Margaret and Jo Vellacott (eds) *Militarism Versus Feminism:
Writings on Women and War*, London: Virago, 1987.

This volume brings together writings by Catherine Marshall and C.K. Ogden and

Mary Sargant Florence on women's opposition to war, introduced and annotated by the editors. The Introduction concedes that feminist pacifism had little political impact in its time, but suggests that understanding of it can illuminate present struggles. Comments on the international character of prewar suffragism, and on the nature of the argument that women's difference implies antipathy to militarism.

See separate entries under Marshall (B100, B101), and Ogden and Florence (B108).

G38   Kennard, Jean 'Feminism, Pacifism and World War 1', *Turn of the Century Women* 2, 2 (1985): 10–21.

Addresses the question as to why the women's peace movement of the early twentieth century failed to sway international politics. Distinguishes between 'negative' and 'positive' approaches to peace. The former is based on the structural opposition of the 'masculine' (i.e. bellicose, power-mongering) by the 'feminine' (focussing on a maternalist essentialism). The latter is concerned with internationalism and opposition to the oppression of individuals. Ultimately turns to Virginia Woolf as one who upholds the link between feminism, pacifism and class oppression, and who supports a flexible and non-oppressive feminist movement.

G39   Krippner, Monica *The Quality of Mercy: Women at War, Serbia 1915–18*, London: David & Charles, 1980.

A study of the women who volunteered for service as doctors and nurses and, having been rejected by the British Army, were enthusiastically received by the Serbs. Documents the history of the Serbian front – the initial appeal for help, the typhus epidemic, invasion and retreat, and the later return – in the light of the experiences of the women who went there. Focusses on Mrs St Clair Stobart, Elsie Inglis, Mabel Dearmer, Lady Paget, Flora Sandes, among others.

G40   Liddington, Jill 'The Women's Peace Crusade: The History of a Forgotten Campaign' in *Over Our Dead Bodies: Women Against the Bomb*, ed. Dorothy Thompson, London: Virago, 1983.

Contextualises the Crusade through discussion of the Hague Congress (1915), the WIL and the Labour Movement. The amount of public information is relatively small, as it was a campaign conducted outside of London, with a mostly grassroots, working-class membership. Describes meetings in Glasgow, which was a major centre of support, and further gatherings in the North of England (Manchester and Nelson). Charlotte Despard was a key speaker.

G41   Liddington, Jill *The Long Road to Greenham: Feminism and Anti-Militarism in Britain Since 1820*, London: Virago, 1989.

An account of women's anti-militarist movements from the early nineteenth century until the late 1980s. Traces particular intellectual or political strands – for example maternalism, equal rights feminism and the association of men with violence – and analyses how they are articulated in given contexts. Spends some time on the Hague Peace Congress (1915), on the IWSA and the formation of the British WIL and also gives an account of the Women's Peace Crusade, a grassroots socialist movement that had greater force outside London than within. Then traces these ideas though later movements, such as the Peace Pledge Union, the Women's

Co-operative Guilds and then into CND, culminating with the Greenham Common Peace Camp. Uses a combination of 'official' histories, auto/biographies and personal testimonies, written and oral.

G42   Liddington, Jill and Jill Norris *One Hand Tied Behind Us: The Rise of the Women's Suffrage Movement*, London: Virago, 1978.

Mostly concerned with the rise of the suffrage movement, but this provides a helpful context for the last chapter which covers the war period. Covers (briefly) the split in the NUWSS, women's war work, relationships between socialist and pacifist organisations. Socialist feminist perspective; concerned with radical suffragists rather than militant suffragettes.

G43   Macdonald, Lyn *The Roses of No Man's Land*, London: Michael Joseph, 1980.

The story of the war from the point of view of the doctors, but predominantly nurses, mostly volunteers, who nursed the wounded in the hospitals and clearing stations behind the frontlines. Based largely on interviews conducted during the late 1970s with surviving volunteers from the UK, USA, New Zealand and Australia, this book contains lengthy quotations from the witnesses in order to give a direct account of the experiences of many of these women, who were struggling to keep men alive without the aid of modern medical technology.

G44   Macdonald, Sharon, Pat Holden and Shirley Ardener (eds) *Images of Women in Peace and War*, Basingstoke and London: Macmillan Education, 1987.

A study of women's relationship to war, peace and revolution, taking examples from Boadicea to the Greenham Common peace camps. The contributors look at women's participation in war and anti-war activities, and also at the symbolic network that surrounds them. Chapter 11 relates to the First World War.

G45   Marwick, Arthur *Women at War 1914–18*, London: Fontana, 1977.

One of the earlier accounts of women and war work, which aims to depict the experience of ordinary women, rather than the more prominent figures alone. The book draws on the archives at the Imperial War Museum (it was published in order to accompany a museum exhibition), the papers of the Ministry of Reconstruction and some of the records of suffrage organisations. It also quotes from government reports, newspapers, novels, autobiographies, and has illustrations on almost every page.

G46   Mitchell, David *Women on the Warpath: The Story of the Women of the First World War*, London: Jonathan Cape, 1966.

Celebratory accounts of the war work of a number of women. Including Sarah Macnaughtan, Phyllis Campbell, Mrs St. Clair Stobart, Mairi Chisholm, Mabel Dearmer, Flora Sandes, L.N. Smith, Vera Brittain, WRAF workers, No-Conscription Fellowship workers, suffragists and a number of other doctors (including Flora Murray and Louisa Garrett Anderson and their Women's Hospital Corps), women police and eccentric aristocratic volunteers.

G47   Oldfield, Sybil *Women Against the Iron Fist: Alternatives to Militarism 1900–1989*, Oxford: Basil Blackwell, 1989.

A book which aims to add to the roll-call of men involved with pacifist thought, the names of women who have played a prominent role in advancing alternatives to Bismarckian 'iron fist' ideology this century. The book doesn't claim a gendered affinity between women and pacifism. The chapters on Kate Courtney, Maude Royden and Virginia Woolf are of particular interest.

G48   Panichas, George A. *Promise of Greatness; The War of 1914–18*, London: Cassell, 1968.

Collection of reminiscences and reflections, mostly by men, but with the occasional female contribution (e.g. by Vera Brittain), and an early essay on Virginia Woolf and the war by J.K. Johnstone.

G49   Pollock, Carolee Ruth 'Against the Tide: The Anti-War Arguments of the British Suffragists During the First World War', MA thesis, University of Calgary, 1989.

An account of suffragist pacifist arguments, including their political/religious orientation: for example, Christian pacifist, radical liberal, anti-physical force, maternalist. (Copy held in the Fawcett Library.)

G50   Popham, Hugh *FANY: The Story of the Women's Transport Service 1907–1984*, London: Leo Cooper in association with Secker & Warburg, 1984.

A more up-to-date history than that by Irene Ward. Provides a brief bibliography, but no detailed footnotes, so gives few leads for those seeking further information on his sources.

G51   Rowbotham, Sheila *Hidden From History*, London: Pluto Press, 1973.

Feminist history of women, and particularly working-class women, whose stories have been obscured by general trends in historical studies. Material on the war covers work practices, trends in the structure of women's employment, aspects of differing needs of middle- and working-class women, unionisation and a brief account of the suffrage movement during 1914–18.

G52   Rowbotham, Sheila *Friends of Alice Wheeldon*, London: Pluto Press, 1986.

This book comprises the text of a play, first performed in 1980, and an extended essay entitled 'Rebel Networks in the First World War'. The essay tells the story of Alice Wheeldon and her daughter Hettie, who were WSPU members in Derby. Alice was convicted of conspiring to poison Lloyd George. The context of industrial espionage, anti-conscription organisations, suffrage and pacifist networks is given, along with an account of the trial itself. (Pat Barker alludes to the story in the second book of her *Regeneration* trilogy, *The Eye in the Door*, London: Viking Penguin, 1993.)

G53   Sanders, M.L. and Philip M. Taylor *British Propaganda During the First World War, 1914–1918*, London and Basingstoke: Macmillan, 1982.

Sets out to refocus the picture of war propaganda as poorly organised and wasteful before the Ministry of Information was established in 1918. Includes accounts of the Parliamentary Recruiting Committee, the Censorship and Press Bureau, the National Press Committee and the War Propaganda Bureau at Wellington House. Little specifically on women, but useful context on, for example, Virginia Woolf's concept of the militarisation of civilian life.

G54   Scott, Joan W. 'Rewriting History', in *Behind the Lines*, eds Margaret Randolph Higonnet, Jane Jenson, Sonya Michel, and Margaret Collins Weitz, New Haven: Yale University Press, 1987.

An essay outlining the general trends in women's histories of war, which tend to concentrate on women's experience, the impact of war upon them, with evidence to affirm or deny that war was a turning point for them. Instead she articulates the need to contrast personal experiences with official pronouncements in order to analyse how and by whom national memory is constructed, how political discourse may be appropriated by people, and how they are shaped by or redefine its meaning.

G55   Shover, Michele J. 'Roles and Images of Women in World War I Propaganda', *Politics and Society* 5, 3 (1975): 469–86.

Examines war poster art, arguing that the governments of the belligerent countries looked to expand the feminine role in order to meet the wartime needs of public policy, and, at the same time, attempted to preserve the traditionally passive feminine role. Includes some illustrations.

G56   Showalter, Elaine *The Female Malady: Women, Madness and English Culture 1830–1980*, New York: Pantheon Books, 1985. London: Virago, 1987.

A cultural history of madness and its relation to femininity. Chapter 7, 'Male Hysteria: W.H.R. Rivers and the Lessons of Shell Shock', provides an account of the psychiatric treatment of 'shell shock', focussing on the contrasting work of Drs Yealland and Rivers. Showalter notes that the symptoms of 'shell shock' are more or less identical to those of hysteria and neurasthenia, attributed to women in the nineteenth century, and draws attention to the parallel situations of powerlessness, loss of control, enforced submission to authority, which are doubly emphasised in the military treatment of shell-shock. She then points out the readiness with which some women writers took on the theme of shell-shock and exemplified the effect of rigid patriarchal values on masculine minds in need of creativity and passion. Rebecca West and Virginia Woolf figure largely in the discussion.

G57   Sillars, Stuart *Art and Survival in First World War Britain*, Basingstoke: Macmillan, 1987.

Takes the year 1916, 'the intellectual and emotional heartland of the war' (9), and examines artistic forms of all kinds (photography, painting, newspaper reportage, film, poetry, music, cartoons, novels, documentary accounts, personal reminiscences) in order to analyse the functions of art in ensuring psychological survival in wartime.

G58   Simkins, Peter *Kitchener's Army*, Manchester: Manchester University Press, 1988.

Little precisely on women's experiences, as the title suggests. But provides useful contextual material on, for example, soldiers' allowances, the 'order of the white feather', which was inaugurated by Admiral Charles Penrose, *not* by a woman, and on some of the more outrageous atrocity stories.

G59   Stiehm, Judith (ed.) *Women's Studies International Forum: Special Issue – Women and Men's Wars 5, 3–4* (1982).

Collection of essays on gender and armed conflict.

G60   Anne Summers *Angels and Citizens. British Women as Military Nurses 1854–1915*, London: Routledge, 1988.

A useful and very interesting history of the military nurse; enlightening not only for the background to and account of the VAD organisation, the QAIMNS and the roles of the Red Cross and the Order of St John of Jerusalem, but for of its analysis of women's citizenship in the Victorian and Edwardian periods. Many women found direct rewards, not as pacifist suffragists, but as part of the army: responding to challenge, to independence, to being abroad and to having a role in the running of the country that was not confined to the private house. Thus, for many, the declaration of war offered the personal validation that the granting of the vote could not hope to achieve.

G61   Swartz, Marvin *The Union of Democratic Control in British Politics During the First World War*, Oxford: Clarendon Press, 1971.

Documents the principles and objectives of the UDC in the context of the movement's effect on the decline of Liberalism and the rise of Labour. Main figures were E.D. Morel, Charles Trevelyan, Arthur Ponsonby. Bertrand Russell was on the committee. It was committed to a negotiated end to the war, and deeply opposed to secret diplomacy. Believed that Britain was ruled by men with selfish nationalistic and class attitudes. Helena Swanwick was a member of the Executive Committee.

G62   Terry, Roy *Women in Khaki: The Story of the British Woman Soldier*, London: Columbus Books, 1988.

An illustrated history of women's changing roles in the army, and of their struggle to be admitted to it in the first place. The first four chapters contain material directly of relevance to period of the First World War.

G63   Thom, Deborah 'The Bundle of Sticks: Women, Trade Unionists and
            Collective Organisation before 1918' in *Unequal Opportunities:
            Women's Employment in England 1900–1918*, ed. Angela John,
            Oxford: Basil Blackwell, 1986.

Considers the question of union leadership, through a study of the very different
styles of Mary Macarthur and Julia Varley.

G64   Thomas, Gill *Life on All Fronts: Women in the First World War*,
            Cambridge: Cambridge Educational, Cambridge University Press,
            1988.

An educational resource book, which draws on interviews, diaries, letters, newspapers and photographs.

G65   Vansittart, Peter *Voices from the Great War*, London: Jonathan Cape,
            1981.

Selection of extracts from war recollections. The voices are predominantly male,
but include Rosa Luxemburg, Rebecca West, Marie Curie, Vera Brittain, Lady
Diana Cooper.

G66   Vellacott, Jo 'Anti-War Suffragists', *History* 62, 206, (1977): 411–25.

An argument against two commonly held assumptions: (a) that the 'nuisance value'
of the suffragettes was prominent in the minds of those who agreed to extend the
vote to women, and (b) that activist women supported the government wholeheart-
edly in fighting the war. Her focus (extended in later papers) is on the non-violent,
constitutional and (often) left-wing suffragists, who linked their cause to that of the
pacifists.

G67   Vellacott, Jo *Bertrand Russell and the Pacifists in the First World War*,
            Brighton: Harvester, 1980.

The subject-matter of the book is explained by its title. It is useful to students of
women's war involvement, however, as a narrative of pacifist organisations,
including the UDC and NCF, in which notable suffragist pacifists were involved.

G68   Vellacott, Jo 'Feminist Consciousness and the First World War', *History
            Workshop* 23, (1987): 81–101.

An account of the impact on British suffragists of the war, and of their various
political and practical responses to it. Discriminates between the suffragettes, the
liberals (such as Mrs Fawcett, Ray Strachey), the pacifists (such as Helena
Swanwick and Catherine Marshall), socialists and Labour Party members.
Comments on the subservient role of most women during the war and on the link
between militarism and women's subordination. Takes as a starting point the split
in the NUWSS in 1915.

G69   Vellacott, Jo 'Historical Reflections on Votes, Brooms and Guns: Admission to Political Structures – On Whose Terms?', *Atlantis* 12, 1, (1987): 36–39.

Brief piece dividing suffragism into three 'stages': militant insistence on access to equal rights; the different sphere of socialist working-class suffragists; the internationalist perspective, intent on undermining patriarchy and belligerence and replacing it with an alternative mentality. Her focus is on the non-militant suffragists associated with labour politics and internationalism: Catherine Marshall, Kathleen Courtney and Helena Swanwick.

G70   Wall, Richard and Jay Winter (eds) *The Upheaval of War: Family Work and Welfare in Europe, 1914–18*, Cambridge: Cambridge University Press, 1988.

Part III of this collection of essays comprises studies of women and work. Jean-Louis Robert, in 'Women and Work in France during the First World War', draws the general conclusion that 1914–18 saw the final climax of increased participation of women in paid work in France. Ute Daniel, in 'Women's Work in Industry and Family: Germany 1914–18', concludes that any increase in women's industrial employment during the war came to an end as war ended. The combination of the collapse of the consumer goods market and a social policy geared towards maintaining women as family workers meant that housework became more burdensome and the rewards for taking industrial work were insufficient. Deborah Thom, in 'Women and Work in Wartime Britain', also concludes that changes were temporary. She comments on the rhetoric, both of the government and of campaigners, aligning women with their potential to be mothers, rather than their capacity as workers. Points out that there were no permanent training schemes or alternations in the organisation of production.

G71   Ward, Irene *FANY Invicta*, London: Hutchinson, 1955.

An account of FANY beginnings, activities during the First and Second World Wars (and intervening period); mentions well-known members, notably Mrs St Clair Stobart and Grace Ashley-Smith (McDougall).

G72   Williams, A. Susan *Women and War*, Hove, East Sussex: Wayland Publishers, 1989.

An educational resource book: a guide to stories of women and war in the twentieth century.

G73   Wiltsher, Anne *Most Dangerous Women. Feminist Peace Campaigners of the Great War*, London: Pandora, 1985.

An account of the work of women peace campaigners such as Rosika Schwimmer, Catherine Marshall, Helena Swanwick, Jane Addams, Carrie Chapman Catt, etc. Takes the Hague Peace Congress, 1915, as a central point and charts the work of the women involved in it and its aftermath.

G74   Woollacott, Angela *On Her Their Lives Depend: Munitions Workers in the Great War*, Berkeley and London: University of California Press, 1994.

A study of women munitions workers, mostly from the working classes, that looks to explore the cultural memory of the experience with all its dangers and discomforts. Aims to examine what was important to the women themselves, to discover and interpret women's range of experiences, rather than to study government or trades union policy.

BIOGRAPHIES

H1   Allen, A.M. *Sophy Sanger. A Pioneer in Internationalism*, Glasgow: Robert Maclehose and Co. Ltd, The University Press, 1958.

An affectionate and admiring portrait by Sanger's companion. Following her education at Newnham (arranged by her brother, the mathematician and barrister C.P. Sanger), she became secretary to the Legal Advice Bureau attached to the Women's Trade Union League, where she met Mary Macarthur and Margaret Bondfield. During the war she helped with the Queen's Work for Women Fund, and campaigned for a reduction in working hours, but her passion was for promoting an international minimum of wellbeing, which she pursued via Labour and pacifist circles, and ultimately by working for the International Labour Organisation, at home and abroad.

H2   Alpers, Anthony *Katherine Mansfield*, London: Jonathan Cape, 1954.

A compatriot's biography, by one who, self-professedly, experienced an ambivalence about his native country similar to that felt by Mansfield. Alpers was assisted in this relatively early study by 'L.M.', and by numerous friends and relations of Mansfield. He did not, however, have access to documentation (letters, diaries, etc.), some of which were published shortly after this book was written. Alpers wrote a later study of Mansfield, her work and her circle: *The Life of Katherine Mansfield*, also published by Jonathan Cape, in 1980.

H3   Benstock, Shari *No Gifts from Chance. A Biography of Edith Wharton*, London: Hamish Hamilton, 1994.

Described as the first full-life biography of Wharton to document published and unpublished sources, this is a detailed, thoroughly researched account. It tells of the New York family Wharton was born into, the expectations that she would become a 'society matron' rather like her mother, her gift for writing, her marriage, her travels. She was a conservative figure, and the war only intensified those attitudes. She spent the war mostly in Paris, from where she wrote articles (propaganda, fiction), raised huge amounts of money for charities and undertook 'tours' of France that would reveal to her the extent of that country's suffering under war conditions. She, inevitably, lost friends to the fighting, and struggled to hold on to her own health.

H4   Benton, Jill *Naomi Mitchison: A Biography*, London: Pandora, 1990.
Reprinted 1992.

A biography written by an author who was well acquainted with her subject. It is a book that intends to honour Naomi Mitchison as a 'Prominent writer, socialist and feminist politician, and advisor to a Botswanan chief'. The part of the book that covers the war years relies on Mitchison's own memoirs, which this author augments with interpretations of, for example, the motivation behind Naomi's restricted young ladyhood (she was being groomed for marriage by her mother, whose standards in this regard, despite her support of the suffrage, were quite conservative). Covers education, marriage, attitudes towards sex and independence.

H5   Berry, Paul and Mark Bostridge *Vera Brittain, a Life*, London:
Chatto & Windus, 1995.

The first full-length biography of Vera Brittain, which aims to illuminate hers as an individual life, rather than one representative of a generation, as was so often her declared intention in her autobiographical writings. Extensive archival materials have been drawn on, and the authors have sought to provide new contexts for Brittain's self-representations, and to expand, where Brittain was reticent, about her more complex relationships.

H6   Boll, Theophilus *Miss May Sinclair: Novelist. A Biographical and
Critical Introduction*, Rutherford: Farleigh Dickinson University Press,
1973.

Part I of this book details her upbringing as the youngest and only daughter in a family of boys. She was influenced by Dorothea Beale, at Cheltenham Ladies College, who stimulated in her an intense interest in philosophy, but failed in impressing on her any religious orthodoxy. As a young woman and struggling writer she was lonely and short of money, but as her writing took off, she made a large number of literary friends, including Katharine Tynan, Ezra Pound, Thomas Hardy, Mrs Belloc-Lowndes, Rose Macaulay, W.L. George, Rebecca West, G.K. Chesterton. Her involvement in the Women Writers' Suffrage League and with the Medico-Psychological clinic were sustaining intellectually and politically. Her experiences in the Munro Ambulance Corps, although brief, had a profound influence on her. Part II accounts for all of her writings, in chronological order. They are described and briefly analysed. This is an intensely admiring study, the fruit of careful, painstaking research. What it may lack in fluency it makes up for in usefulness as a resource.

H7   Brittain, Vera *Testament of Friendship*, London: Macmillan & Co.,
1940. Reprinted London: Virago, 1980.

Vera Brittain's loving portrait of and public tribute to her friend, who died aged 37. Delineates Winifred Holtby's warmth, versatility and productiveness, in the context of her life, her writings and her social and political interests.

H8   Burgess, Alan *The Lovely Sargeant: A Biography of Flora Sandes*,
London: Heinemann, 1963.

An account of the life of Flora Sandes, an English Red Cross Nurse who joined
the Serbian army and fought against the Bulgars, rising to the rank of sergeant-
major.

H9   Cline, Sally *Radclyffe Hall: A Woman Called John*, London:
John Murray, 1997.

A full study of the life of Radclyffe Hall, which aims to analyse the entirety of her
life and works, without unduly privileging the book that made her into a legend:
The Well of Loneliness. The author has drawn on materials unavailable to
previous biographers, and is openly cautious about accepting the veracity of Una
Troubridge's accounts at face value. Covers Hall's reaction to the war, her frustration, her jealousy of those who had an active role in it, her recruitment campaigns.

H10   Colenbrander, Joanna *A Portrait of Fryn: A Biography of F. Tennyson
Jesse*, London: Andre Deutsch, 1984.

Written by her secretary, this account of F. Tennyson Jesse's life covers her child-
hood (she was born into a Naval family) and early break in Fleet Street, where she
was taken on by *The Times* and *The Daily Mail*, and had a short story published in
The English Review. She went out to Belgium at the begining of the war as a *Daily
Mail* correspondent, using Ostend as a base from which to send reports about
Ghent, Antwerp, Termonde, etc. She left Antwerp just before the Germans arrived.
In January 1915 she went to Holland as the guest of the Commission for Relief in
Belgium, and did some fundraising work for them. She wrote a novel, and some
articles for *Vogue* and, on the basis of the latter, she was invited by the Ministry of
Information to do a full study of women's war work in France – *The Sword of
Deborah*. The account goes on to cover her postwar marriage to Tottie Harwood
(with whom she wrote plays, including the war play *Billeted*), her travels, her
addiction to morphine (as a result of numerous operations on a hand injury), her
novel writing and her Second World War experience.

H11   Darroch, Sandra Jobson *Ottoline: The life of Lady Ottoline Morrell*,
London: Chatto & Windus, 1976.

The first biography of Ottoline Morrell, drawing on a considerable archive of
unpublished letters. Strikes a general, even tone. The section on Garsington is the
one most relevant to the war, and this covers the numerous visitors, conscientious
objectors and their friends, attempts to reason with Asquith, relationships with
Russell, Strachey, Carrington, etc.

H12   Emery, Jane *Rose Macaulay: A Writer's Life*, London: John Murray,
1991.

A critical biography of Rose Macaulay that seeks to illuminate the relationships
between her fiction and her lived experience, and to delve into the hidden corners
of her complex, resilient character. Covers her whole life, but the section relevant
to the war appears in Chapters 8 and 9. She grieved at the death of Rupert Brooke,
took up first VAD work, then land work, and finally became a civil servant, a job

that was to provide material for some of her more satirical novels and introduced her to Gerald O'Donovan.

H13   Fisher, John *That Miss Hobhouse*, London: Secker & Warburg, 1971.

The story of Emily Hobhouse, cousin of Stephen Hobhouse, the conscientious objector, son of Margaret (of '*I Appeal Unto Caesar*') and Rt Hon. Henry Hobhouse. Emily had experience of the South African war, and wrote an account of the fate of women and children, many of whom died as a result of farm burning. Joined the Quaker Relief Detachment in 1915 and went to Paris. Decided to mobilise the women of Italy and Switzerland against war. Acted as temporary secretary to the International Committee of Women for Permanent Peace. The Foreign Office was keen to keep her in the UK, to prevent her from spreading pacifist propaganda abroad.

H14   Glendinning, Victoria *Edith Sitwell: A Unicorn Among Lions*, n.p.: Phoenix, 1980.

Little directly about the war, but the years 1914–18 coincide with Sitwell's growing independence from her parents, and with her increasing confidence and acclaim as a poet and as a member of the London literary scene.

H15   Glendinning, Victoria *Rebecca West: A Life*, London: Weidenfeld & Nicholson, 1987.

A lively account of West's long and eventful life, written and researched with full family co-operation. Glendinning notes that on 4 August 1914 Rebecca West gave birth to her and H.G. Wells's son, Anthony. She spent the war years caring for her son, maintaining a relationship with Wells and writing. This arrangement was not always particularly harmonious, but she nevertheless produced *The Return of the Soldier* and continued friendships with Dora Marsden, G.B. Stern, F. Tennyson Jesse and Marie Belloc-Lowndes, among others.

H16   Grant, Joy *Stella Benson: A Biography*, London and Basingstoke: Macmillan, 1987.

This biography is based on Benson's diaries, upon which there was an embargo for some years following her death. It describes her life fully, often quoting from the diary. The war years are characterised by bad health, which was never to leave Benson, and a determination to fight the suffrage corner and help those suffering in the war. Thus she worked in the Literary Department of the Women Writers Suffrage League, joined the United Suffragists and signed up with the Women's Emergency Corps, which sent her to the East End, to work with the Charity Organisation Society. She became the organising secretary of a Queen Mary's Workroom, witnessed anti-German riots, zeppelin raids and did what she could for the poor, deserving and otherwise. In between these activities, she wrote novels: *I Pose* and *This is the End* were well received during the war years, and *Living Alone* satirises some of her experiences in charity work. She also did some land work. But this was all punctuated by instances of poor health. In July 1918 she sailed for America.

H17   Hardwick, Joan *An Immodest Violet: The Life of Violet Hunt*, London: Andre Deutsch, 1990.

The story of the life of Violet Hunt, from the pre-Raphaelite influences on her childhood, to her death in 1942. A strong emphasis is placed on her relationship with Ford Madox Ford, which came to an end during the war years, and which is depicted in Ford's *Parade's End* tetralogy. May Sinclair was a contemporary and close friend; Rebecca West was a younger friend and the circles in which Hunt moved included Henry James, Wyndham Lewis, the Lawrences, the Meynells and Mary Borden. She and Ford were treated with suspicion by local residents during the early war years, as possible spies or enemy aliens (Ford, of course, had German relatives), and, on the whole, Hunt felt too old to do war work: she was caught between the older Victorian and the younger modern generations.

H18   Izzard, Molly *A Heroine in her Time: the Life of Helen Gwynne-Vaughan (1879–1967)*, London: Macmillan, 1969.

The story of the widowed botanist, who joined Mona Chalmers Watson to head the WAAC in France.

H19   Lawrence, Margot *Shadow of Swords. A Biography of Elsie Inglis*, London: Michael Joseph, 1971.

Full portrait of the life of Elsie Inglis, who secured fame for initiating the SWH and for her heroic work in Serbia and Russia. The author drew on unpublished material to shed light on events left obscure in previous biographies.

H20   Lee, Hermione *Virginia Woolf*, London: Chatto & Windus, 1996.

This biography of Virginia Woolf, unlike those by James King and Quentin Bell, for example, registers the war as an important event in her life. Our attention is drawn towards the imagery of war in Woolf's books, the narrative position it occupies in her fiction, and the importance, in her day-to-day life, of the events surrounding conscription, and of Leonard's increasing involvement with Labour and Fabian politicians. This is a full and well-balanced study, which takes into account the recent debates surrounding Woolf's life and work.

H21   Liddington, Jill *The Life and Times of a Respectable Rebel: Selina Cooper 1864–1946*, London: Virago, 1984.

The biography of an almost forgotten working woman from Nelson in Lancashire, who embraced socialism, suffragism and pacifism. A passionate speaker and gifted organiser, she was a leading figure in Labour and suffragist circles in the cotton towns of the North. Chapters 15 and 16 deal specifically with the war. This is a biography built up from oral testimony, and a discovered box of documents kept, in an attic, by Cooper's daughter.

H22   Linklater, Andro *An Unhusbanded Life. Charlotte Despard: Suffragette, Socialist and Sinn Feiner*, London: Hutchinson, 1980.

Covers her childhood (she was the sister of Sir John French), her marriage to Max Despard, widowhood and slow emergence from grief to political activity. She is best known for her suffragette activity, for which she was imprisoned. She broke from the Pankhursts to form the Women's Freedom League, and continued her suffrage work during the war. Despard was also involved in relief work, and in the protests against the discriminatory regulation and police surveillance of working women. She welcomed the Russian Revolution, 1917. This biography emphasises her spiritual life alongside her political commitments.

H23   Oldfield, Sybil *Spinsters of this Parish: The Life and Times of F.M. Mayor and Mary Sheepshanks*, London: Virago, 1984.

Two separate life stories, one of the novelist F.M. Mayor, the other of Mary Sheepshanks, editor of *Jus Suffragii* and Secretary of the International Woman Suffrage Alliance. Sheepshanks taught at Morley College for Working Men and Women (as did Virginia Woolf) and became its Vice Principal. She attended the Stephens' Thursday evenings in Gordon Square.

H24   Roberts, R. Ellis *Portrait of Stella Benson*, London: Macmillan, 1939.

Memoir of the author, by a friend. Based on letters, reminiscences, the help of friends and family, but with no recourse to Stella Benson's diary.

See Joy Grant, *Stella Benson: A Biography* (H16).

H25   Romero, Patricia W. *E. Sylvia Pankhurst: Portrait of a Radical*, New Haven and London: Yale University Press, 1990.

A full portrait of Sylvia Pankhurst, which, in Part II, details her relationship with her mother and sisters, her relationship with Keir Hardie, her work for the East London Federation of Suffragettes, and her espousal of a sequence of radical causes.

H26   Sebba, Anne *Enid Bagnold – A Biography*, London: Weidenfeld & Nicholson, 1986.

Follows her through her upbringing in a military household, study under Walter Sickert, friendships with Irene Cooper Willis, Antoine Bibesco and Desmond McCarthy. It was Bibesco who recommended that she write down her experiences in the Royal Herbert Military Hospital, Woolwich, where she was a voluntary nurse. McCarthy read it for the publisher William Heinemann, 15,000 copies of *Diary Without Dates* were published and Bagnold was sacked for breach of military discipline. This came about because some of her descriptions of unfeeling hospital routine were used by the *Daily Mail* in a piece on a scandal in a Rouen hospital. Her novel, *The Happy Foreigner*, derives from her experiences as an ambulance driver at the end of the war. In 1920 she married Sir Roderick Jones, the proprietor of Reuters. They had four children, and she went on to write, among other plays, poems and novels, *National Velvet*.

H27   Shaw, Marion *The Clear Stream: A Life of Winifred Holtby*, London: Virago, 1999.

The forthcoming, full-length study of Winifred Holtby's life and work.

H28   Sutherland, John *Mrs Humphry Ward. Eminent Victorian, Pre-eminent Edwardian*, Oxford: Clarendon Press, 1990.

Mary Augusta Arnold, grand-daughter of Thomas Arnold of Rugby and niece of Matthew Arnold, had a considerable family tradition to live up to. She married Humphry Ward and became known, in the late Victorian period, for her philan-thropic and educational work, as well as for writing best-selling novels, which were quite a hit in America as well as in England. As war approached, her career seemed on the wane; her son, a compulsive gambler, used up a great deal of the family money and her reputation as an anti-suffragist seemed rather to undercut her earlier success in helping to found Somerville College. Her 'old friend', the former US President Roosevelt, precipitated a late revival in her fortunes by suggesting that she write to him about England's experiences of war. She cleared the proposal with Wellington House (soon to be the Ministry of Information) and set off on a 'tour' of munitions factories, naval fleets and behind-the-lines France which resulted in a work of propaganda said to have been important in persuading the USA to enter the European War. She wrote two further volumes of this and three war novels before her death, at the age of 68, in 1920.

H29   Tomalin, Claire *Katherine Mansfield: A Secret Life*, London: Viking Penguin, 1987.

A biography that departs from the interpretation offered by Alpers, by paying greater attention to the relationship between Mansfield and Lawrence, and by placing a new emphasis on her sexual and medical history.

H30   Vernon, Betty D. *Ellen Wilkinson 1891–1947*, London: Croom Helm, 1982.

Covers the life of Ellen Wilkinson from her birth, in Manchester, into a working-class family, to her death while serving as a cabinet member of a Labour government. It is the story of a socialist, a suffragist and a pacifist, who dedicated her life to the trades union movement and to bettering the conditions of working people. During the war she was a member of the WIL, she was seconded by the NUWSS to organise relief workrooms for the women of Stockport, and in 1915, at a time when female involvement in trades unions was rare, she was appointed National Woman Organiser to the Amalgamated Union of Co-operative Employees (AUCE) which later became the National Union of Distributive and Allied Workers. Her war work was thus mainly union work, and involved recruiting women into the union, negotiating rates of pay (she was heavily involved in the 'equal pay' battles), conditions of employment and union policy on substitute labour. She also wrote novels, took part in the Jarrow Crusade, and was elected in 1924, as part of the first Labour government.

H31   Waagenaar, Sam *The Murder of Mata Hari*, London: Arthur Barker Ltd., 1964.

Aims to tell the true story of Mata Hari, liberated from myth and fantasy. Told with the help of Mata Hari's maid, companion and confidante, who claims expressly that 'she was not a spy'.

H32   Wenzel, Marian and John Cornish *Auntie Mabel's War: An Account of Her Part in the Hostilities of 1914–18*, London: Allen Lane, 1980.

A scrapbook with connecting narrative rather than a conventional biography, this book presents photographs, illustrations and extracts from Mabel Jeffery's papers, along with the memories of her niece, Mrs Turner, to build up a narrative of a nurse who served with the SWH at Royaumont, elsewhere in France, and in Serbia.

H33   Whitelaw, Lis *The Life and Rebellious Times of Cicely Hamilton, Actress, Writer, Suffragist*, London: The Women's Press, 1990.

A biography written in a feminist framework that acknowledges the gaps and silences that result from a subject's disappearing from history. The part of her life that relates to the war sees Cicely Hamilton at Royaumont with the SWH, and in France with Lena Ashwell's organisation 'Concerts at the Front'. She also spent time at Senlis, whence comes the description in the book of that name, and the related images in *William – An Englishman*.

H34   Wilson, Francesca *Eglantyne Jebb, Rebel Daughter of a Country House*, London: Allen & Unwin, 1967.

The life story of the founder of the Save the Children Fund. Jebb came from a close-knit family, and she was particularly close to her sister Dorothy, whose marriage to Charles Buxton put her in close touch with the *Cambridge Magazine* and a body of thinkers who were critical of the bellicose attitudes that seemed to dominate the conduct of the war. Jebb oversaw the translation of foreign language materials for the *Cambridge Magazine*. She had always been involved in philanthropic work, had visited Serbia in 1913, became a pacifist at the outbreak of war, and, as a result of the peace, became a co-founder of the Fight the Famine Council. This was for the relief of 'enemy' civilians suffering from the blockade. Dr Hector Munro accompanied Jebb on a visit to Vienna and helped raise funds and support for the Save the Children Fund.

BIBLIOGRAPHIES
AND REFERENCE
WORKS

I1   Barrow, Margaret. *Women 1870–1928. A Select Guide to Printed and Archival Sources in the United Kingdom*, New York: Mansell Publishing, Garland Publishing, 1981.

I2   Bayliss, Gwyn M. *Bibliographic Guide to the Two World Wars. An Annotated Survey of English-Language Reference Materials*, London and New York: Bowker, 1977.

I3   Blunden, Edmund and Cyril Falls, H.M. Tomlinson and R. Wright *The War, 1914–18: A Booklist*, London: The Reader, 1929.

I4   British Museum, Department of Printed Books *Subject Index of Books Relating to the European War, 1914–18, Acquired by the British Museum, 1914–1920*, London: Longmans, Bernard Quaritch, Humphrey Milford, 1922.

I5   Brown, Loulou, Helen Collins, Pat Green, Maggie Humm, Mel Landells, (eds) *W.I.S.H. The International Handbook of Women's Studies*, Hemel Hempstead: Harvester Wheatsheaf, 1993.

I6   Bulkley, Mildred Emily *Bibliographical Survey of Contemporary Sources for the Economic and Social History of the War*, Oxford: Clarendon Press, 1922.

I7   Burnett, John, David Vincent and David Mayall (eds) *The Autobiography of the Working Class. An Annotated Critical Bibliography*, 3 vols, Brighton: Harvester, 1984–9.

I8   Cassis, A.F. *The Twentieth Century English Novel: An Annotated Bibliography of General Criticism*, New York and London: Garland Publishing, 1977.

I9   Carroll, Berenice *et al. Peace and War: A Guide to Bibliographies*, War-Peace bibliography series no. 16, Santa Barbara: ABC Clio 1983.

I10   Cline, Cheryl *Women's Diaries, Journals and Letters. An Annotated Bibliography*, New York and London: Garland, 1989.

I11   Doughan, David and Denise Sanchez *Feminist Periodicals, 1855–1984: Annotated Critical Bibliography of British, Irish, Commonwealth and International Titles*, Brighton: Harvester, 1987.

I12   Enser, A.G.S. *A Subject Bibliography of the First World War. Books in English 1914–1978*, London: Andre Deutsch, 1979.

I13   Falls, Cyril *War Books: A Critical Guide*, London: Peter Davies, 1930.

I14   Gilbert, V.F. and D.S. Tatla *Women's Studies. A Bibliography of Dissertations 1970–1982*, Oxford: Blackwell, 1985.

I15   Gray, Randal with Christopher Argyle *Chronicle of the First World War. Vol. 1: 1914–1916*, Oxford: Facts on File Ltd, 1990.

I16   Gray, Randal with Christopher Argyle *Chronicle of the First World War. Vol. II: 1916–1918*, Oxford: Facts on File Ltd, 1991.

I17   Hager, Philip E. and D. Taylor *The Novels of World War 1: An Annotated Bibliography*, New York: Garland, 1981.

I18   Commission for the Teaching of History, *The Two World Wars: Selective Bibliography*, Oxford: Pergamon Press, 1964.

I19   *The Libraries Directory*, Cambridge: James Clarke & Co Ltd, 1998.

I20   Lynn, Naomi B., Ann B. Matsar and Marie Barovic Rosenberg *Research Guide in Women's Studies*, Morristown, NJ: General Learning Press, 1974.

I21   Markmann, Sigrid and Dagmar Lange *Frauen und Erster Weltkrieg in England. Auswahlbibliographie*, Osnabrück: H. Th. Wenner, 1988.

I22   Matthews, William *British Diaries: An Annotated Bibliography of British Diaries Written Between 1442 and 1942*, Gloucester, MA: P. Smith, 1967.

I23   Matthews, William *British Autobiographies: An Annotated Bibliography of British Autobiographies Published or Written before 1951*, Hamden, CT: Archon Books, 1968.

I24   Mayer, S.L. and W.J. Koenig *The Two World Wars. A Guide to Manuscript Collections in the United Kingdom*, London and New York: Bowker, 1976.

I25   Murdoch, H., Hilda Spear and D. Valentine *A Catalogue of Books Relating to the Great War held in the Library of the University of Dundee*, Dundee: Blackness, 1980.

I26   Papworth, Lucy Wyatt and Dorothy M. Zimmern *Women in Industry: A Bibliography*, London: Women's Industrial Council, 1915.

I27   Phillips, Jill M. *The Darkling Plain: A Bibliography of Books about World War 1*, New York: Gorden Press 1980.

I28   Reilly, Catherine *English Poetry of the First World War: A Bibliography*, London: Prior, 1978.

I29   Ritchie, Maureen *Women's Studies: A Checklist of Bibliographies*, London: Mansell, 1980.

I30   Rosenberg, Marie and Len Bergstrom *Women and Society: A Critical Review of the Literature with a Selected Annotated Bibliography*, Beverley Hills: Sage Publications, 1975.

I31   Uglow, Jennifer *The Macmillan Dictionary of Women's Biography*, 2nd edn, London: Macmillan, 1989.

INDEX